How to Manage a
Successful Software Project
With Microsoft® Project 2000

Second Edition

Sanjiv Purba
Bharat Shah

Wiley Computer Publishing

John Wiley & Sons, Inc.

NEW YORK • CHICHESTER • WEINHEIM • BRISBANE • SINGAPORE • TORONTO

This book is dedicated to family and friends.

Publisher: Robert Ipsen
Editor: Robert M. Elliott
Assistant Editor: Emilie Herman
Managing Editor: John Atkins
Associate New Media Editor: Brian Snapp
Text Design & Composition: Publishers' Design and Production Services

Library of Congress Cataloging-in-Publication Data

Purba, Sanjiv.
    How to manage a successful software project : with Microsoft Project 2000 / Sanjiv Purba, Bharat Shah. — 2nd ed.
        p. cm.
    Includes bibliographical references and index.
    ISBN 0-471-39339-8 (paper : alk. paper)
    1. Computer software—Development—Management. I. Shah, Bharat. II. Title.

QA76.76.D47 P855 2000
005.1′068′4—dc21   00-063346

Printed in the United States of America.

10 9 8 7 6 5 4 3 2 1

Contents

Acknowledgments

Special thanks go to David Sawh, who wrote the Microsoft Project tutorial in the first edition of this book. Due to other commitments that have kept him hopping and billing quite nicely, he was unable to develop it for this edition. Nevertheless, he helped out with the survey and acted as an excellent sounding board.

Thanks also go to Emilie Herman for keeping this book on track. Emilie is excellent to work with, highly detailed, and very patient.

Thanks also to the following colleagues who have helped out in one way or another over the years: Christine Stephens, Ian Tait, Gordon Shields, Terry Stuart, Wayne Thomas, Wayne Martin, Franca Del Bel Belluz, Peter Fernie, and Katie Comerford.

We would also like to thank the following project managers who took the time to share their experiences with us and/or filled out our survey:

Lorenzo Artuso, Johnny Agsalog, Santiago Astray, Ron Bates, Charles Banyay, David Brassor, Dorin Brebeanu, Angela Bridge, Carole Chauncey, Bosco Cheung, Antoinette Chong, Dennis Choptiany, Tim Christmann, Ivan Church, Maria Churchill, Jaya Chopra, Claudia Cifelli, Carl Clutton, Katie Comerford, Forrest

Danson, Dinesh Dattani, Rhiannon Davies, Bob Delaney, Alex Dhanjal, Gulab Dhole, Judy Dinn, Len Dvorkin, Selim El Raheb, Jeffrey Feldman, Perry Finklestein, Noela Fowler, Todd Genton, Vivian Gibson, Ido Gileadi, Sharad Goel, Dora Gugliotta, Amlan Gupta, George Hart, Roger Hauk, Dipak Karia, Jim Kilpatrick, Craig King, John Koopmans, Joe Lee, Danny Leung, Pete Lyons, Abe Mathew, Barb McCann, Dave Middleton, Stephen Missirlis, Srinivas Padmanabharao, Elena Pastekova, Yogesh Patel, Mike Pickering, Peter Pille, Harry Price, Gerald Roddau, Paul Rogers, Allan Salek, Gordon Sandford, Shiraz Sarangi, Dave Sawh, Manjit Sidhu, Michael Simonyi, Monty Spivak, Karen Schwichtenberg, Eric Steinberg, Mike Sutton, Karen Roger Tanjuakio, Ashok Tandon, Jim Tessmer, Huneid Vakharia, Kan Wadehra, David Wadsworth, Dick Watada, Fred Yagi, Miles Au Yeung, Tanya Zablishinsky.

From Sanjiv Purba

Special thanks to my wife Kulwinder Purba for her support during this long process and the many long weekends she waited for me patiently to write this book. I also want to thank my two sons, Naveen and Neil, for their patience, support, and understanding. Thanks also go to my parents, Parkash Purba and Inderjit Purba. I also want to thank my grandparents Amrit Gurcharan Singh and Rajwant Kaur Puri.

From Bharat Shah

Special thanks to my wife Barbara and my three sons, Kieran, Timothy, and Trevor, for their patience, support, and understanding.

Preface

Information technology (IT) organizations are affected by three types of change: ever-evolving technology, changing business expectations, and changes to core business models. Since we wrote the first edition of this book, the business and technology landscape has changed dramatically. Downsizing and rightsizing corporate objectives have been replaced by the need to adopt eBusiness practices. The need to catch up to competitors already using the Internet has made project delivery more important than budgets in some cases. In other cases, functionality and content availability have become the most important components of the "project success" definition. Other hot technology areas include the proliferation of personal device assistants (PDAs), voice application, and wireless technology. New solutions will undoubtedly be added to this list.

Since we started writing this edition, eBusiness has gone from being a panacea to the business community with literally billions of dollars of venture capital backing to a much more cautious and traditional corporate undertaking. What would have been considered a successful dot-com project only three months ago would today make the same business owners extremely nervous. In another ironic twist, what was once bleeding-edge client/server architecture is now just a tiny bit short of getting the dreaded "legacy" title. There is little doubt that the intensity of change—technical, organizational, and business—will continue well into the future.

However, many project histories show that a large number of project outcomes—successful or not—are still the result of applying traditional management practices such as issue resolution, testing, architecture, and organizational personalities. This book examines experiences across many types of projects and finds a common layer that is more or less consistent across initiatives. The common layer contains approaches, techniques, experiences, and tools that are needed to deliver almost any type of project successfully based on pragmatic principles. However, this is not the whole picture. This book also extends the basic framework by incorporating the fundamental requirements of any given marketplace as an add-on to the common management layer. Addressing both the old and the new in this way provides a flexible, effective management framework—regardless of the technology or business models that are popular at the time of reading.

The Role of IT Management

Most parts of any organization are involved in meeting the challenge of constantly changing business requirements. Because technology is often the enabler of change, IT becomes the workhorse for meeting the new requirements. Projects with firm start and end dates, resources, and objectives will help ensure success. Since project managers are responsible for project delivery, their role in the new economy is critical.

IT Management is once again undergoing profound change in terms of organization, mandate, and business expectations. Their mandate is getting projects completed on time, within budget, and to the satisfaction of the business community. The relentless evolution in new technology increases business expectations, making this job even more difficult. Intense international pressure, rightsizing, and large investments in IT infrastructure are some of the factors that have fueled high expectations of the business community from their IT organizations in the past. IT is viewed as a key enabler that must be prepared to meet new business expectations, specifically in the following areas:

☐ Quick response to new business requirements

☐ Lower development and maintenance costs

- ☐ High-systems development
- ☐ Independence from the hardware/software infrastructure so that business systems are not locked into a specific environment (e.g., portability and interoperability)
- ☐ Ability for application systems to manage increased data traffic and users without decreasing reliability or response time (e.g., scalability)
- ☐ E-enablement (and whatever letter is popular at the time)
- ☐ Intuitive interfaces with corresponding reduced training requirements
- ☐ Direct support for business users to enter their own business rules

The project managers are the link between the business community and the IT reality who meet these expectations and deliver projects successfully to their clients. Organizations measure project success in one of two ways: by budget and by time. These are also measured in the context of functionality and user satisfaction. Additional measures include team satisfaction, team growth, increased investment in team skills, and overall team happiness.

There are specific dependencies among some of these dimensions. For example, projects with large budgets tend to have large staff complements. In general, larger numbers result in more complex projects. This requires the project manager to ensure that an adequate organization and project plan is in place to handle the specific permutations resulting from the specific project dimensions. In general, the specific value of the dimensions on a given project drive specific behaviors from the team members. For example, longer projects tend to make team members more process-oriented than results-oriented. If this is not balanced adequately, the project focus shifts away from producing deliverables and more toward how things are done—without actually getting anything done. Managers must assess the makeup of their projects and take appropriate action in building and allocating resources to their projects.

Purpose of This Book

This book is about management approaches, techniques, and experiences at the project level. It is intended to provide information to project managers, or aspiring project managers, to allow them to deliver IT projects successfully. Guidelines and techniques presented in this book are based on the actual work experiences of the authors, and supported by advice that was provided by more than a hundred managers who were interviewed or surveyed for this book.

This book essentially provides a survival framework for project managers to deliver their projects successfully or with the best possible results that can be achieved in a given situation. It considers that the definition of success may be elusive and highly dependent on how a particular result is packaged. Sometimes a project manager must be flexible in understanding and communicating what an organization may actually need to be successful while accepting a lack of success in some other measures (e.g., cost or budget).

The survival framework traverses the phases of the standard project development lifecycle. Beginning with a high-level project portfolio that satisfies a corporate strategy, the framework describes the techniques, tools, and approaches that a project manager should consider following. The process starts with a high-level project portfolio that is used to schedule projects for delivery. These are planned in a consistent and manageable manner so that the projects are driven by demonstrated and accepted business needs. This book can also be used as a handbook to initiate, develop, and implement projects on time and within budget. A project development framework or methodology titled the iterative project development framework (IPDM) is introduced in this book. IPDM has been successfully used on a broad range of projects, including n-tier architecture, mainframe applications, open systems, Web-based/killer applications, and eBusiness solutions. This new methodology framework has evolved from the iterative project development methodology (version 1) that was introduced in the first edition of this book. Its core elements have remained the same; however, it is updated with recent technology architectures.

A Microsoft Project tutorial is included in this book to demonstrate the key project lifecycle concepts and some of the components in the Project Management Toolkit. This tutorial is not intended to be exhaustive. Microsoft Project is not reviewed in this book for functionality, but instead to serve as a physical demonstration of the management concepts covered in the book. Microsoft Project was selected as the tool to do this because of its market presence, ease of use, and substantial functionality. We have used it to manage projects with budgets in excess of

$10 million, resources exceeding $150 million, and with multiyear duration. On the flip side, we have also used it to manage small projects.

The authors have written this book with the hope that it will stimulate critical thinking and provide an opportunity to analyze business needs and objectives, assess risks and benefits, and understand the total life-cycle costs of a project before it is actually undertaken. Within this framework, this book demonstrates how typical problems associated with information technology projects—such as changing business requirements and specifications, cost overrun, projects behind schedule, and poor product quality—can be significantly minimized.

Organization of the Book

Organizing a book on project management can be done in a variety of ways. For example, chapters can be ordered according to a project manager's roles and responsibilities over some sort of project development lifecycle. Another approach would be to organize the chapters according to key management responsibilities and techniques without reference to a timeframe. Another possibility is to leverage a combination of these two formats. This latter hybrid approach is used in this book to allow project managers to focus on vital goals from start to finish on most projects by reading and applying chapters in the book, which are collected into a series of key blocks.

The approach to project management in this book is based on understanding the fundamental building blocks (shown in Figure P.1): executive mandate and justification, experiences, methodologies, team

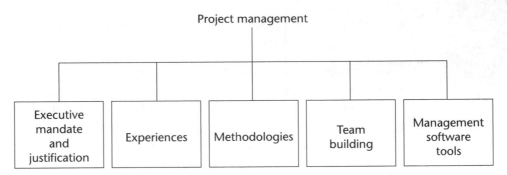

Figure P.1 Building blocks of project management.

building, and management software tools. These building blocks should not be viewed as a methodology in themselves, but rather as a checklist or toolkit that describes the broad areas that a project manager must address for a given project—although not necessarily in this order.

Chapter 1 describes the roles and responsibilities of the project manager in the context of the management pyramid in most organizations. Concepts such as team empowerment, project team structure, and project management offices (PMOs) are also examined. Chapter 4 examines project planning and scheduling concepts that are needed after a project is initiated. It reviews the impact of some basic project planning constraints, such as budget, time, and resources, on the planning activities.

The primary objective and the relevant chapters for each building block are described in the following list:

1. **Executive mandate and justification.** Receive executive approval to initiate a project and a mechanism to resolve obstacles and clashing priorities in the organization. Establish regular access to the executive sponsor.

   Chapter 2 examines project management concepts suitable for overall project definition, and Chapter 3 looks at project initiation and justification. The key roles, responsibilities, and contacts that a project manager must assume before a project begins are covered here. The chapter also examines project risk, control, and communication.

2. **Experiences.** Examine past project experiences to build a high-level project plan, risk analysis, status reporting requirements, and quality expectations. The project manager can draw on internal or external project experiences. This can be combined with the methodology block, defined next.

   Chapter 5 provides a definition of project failure and then describes key categories that are commonly responsible for this event. This chapter includes a lot of vital survival information for project managers, including how to identify projects that are going to fail. Chapter 6 offers a definition of a successful project and methods to achieve it. It enhances the project manager's toolkit by adding interpersonal skills, knowledge-based management, status reporting, standards, templates, and other practices and techniques. Case studies are included in both chapters.

3. **Methodologies.** Incorporate the organization's project methodology or framework to add significant detail to the project plan. Ensure the identification of key deliverables throughout the project plan. Use estimating tools or knowledge of available resources to draft a timeline. Use the methodology to identify roles and responsibilities for the project.

   Chapter 7 defines an iterative project development methodology (IPDM) that has been used successfully on many different types of projects in the past. It contains key features such as a strong deliverables focus, iterative development, strong user involvement, and highly flexible activities. It leverages techniques such as prototyping, proof of concepts, risk assessments, and extensive testing to ensure strong deliverable quality. Chapter 9 examines outsourcing as an alternative to staffing projects internally. Recent trends, such as Application Service Providers (ASPs) are reviewed.

4. **Team building.** Resources—such as team leader, architects, testers, and coders—should be allocated as soon as possible. A strategy to fill the remaining roles and responsibilities defined on the project plan should be defined and implemented. A strategy for building the team, communication approaches, mentoring/coaching approaches, and team-building exercises should be defined.

   Chapter 8 examines techniques for meeting a project's resourcing requirements. It examines common roles and responsibilities on a diverse base of projects.

5. **Management software tools.** Identification and implementation of tool sets for managing a project, including project management software, project estimating tools, presentation software, and document creation/management software.

   Chapters 10 through 12 use Microsoft Project to demonstrate physical applications of the concepts discussed in the book, including creating project plans, enhancements, project tracking and reporting, and customization.

The appendices provide examples of sample project plans, the management questionnaire, survey results, management forms, and a generic project lifecycle.

What's New in This Edition

Most of the chapters in this book have been revised with information that is more current and based on relatively recent project experiences. Reusable templates, checklists, and examples that demonstrate the concepts in the chapters are included to provide readers with a head start in designing their own management processes. The Microsoft Project tutorial chapters have also been replaced with examples built under the newest release of this popular tool. The appendices have also been reworked with substantially more reusable information for readers to leverage. In particular, the following changes are included in this edition of the book:

- Definition of a project management toolkit
- Web and Internet project management
- Increased case studies
- Improvements to the streamlined methodology
- Project templates
- Comparison of estimating and project management tools
- Expanded Microsoft Project 2000 examples
- Richer examples in the appendices
- Expanded bibliography
- Reissued project management survey

Project Management Survey

For this edition, we updated the project management survey questions and gathered responses from more than a hundred Information Systems managers. The survey covers a variety of management-oriented questions that provide empirical evidence to support key conclusions presented throughout this book. Some of the interesting discoveries that were made or confirmed through the survey include the following:

- Projects based on eBusiness solutions have a different set of success criteria—at least for the current time—than previous types of architectures. Many of these projects are evaluated on timely delivery and functional content. Success is measured in terms of market penetration instead of financial costs or profit. Until this returns to the traditional economical model, project managers must recognize when to shift their thinking on how to manage their resources on a given project.

☐ There is a strong requirement for usability and end-to-end testing on Web-based solutions. Similarly, stress and concurrent user testing is critical because it is difficult to accurately predict the number of hits against a Web site.

☐ Project development methodologies are being replaced with project development frameworks that support flexible approaches to a project. Projects should be structured to deliver something that is measurable and production usable every five to seven months in a project lifecycle.

☐ Responsibility for delivering projects is shared equally between information systems and business users. Many respondents feel that the business should retain overall project management in most initiatives that cross functional divisions.

☐ There is strong consensus among managers that common, quantifiable factors derail projects, such as bad planning, changing requirements, and poor communication.

What's on the Web Site?

The companion Web site contains project plans and management templates that readers can use directly or customize for their own projects. These include:

☐ **Project initiation.** This template bundle contains a project charter, estimate by components, project risk, streamlined quality plan, resource needs table, and role requirements across systems.

☐ **Project management.** This template bundle contains a milestone checklist (lifecycle), a data conversion project plan, a weekly status report, a monthly status report, a monthly timesheet, an issue and concern log, an issues list, an issues log, a planning checklist, and a status meeting agenda.

☐ **Change requests.** This template bundle contains a scope change and a project change request.

- □ **Testing.** This template bundle contains a testing variance, test scenario, and problem report.

- □ **Requirements.** This template bundle contains a requirements checklist and a requirements statement.

- □ **Architecture.** This template bundle contains architecture checklists.

- □ **Communication.** This template bundle contains a letter for wide distribution before implementing a project, an issue memo, and a project newsletter.

- □ **Signoffs.** This template bundle contains a project deliverable and a project acceptance form.

- □ **Costing.** This template bundle contains estimating project costs, a deliverables-based project cost report, a project cost report for resources, and calculating a budget.

- □ **Other.** This template bundle contains a resource evaluation, a short evaluation form, a project evaluation matrix, and a project history form.

Audience

This book is specifically aimed at project managers, systems developers, users, project leaders, executives who pay for the development and implementation of projects, computer software and hardware vendors, information technology planners, business and systems analysts, and university students. Readers new to project management should read the book sequentially, as the chapters build on one another. Experienced project managers may want to start out with chapters 5, 6, and 7 to get management suggestions they can leverage immediately. They should then proceed sequentially from the beginning of the book.

CHAPTER 1

The Role of a Project Manager

This chapter introduces the reader to general project management concepts, focusing on the characteristics, roles, and responsibilities of the hands-on project manager. Prerequisites for this effective style of managing projects include an end-to-end understanding of the underlying technology, processes, and business requirements related to a proposed solution. Project managers can leverage a basic toolkit that defines tools, methodologies, frameworks, standards, and experiences to meet these prerequisites. The reader will learn about the following topics:

- Management approaches
- Hands-on project management
- Management pyramid
- Management authority flows
- Management roles and responsibilities
- Project management office (PMO)
- Project manager's toolkit
- Project management styles

The Hands-on Project Manager: Returning to the Front Lines

This book focuses on managers who occupy the space at the base of the organizational management pyramid shown in Figure 1.1. These managers are directly responsible for the delivery of information technology (IT) projects from the start of the project lifecycle through final delivery and the ongoing operations implemented by the solution. These project managers have authority over project resources, project plans, and project deliverables. They are generally accountable to both the business clients and executive management. Most of their time is not spent on operational activities pertaining to existing systems, but rather on delivering new projects. The issues that confront project managers are very different from the ones confronting operational managers or others who are closer to the top of the management pyramid.

Traditionally, project managers have focused on such duties as time collection, team evaluations, and status reporting. This involved tracking the deliverables that were completed, but not necessarily having any input or direct knowledge of the details of each deliverable. Some project managers have increasingly adapted a more tactical or hands-on approach to project management that gets them directly involved in crafting the details of the solution they are managing. They also have increasingly aligned themselves with specific technology solutions (e.g., Internet-enabled solutions, Web hosting, or XML experience). While this narrows the types of environments that project managers can operate in and support, it also allows them to contribute more to the solution. Some of the benefits of the "hands-on" management approach include:

☐ The ability to act as a knowledgeable integrator between all the different resource groups contributing to the project

☐ The ability to comment on and evaluate the quality and contents of the deliverables that are produced by the project team(s)

☐ Higher confidence in deliverables that are reported to be complete

☐ The ability to jump in on the ground floor with a good knowledge of the details when problems begin to arise on a project

☐ The knowledge to act as an impartial referee in discussions between the business and the development teams

☐ The knowledge to present the project details outside the core team with an improved ability to overcome outside obstacles or objections

☐ The knowledge necessary to win the respect of team members

☐ The ability to know when you are not being given all the facts by anyone in the extended team

The term "hands-on" project manager is used in this book to distinguish a style of project management that provides better results than the alternate methods. Hands-on means daily involvement in a project, an understanding of the key issues, and the mandate to remove obstacles. The hands-on manager may delegate responsibility for key activities in a project to other managers, project leaders, architects, or analysts , but must stay closely involved in pulling all the pieces of the project together. The manager must continue to assume full responsibility for the ultimate implementation of the project.

The Management Pyramid

Management within an organization can be divided into many roles and responsibilities, as shown in Figure 1.1. To understand how the management pyramid works, let's briefly examine the levels above the project manager. Authority flows down from the top of the pyramid, beginning with the board of directors, shareholders, or owners of the company. The top level of the pyramid is concerned with issues such as stock prices, corporate expenditures, and profitability. The board generally empowers other officers of the company to control the corporate direction and operations.

The next level down in the pyramid is executive management. Executive management is concerned with acquisitions, corporate profitability, sales, stock prices, hostile takeovers, and corporate costs. Their involvement in IT projects tends to be restricted to receiving the information that an infrastructure is in place for a corporate initiative when it is needed. The CIO (chief information officer), the COO (chief operations officer), or the CTO (chief technology officer) are specifically involved in establishing a robust and reliable standard technical infrastructure across the organization. In practice, the infrastructure expands to include individual project technology requirements where they are different from the corporate standard.

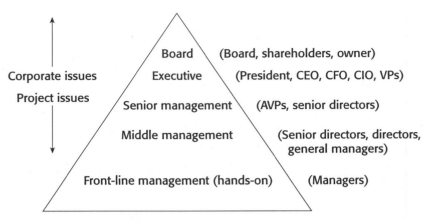

Figure 1.1   Management pyramid.

Senior management, the third level from the top of the pyramid, generally holds responsibility for a group of departments and projects. In many organizations, senior management sets direction, allocates a budget to a project, empowers a manager, brings in outside assistance (e.g., auditors), and chairs steering committee meetings. They also get involved in extending additional funding, removing impediments to a project, and, in some cases, terminating a project.

Although this group is affected by the success or failure of a project, the managers occupying these rungs of the management pyramid are not close enough to directly influence project results on a daily basis. Their presence at steering committee meetings gives them an intermittent opportunity to react to what is happening on a project and makes them accountable if they do not take appropriate action in response to the information they receive. It is important to recognize that lower levels of management generally provide this information and that many of the details of a project may be lost through filtration to the upper levels. The project management office (PMO), a structure that is discussed later in this chapter, offers a vehicle to reduce the level of information filtration that occurs at these levels.

The lower levels of the pyramid shown in Figure 1.1 consist of middle and front-line management. There can be a certain amount of overlap between these groups, since some directors and general managers become directly involved in project delivery. However, this is not the norm. In most cases, middle management is involved in attending steering committee meetings and providing guidance or resolving problems. Their responsibilities also span multiple projects, so although they are closer to projects than the management groups already discussed, and they do have some direct influence on projects, they are still too far away to know precise details (e.g., few senior directors will need to know what version of the C++ language is being used on a project).

Front-line (or hands-on) management, which includes information technology (IT) project managers, is involved directly in the delivery of projects. Project managers are empowered to control and deliver a project for an organization—and they are fully accountable for its success or failure. We focus on this level of management throughout this book. Project managers can be drawn from different parts of the organization to lead a project, including the business, operations, and technology areas.

There is a certain amount of confusion about the difference between an operational manager and a project manager in terms of their responsibilities. Operational managers' chief mandate is to support operational, "support-the-business" types of systems. Their organization consists of help desk resources, operations staff, users, and some technical resources for infrastructure support. Operational managers are sometimes seconded to act as project managers on specific projects. However, it is difficult for an operational manager to do double-duty as a project manager, although this happens quite frequently to the detriment of projects. In cases where operational managers split their time between a project and their operational duties, it generally appears that most of their time gets spent on the operational demands that have an immediate and visible impact on the organization. Unless a project is small, it is preferable to assign a full-time project manager or project leader to head the project initiative.

Flow of Management Authority

Project management authority and influence flows in several directions within an organization. As shown in Figure 1.2, project managers occupy a middle ground that allows them to access these flows in order to deliver their projects—hopefully successfully. They manage their own project teams, technology, and other resources, while being managed by other factors (e.g., executive management) in the organization. They can also use their key, central position on a project(s) to influence demands made by business clients and to negate competition raised by other projects. For example, if a project is heading towards disaster, a project manager can influence business users to compromise by reducing expected functionality, extending a deadline, or providing additional resources as potential ways to turn things around.

Project managers receive a mandate from higher levels of management to deliver one or more projects successfully. In order to achieve this, they are empowered with a budget and broad authority to organize and deliver the project. Some managers hold total control over a budget, while others have access to a budget but no flexibility in how it is spent. Managers in the latter group generally do not feel as strong or in control of their destinies as those positioned in the former. Project managers are also responsible for the direct management of staff resources such as developers, analysts, architects, designers, users, and project leaders. Managers can often purchase and implement technology such as computer platforms, network devices, and software packages. They also control the use of physical resources such as office space, telephones, and other miscellaneous items.

Figure 1.2 Flow of management authority.

In addition to the controls placed on them by executive management, project managers are managed from several other sources. External constraints, such as laws and regulations, limit what the manager can do within a project. For example, employment laws in some places limit how many hours an employee can be made to work and establish guidelines for physical working conditions. Business clients, also called users, typically determine the business requirements and, consequently, the details of a project solution. Other policies in the organization place various constraints on a manager. One of these is the need to maintain consistent technology or software standards across an organization. Another constraint on the manager is the frequent competition between projects for relevant but limited resources within a company.

From the middle ground that project managers occupy in the management pyramid, they have significant influence over their business clients and the executive management of the company. In the former case, managers are expected to work cooperatively with their business clients to fulfill a requirement identified by someone in higher management. In practical terms, the manager must build a relationship that allows the business clients to contribute their relevant expertise to the project. Managers sometimes need to strongly negotiate with clients in establishing communication methods with the project team. This should be done with tact (see chapter 6) so that the working relationships are left intact. In order to deliver a project successfully, managers must usually manage their own bosses.

Managers also have a great deal of influence over executive management through a regular reporting process and in steering committee meetings. Project managers serve as the most common pipeline through which information flows from a project upwards into management pyramid's upper layers. Through this information, executive management can be influenced to increase budgets, allocate additional resources, shift deadlines, change standards, and remove obstacles.

Managers can also influence other projects within the company, either through executive management or through their personal contacts with other managers. The likelihood of success depends on the importance of their project and their ability to persuade others to their own way of thinking.

A Hands-on Project Manager's Roles and Responsibilities

Managers are fully responsible for the success or failure of an IT project. If the project succeeds, the manager should willingly share credit for its success with other members of the project team. This will help to build a win-win relationship that will be useful on future projects. Figure 1.3 shows the multiple roles and multiple responsibilities that the typical manager holds on a project. These are listed in order of decreasing importance (e.g., vision is the most important). It can be argued that managers are responsible for assuming any role that is required to make a project a success. Project success is defined in chapters 5 and 6. This makes the manager the person on the project team that is most capable of affecting the outcome of the project.

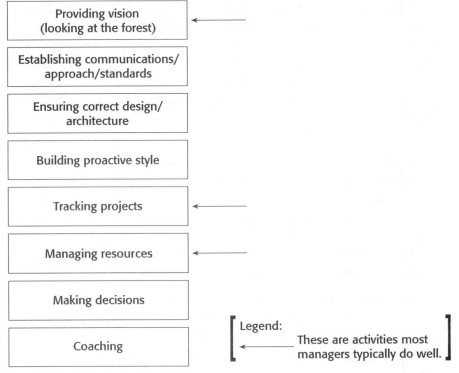

Figure 1.3   A manager's responsibilities.

The responsibilities identified in Figure 1.3 are described in further detail in this section. Some of these responsibilities are of greater importance than others on a given project. However, it is not unusual for some managers to focus on what they do well and neglect other areas, putting the delivery of some projects at risk.

Providing Vision

The most important role a manager can play on a project is that of visionary. A manager must have an instinctive understanding of the importance of a project to the organization. This vision must remain consistent for the duration of the project, and it must be shared with others in the company—especially the project team.

A manager must also have a global vision of the project. Typical projects are like living organisms that can contain thousands or millions of tiny, dynamic details, each of which requires anywhere from an hour to years of person-days of effort for completion. The manager is in a position to view these details in context, to ensure that each piece fits into the master puzzle called the project, and to make appropriate adjustments to protect the integrity of the vision.

Establishing a Communication Strategy

Communication on a project involves the exchange of information, ideas, and status between the core and extended project teams. The core team includes the project manager, project resources dedicated to the project, and resources seconded to the project (e.g., dedicated users). The extended project team involves any other resources that have an interest in the project. This includes other groups contributing deliverables to the project (e.g., vendors), stakeholders, executives, business users, and other project teams that are affected by the results. Communication between all of these groups can be compromised by numerous factors, as follows:

☐ **Geography.** Resources may be located in different offices, separated by great distances. Different time zones can also complicate communication strategies.

☐ **Personalities.** Some resources do not want to share information with others on the project. Some resources feel they are too busy to communicate with others.

☐ **Information complexity.** It is not always clear how to distill a lot of information into a documented subset.

☐ **Accessibility.** In many cases, information is available, but not accessible to everyone. Its existence may not be known by everyone either.

Despite these factors, the project manager must ensure that relevant groups communicate appropriate information to each other in a timely manner. This involves establishing guidelines for what to communicate (e.g., meeting minutes, status), how to document it (standards), how to distribute it (email, Web site, central repository), and timing (e.g., some weekly, some daily, some monthly).

Managers must also ensure that information is shared freely between a broad base of resources involved in the project. It is not unusual for information to be guarded and withheld on projects. This can lead to counterproductive behavior that is justified by some method or other that can often be overruled by management. Proven techniques for free information exchange on projects are discussed in chapter 4.

Establishing Project Approaches and Standards

A manager is responsible for defining an acceptable approach and expectations for a given project. The approach may be driven by the organization, based on personal experience, or be an acceptable combination of the two. After determining an approach for the project, the manager must ensure that it is communicated to the project team, interpreted accurately, and then followed correctly. The information to be communicated can include regular status meeting times, available training programs, billing methods, core working hours, and so on.

Project standards effectively implement the approach determined by the project manager. These standards should be communicated at the same time as the project approach is rolled out to the team. Standards should be defined for the items shown in the following list:

☐ **Status meetings.** This includes the time, location, expectations, and attendees at each status meeting. It also includes methods for participating in the meeting, such as a common teleconference number that absent attendees can use to dial into the meeting.

☐ **Status reports.** This includes who should submit a report, the format of the report, and the distribution schedule.

☐ **Issue lists and logs.** This includes a format and method for reporting issues and concerns. It also includes a method of categorizing and tracking the lists.

☐ **Documentation standards.** This includes formats and content for other project documentation based on the lifecycle. This can include business requirements, architecture, designs, component specifications, and test plans.

☐ **Project schedules.** This includes the format and deliverables to be tracked by individual team leaders on the project.

☐ **Other.** This includes such things as personal plans for team members and celebration ideas.

Other standards that the project manager should consider introducing at this stage include the following:

☐ The methods used for writing programming code, naming standards, testing, issue tracking, reporting, and source control

☐ Software packages (e.g., WordPerfect for documentation, Microsoft Project for project management, Lotus for spreadsheets, and Microsoft Access for quick database retrieval. This should not be confused with the technology infrastructure or standards that are established during the technical design phase)

☐ Identification of documentation repositories (e.g., paper, Web-based, file-based)

Ensuring Correct Architecture/Design

Core architecture is a fundamental building block of any application, and must be sound for anything meaningful to be developed. Soundly designed architecture wins points in an organization and can buy goodwill when it is needed if things start going wrong. Managers may not necessarily have the skills to design an architecture for a business solution, but they are responsible for ensuring that it gets done properly. This is not as easy as it sounds. On many projects, one of two things happens: the application is so complex that no one wants to tackle the design work or everyone on the team wants to take credit for completing the design work.

The first event occurs because there are usually so many things happening on a project that most people naturally prefer to spend their time doing the easy things first. Sometimes, as long as his or her staff is busy, a manager does not insist that the more difficult activities be completed. This situation could go on for years.

The second situation occurs when those who are clearly unqualified to do the work compete to assume responsibilities for which they are unprepared. These persons can hinder qualified individuals from doing the real work. The potential for more insidious repercussions also exists. A project can degenerate because of all sorts of internal problems (see chapter 5).

Managers should not tolerate either of these two situations, which have derailed many straightforward projects. Instead, they should hire capable, experienced professionals (staff or consultants) to do this extremely important work correctly. Managers should also rely on skills transfer to train staff who have the ability, but lack the experience, to do the kind of work needed to build a sound architectural infrastructure. It is important to be clear and direct with the design team regarding who is really leading the effort and who is following under these circumstances.

Managers should invest the time to understand and approve the design and architecture of a project solution. This should not be a quick review of a design document, but should be a detailed review of the system design and architecture with the design team. For mission-critical applications, the architecture should be validated with a proof-of-concept initiative that examines capacity, response time, and core design. Questions should be asked during the review process to ensure that the manager can track the remainder of the project against this design.

Building a Proactive Management Style

Proactive resolution occurs when managers anticipate and resolve problems before they actually happen. Failure to do this can place managers in a position where they have to become reactive instead, so that they are continually trying to catch up. The end result is that the project is never under control.

Some managers succeed in building a proactive style of management. They are the ones who move from one successful project to the next. They are also the managers parachuted into problematic projects, which they are usually able to turn around and deliver successfully.

Proactive managers are easy to identify at meetings. They are the ones who ask questions that lead the project team toward actual deliverables (e.g., producing the measurable objectives of a project). They use their experience, judgment, and intelligence to stay a few steps ahead of the project team. While their staff is working on a problem, the proactive manager ensures that resolution occurs, avoids procrastination, and plans the next few steps in detail. Proactive managers have an uncanny knack for staying on top of important issues. They also fit all the pieces of the project together and retain a global view. Proactive managers tend to retain the respect and esteem of their team and ultimately encourage others to be proactive.

Planning and Tracking Projects

Planning involves a recurring set of activities that are not finished until the entire system development lifecycle for the project is finished. Poor planning can have insidious results that are not readily visible until the end of a project. These results may include failure to implement a system, satisfy users, or complete a deliverable satisfactorily. Poor planning can be recognized by a lack of precise details in the project plan as well as by the absence of key users or the sign-off of key deliverables. Another key indicator of poor planning is that deliverables are expected to be produced too close together. For example, if the project plan is constructed to produce all deliverables near the end of the lifecycle, chances are that there will be an insufficient opportunity to correct mistakes and incorporate the improvements that are inevitably requested by the business community. Another sure sign of bad planning is a lack of consultation with key users, stakeholders, and experts on a regular basis throughout the project lifecycle.

Project tracking can become an administrative management role in which a manager compares estimates of the time required to complete project activities to the actual time spent by project team members. Project tracking should be a value-added activity that resolves conflicts and problems. There is a risk, however, that it can become a thankless job involving reading numbers off a timesheet and entering them into a spreadsheet or a project management tool.

Managers tend to spend a great deal of time in this role. They should ensure that they are receiving value for their efforts. Project tracking should be used to monitor the progress of a project at regular intervals, allowing enough time for adjustment and correction. It should not be used simply as a procedure, since this adds no value to the bottom line of a project.

Managing Resources

Managers must supervise all types of resources (e.g., office space), with an emphasis on human resources. Managers are responsible for hiring, firing, promoting, and training their staff. Since individuals who tend to gravitate toward management enjoy working with people in some capacity, managers tend to spend a great deal of time in this role as well. The success of the project manager is entirely dependent on other resources in the organization. Project managers must have solid interpersonal skills to do their jobs effectively.

Some of the decisions that project managers are called on to make are:

☐ Should Joe be hired?

☐ Should Bob be counseled out?

☐ Who is right or wrong in a conflict of opinion?

☐ Can Jorge take Friday off?

☐ Should another $5,000 be spent upgrading PC software?

☐ Should Amanda be promoted?

☐ Should Tony be given a raise?

☐ How should Beth's career aspirations be satisfied within the context of a project?

☐ Who should work overtime to improve the chances for the project's success?

☐ What training is needed on the project?

☐ Do we have enough testers?

    ☐ Will letting some of the developers work from home improve their efficiency?

    ☐ How do we celebrate a success?

Coaching and Mentoring Resources

A manager can also serve as a mentor or coach to keep team members happy, productive, and successful. This may be a value-added activity for the current project, since contented team members tend to stay around longer and work more productively. Managers should be careful to strike a balance between resource improvement and deliverable production to ensure that this role does not get in the way of completing the project successfully.

Managers can also delegate coaching and mentoring responsibilities to other members of the project team. It is useful to establish a process upfront so that both mentors and those team members being mentored can benefit from these roles. The manager should ensure that every team resource establishes project and career goals up front.

Matrix of Roles/Responsibilities

Table 1.1 contrasts the manager's roles and responsibilities with how well they are generally performed on various projects, based on information gathered on our management survey. The Role/Responsibility column identifies a cross-section of areas on which project managers should focus their day-to-day activities. The Attempted column identifies how well they fare on most projects, based on the results of our management survey. The Successfully Completed column identifies their perceived level of success. The key values from best to worst are: Yes, Not always, Sometimes, Never.

Based on the information in this table, managers should concentrate on developing skills in at least the following areas: communications, approaches, and standards; proactive resolution; decision making; and coaching. This can be done using the following techniques:

    ☐ Reading management books and journals

    ☐ Receiving constructive criticism from knowledgeable sources (e.g., colleagues, mentors)

Table 1.1 The Manager's Roles and Responsibilities

ROLE/RESPONSIBILITY	ATTEMPTED	SUCCESSFULLY COMPLETED
1. Providing vision (looking at the forest)	Yes	Sometimes
2. Establishing communications	Not always	Not always
3. Establishing standards	Not always	Not always
4. Ensuring correct design/architecture	Yes	Sometimes
5. Building a proactive management style	Yes	Not always
6. Tracking projects	Yes	Usually
7. Managing resources	Yes	Usually
8. Making decisions	Yes	Not always
9. Coaching	Not always	Not always
10. Resolving obstacles	Not always	Not always
11. Ensuring business buy-in	Not always	Not always

- ☐ Attending management seminars
- ☐ Discussions with colleagues
- ☐ Personal reflection and goal setting
- ☐ Attending courses at universities and colleges

Empowering Teams

A project manager is arguably the most vital person on a team by virtue of his or her authority and responsibility for delivering the project successfully; conversely, the other members of the project team are vital to the manager. A project manager cannot deliver any sizable project without the efforts and dedication of talented team members. A symbiotic relationship between these groups clearly exists and must be nurtured.

The traditional hierarchical approach to project management is being replaced by another approach, known as team empowerment. Just as project managers are empowered by their superiors to deliver a project, project managers empower various members of their project team to deliver parts of a project. Figure 1.4 shows that in return for being empowered, members of a project team must return meaningful information to the project manager. If this information is not forthcoming, project managers themselves must get involved and become more proactive in getting things done. Clearly, the level of empowerment will change with the success or lack thereof achieved by the project team. At no time should a project manager simply empower (or delegate) and forget to monitor.

Managers must deal with people in the real world. Some people take well to being empowered, others do not. It is the manager's responsibility to ensure that empowerment is used effectively so as not to threaten the success of the project. Resources that do not perform well when empowered to do too much must be managed more closely. One approach is to limit the degree to which they are empowered, perhaps with a limit at the task level, and then increase this limit over time and with success.

Some managers are ineffective because they refuse to empower their staff, choosing instead to stay directly involved in even the smallest details of a process. These managers find themselves chronically short of time and unable to meet deadlines. They also find that their most talented employees are constantly moving on to other opportunities in search of better working conditions and an opportunity to grow professionally. At the other extreme, some managers never get a project under control because they empower ineffective staff. They then compound the error by not correcting their earlier lack of judgment.

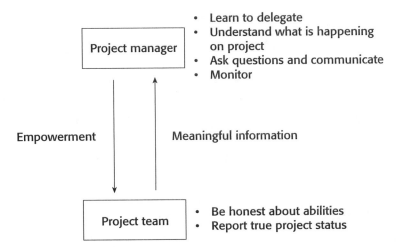

Figure 1.4   Team empowerment.

Structure of Project Teams

The composition of project teams is naturally diverse. Project managers generally have a great deal of control over the combined skill sets of their teams. They should ensure that there is a broad mix of skills and enough overlap to buffer staff turnover. Another consideration is striking a balance between leaders and workers. There will always be the need for short-term skills or expertise. This can be obtained by training current staff or bringing in contract or consulting personnel for the duration. Project managers also have the option of tapping into outsourcing firms or contracting out components of a project, as discussed in chapter 9.

Figure 1.5 shows a recommended generic composition for a project team. The project manager can draw on short-term expertise through architects, consultants, and experts. Consultants can be those with special short-term skills, such as facilitators, auditors, data modelers, and network specialists. Many of these skills are available in full-time staff; however, if there is a spike in demand for resources or specific expertise, consultants can be used on an as-needed basis. Some management responsibility can be delegated to project leaders or other team members with the "senior" prefix in their job titles—for example, senior systems analyst or senior business analyst. Business and technical requirements are supported by business/technical analysts. Developers

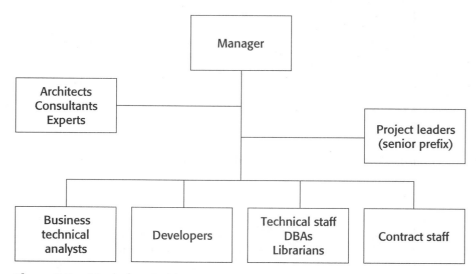

Figure 1.5   A typical project team.

are required for a range of software products (e.g., database, programming, network software, operating systems) that are used on the project. Projects also require those with specialized roles such as database administrators (DBAs) for database control, network administrators for backup/recovery and security, and librarians for standards. Contract staff can provide any skills that are in short supply. They offer the advantage of being temporary expense items that will automatically disappear at the end of the project. These roles are discussed further in chapter 8.

Project Management Office (PMO)

A project management office (PMO) is an independent structure that coordinates multiple projects within an organization. It is usually operated by one or more dedicated resources that report to the executive level within a company. At least one of the PMO resources is generally at a senior manager level. PMO responsibilities include collecting status information from project managers and providing them with information from the collective project teams. PMOs are also involved in tracking and resolving major issues between projects that are at a high enough level to warrant the attention of the executive level. Other responsibilities include leveling resources, organizing meetings, coordinating funding, and accounts payable.

PMO structures have an inherent operational overhead and have the potential to get out of control and end up adding significant overhead to an organization. They can vary in size quite dramatically. Organizations that have lots of distributed projects require larger PMOs—measured in operating budget and resources—than organizations with a few local projects. Establishing a PMO can be a challenging proposition. Finding a qualified senior resource with the right temperament to run a potentially politicized PMO usually involves some reshuffling of internal resource responsibilities. Newly established PMOs must also gather and organize a large amount of information to get started. When the PMO begins to get involved in the affairs of individual projects, there is a widespread belief that the PMO is imposing their authority on the project's management and duplicating administration costs.

It always takes time for a PMO to prove its value to an organization. Their support can prove to be critical on any project than is dependent on resources or areas outside the direct control of the project team. A streamlined PMO that scales with the number and complexity of projects is a proven approach for implementing a PMO from scratch. If a PMO exists, project managers should insist on having regular involvement with and access to it. Here are some guidelines for setting up a streamlined PMO:

☐ PMO meetings must be attended by at least one project sponsor to demonstrate executive-level commitment to the other attendees.

☐ PMOs should meet formally at least once a month. It is not useful to have the meetings too frequently, because this is viewed as administrative overhead by the project teams.

☐ Issues should be regularly tracked at the PMO level. Status reports and issues should be sent to the PMO on a regular basis—perhaps weekly.

☐ The PMO should sponsor regular risk reviews of projects within its mandate.

☐ The PMO should have its own organization. It should be headed by a senior resource within the organization and one who has widespread respect. A few assistants should also be in the PMO to ensure that meetings are set up, status reports are collected, and issues are tracked and resolved.

Project Manager's Toolkit

The manager's toolkit consists of a set of tools to plan the project, track activities, report status, and share other information with the organization. These tools, combined with processes, techniques and best practices, are required to get the management job done. Tools are used at all levels of the project development lifecycle. Some of the major project management tools that you should consider using are discussed in this section.

Project Planning and Tracking Tools

Project management software that supports a Gantt chart, resource allocation at the task level, and various reporting views should be adopted by the organization as a standard and should be used by the project manager to build the project plan. It may be useful to have a high-level major project plan with links to subplans that cover limited portions of an initiative. Subplans can also be built for different streams within the project, including the architecture, management, testing, and quality. It is a good idea to have access to a standard project management tool in an organization to allow project plans from different projects to be integrated.

Estimating Tools

Estimating tools are commonly closely related to development methodologies. They use best practices, metrics, and an experience base to estimate task durations according to a variety of project criteria (e.g., experience of the development team, complexity of the project, length of the project). This allows project managers to build realistic work estimates for the first draft of the project plan. Some estimating tools are integrated with project planning tools.

Methodologies

Development methodologies sometimes get a bad reputation because they are misused or overused. A comprehensive methodology that contains sample project plan templates, sample deliverables, and descriptions of how to conduct tasks offers an invaluable quick-start to the planning process. Good methodologies are commonly available in the marketplace and should be sought out and implemented as a corporate standard. Some sources to search include the knowledge accompanying project tools, the Internet, and consulting firms. Choosing a suitable methodology requires a selection process similar to the one described in chapter 10 for selecting a project management tool. Project managers should become intimate with at least one project development methodology.

Frameworks

Frameworks are prebuilt industry- or technology-specific solutions that offer several advantages, namely: reusable code, a quick start to development, and reduced development risk. The project manager should ensure that frameworks are evaluated against criteria that include the popularity of the project, project success stories, costs, vendor commitments, and specific benefits available in the context of the project.

Word-Processing Tools

Integrated word-processing tools are needed to capture project documentation, report project status, and communicate information to the rest of the project team. The project deliverables will also be documented using these tools. The tools should be consistent with the standard word-processing software that is used by the rest of the organization.

Spreadsheet

An integrated spreadsheet can be used to track such items as the project budget, team vacations, and project risks. The spreadsheet should be compatible with the word-processing software so that activities and descriptions can be copied from one source to another using a clipboard or an export/import feature.

Presentation Software

Project managers are involved in many presentations to the team, other project teams, project sponsors, and the steering committee. Presentation software should support a variety of graphical formats and slide views.

Document Repositories

All project documentation should be stored in a document repository to provide access to the distributed members of the organization. Working files can be protected by system or manual security until they are ready for viewing by a wider audience. These repositories can be positioned on the Web, on LANs, or in other locations.

Deliverable Templates

Reusable templates of deliverables provide a head start for the project team and the manager by allowing them to see a sample of the final products to be developed. It is useful to have templates for such things as: the project plan, status reports, issue items, issue logs, team memos, business requirements, system requirements, and architectures. Some examples are contained in Appendix E.

Best Practices

A central database containing the best practices of similar projects is useful to browse in order to learn important lessons and risks. It is useful to actively add deliverables from completed projects to the database on an ongoing basis. Best practices can also be reflected in the standard project development methodology used in an organization.

Project Management Style

A great deal has been written about management styles and the types of responses they elicit from team members. IT professionals, as a group, are not shy about stating their expectations, and are willing to leave in search of greener pastures if they are not treated professionally. This is certainly not beneficial to the success of a project. Managers must examine their own styles to ensure that they are nurturing their project teams. The following management styles are commonly used by managers on IT projects. You may want to consider the impact of the different styles and then develop a hybrid solution that is appropriate to your specific environment.

Visionary

Visionaries think long-term and focus on bleeding-edge solutions. They typically find elegant, if impractical, solutions to business problems. An isolated visionary often lacks the specific skills to successfully implement a solution. A visionary generally needs the support of a strong and practical project leader or architect to be effective in the context of a project that needs to be delivered. With the proper balance of other styles or additional resources, the visionary can add value to the infrastructure of a project.

Politician

The politician remains unscathed, no matter how difficult an assignment is, no matter how negative the final results. This style does not view a specific project as an end, only as a place to stop on the way to something greater. Every resource and system is perceived to be a tool for the improvement of the project manager. The advantage of this style is that it allows a project manager to succeed in diverse environments and may allow a manager to draw value from different individuals through political means. The weakness with this style is that it may not result in any meaningful project deliverables. The project manager may spend an inordinate amount of time playing politics. At some point, this technique begins to adversely affect project teams, who tire of the politics or become adept players themselves.

Sweatshop Owner

This style views IT professionals as commodities to be exploited down to the very last penny and minute. Every line of code is valued as a portion of billable time. The idea is that local IT professionals are fortunate to have jobs—after all, with the Internet, wide area networks, and even floppy disks, there are thousands of offshore professionals waiting to do the job for a fraction of the cost. The strength of this approach is that it can produce results in the short term with certain types of human personalities.

The weakness of this management style is that talented IT professionals are not easy to find—and are no longer simply commodities to replace at will. In fact, the best IT resources have been in high demand for decades and are currently able to have their demands and expectations met by dozens of other suitors. The sweatshop approach encourages the best resources to leave an organization or to burn out. The ultimate cost to the organization is difficult to measure in advance, but will be harsh when it is felt in the end.

Motivator or Teacher

This style is like a sports coach, therapist, and expert all rolled into one. The motivator works with every member of the team and inspires them to be their best. The advantage of this approach is the improvement of the development team as individuals and their potential loyalty. The weakness is that it requires a great deal of energy and may, at times, affect the project schedule.

Dictator or Emperor

This style views the development team as part of a personal empire. The bigger the hierarchical pyramid the better. The team is there to serve the ruler. The manager rewards those who play and punishes those who do not. There appears to be few strengths offered by this style, but a great number of weaknesses. The setup is designed to elevate the ruler, while, perhaps, providing the organization with only the minimal value necessary to maintain support for the ruler.

Negotiator

The negotiator works well with different personality types. This manager identifies the interests of all parties relevant to the project and finds the middle ground in disputes. The strength of this approach is its ability to reconcile divided camps. The weakness with this approach is that it can lead to politics, which can be severely detrimental to a project's success.

Follower

This style can also be described as a collaborator. The follower typically identifies the perceived source of power, be it an executive or a client sponsor, and sets out to please him or her. The strength of this approach is that it provides a clear acceptance procedure. The weakness is that it can lead to less than ideal solutions, if the source of power was misidentified or incapable in the first place.

Leader

Leading is what successful managing is all about. The leader inspires the core project team and the extended project team. Whenever anyone has doubts, they should only have to look at the leader to be inspired. The leader understands the project requirements, the importance to the organization, and the issues involved. He or she should be able to articulate a vision, dependencies, and the role of the project in the larger picture of the organization and the profession. The leader's presence eliminates conflict between team members and brings clarity to the project.

The project manager who can learn to use more than one style at a time, and know which one to apply in a given situation, will be more effective as a manager.

Summary

Project managers have traditionally been responsible for what can be described as operational activities, including filling out time reports; tracking project budgets; hiring, firing, and promoting resources; filing status reports; hosting team meetings; rewarding teams; and ensuring that project documentation is constructed and shared. These collective activities, of course, must continue to be completed by project managers. Although productivity tools can be helpful in minimizing the time commitment required to fulfill these responsibilities, the reality is that a manager's operational responsibilities can become so time-consuming that the manager cannot address the other areas in the toolkit. The first items to be ignored by busy project managers are often "planning" or "leadership" activities. Furthermore, time-related stress can result in adopting poor management styles. The manager must be willing to delegate some management responsibilities to other members of the team. This would ideally include the more routine responsibilities, such as status reporting, timesheet collection, and analysis. Other operational responsibilities include the following: defining the productivity expectations for the project team, defining career paths, defining quality expectations, defining working conditions (e.g., flextime, equipment ergonomics, dress code), and celebrating and recognizing project successes.

This chapter also focused on the roles that managers play within the management pyramid and within the general organization of a company. A distinction was made between front-line functional project managers and other types of managers. It was discovered that the former were empowered with budgets and authority for the singular purpose of successfully completing projects. Those above the base of the management pyramid are thought to be too far removed from the everyday details of a project to remain as effective as the project manager in influencing projects.

This chapter defined projects as living organisms with many details that must be integrated and monitored. In this context, the project manager is deemed to be the most important person on a project team because of his or her authority and close proximity to the project. Project managers must enter into a symbiotic relationship with their staff in order to successfully deliver IT projects.

Project managers have a broad range of roles and responsibilities on a project. These include providing vision; establishing communications, approaches, and standards; ensuring the correct design and architecture; building a proactive style; tracking projects; managing resources; making decisions; and coaching. Other roles and responsibilities can be added to this list as the need arises. Essentially, the project manager is responsible for the successful delivery of a project and will consequently assume the roles that are necessary to ensure that this occurs. A project management toolkit was also defined in this chapter to assist managers. This toolkit includes such items as project management tools, methodologies, frameworks, and best practices. Project managers can work through this list and ensure that they are properly equipped to manage projects.

This chapter examined an approach for increasing the support received from project teams on an engagement. Empowered teams, where managers delegate their authority to key individuals with the provision that they are provided with information, were presented as an alternative to the hierarchical organization. The information received allows project managers to react to events on a project and still remain "hands-on."

CHAPTER 2

Project Management Concepts

This chapter provides an overview of basic project management concepts and applications. It covers commonly used project management terminology, the relationships between these terms, and their significance in undertaking and completing projects. Although project management concepts and methodologies can be applied to any type of project, this chapter emphasizes information technology projects in a business environment. This chapter also focuses on developing an understanding of the project management process by describing how strategic and tactical planning processes can be used to build a portfolio of projects based on business needs. It goes on to describe project fundamentals such as project definition, an overview of the activities and tasks of a project and the relationship between them, and the different types of projects that can be undertaken by consumers or businesses to achieve their objectives. In this chapter a reader will learn about:

- Project management concepts
- The project management process
- Project fundamentals
- Project definition
- Project stakeholders

- Project methodology
- The strategic planning process
- Tactical and operational plans

Project Conceptualization

Many of us have engaged in initiating and completing projects several times in a typical year. We have sometimes wondered about some of the following questions: How did this project get executive support? Why is this project being initiated, instead of the eleven others in the strategic plan? What kind of information is needed about the project to get started? What resources are required to complete the project? What is the duration of the project? What are the likely outcomes of the project? How is this project different from other projects? Is it related to other projects?

Projects are typically initiated because certain activities need to be undertaken for any number of reasons, including technology evolution, business changes, or legislative changes. For example, an IT project can be undertaken because a new software version needs to be acquired, or a new wireless system is required to help the mobile user, or a new Web-based order management system is required.

The IT industry continues to evolve, delivering newer products and solutions at a lower cost and with improved performance. With every new hardware or software product, there is usually a project team of developers, engineers, and marketers who are committed to providing improved functionality and who are also responsible for successfully bringing these products to the marketplace. These rapid changes in the industry are the result of a number of factors, as depicted in Figure 2.1.

These developments are requiring larger investments, from both the consumer and business communities, to capitalize on the benefits of newer technology and to achieve improved productivity. Projects are typically undertaken to translate these investments in computer technology into the desired objectives. These projects translate the business and investment opportunities into operational items and provide tangible and intangible benefits to the organization. A project can not only have a significant impact on a given business process, but may also have

Time

Potential of realizing value-added solutions through the use of computer technology

Computers becoming more pervasive in society—use of computers in everyday living such as kitchen appliances, watches, home security systems, and automobiles

Rapid obsolescence of hardware and software

Push by computer vendors to offer nonproprietary products with enhanced functionality at a lower cost

Increasing sophistication of end-users and expectations from the computer industry

Pressures on business to stay competitive and improve their profitability

Figure 2.1   Evolution of the computer industry.

a dramatic impact on the operation of the organization. For instance, an electronic commerce project can fundamentally change the old business model from providing a specific service, such as processing a customer order, to managing the overall customer relationship. It is important that the manager recognize that the project effectively utilizes information technology to achieve cost-effective results within the framework of servicing and enhancing the customer relationship.

Like any business investment, resources committed to a project should undergo scrutiny to ensure that there are benefits derived from them. An organization should address some of the issues concerning project initiation by evaluating how this project would help to achieve business goals.

Here are some typical questions about project initiation and the ultimate results to be achieved by the project:

☐ Who is paying for the project and what is the rationale for supporting it?

☐ What specific objectives are being addressed by this project?

☐ How will the project be monitored and reported so that there are virtually no surprises during the project development lifecycle?

☐ What management tools are required so that the expected benefits will be realized?

☐ What management skills are necessary to complete projects on time and within budget?

☐ What essential attributes are required from the project team members to ensure that they are working together toward a common goal?

☐ What are the risks of project failure?

☐ Were these project risks addressed with the client?

☐ Will the project have the right combination of technology and human resources to be completed successfully?

☐ What mechanisms will be in place to ensure that project requirements are understood, communicated, and accepted by the client?

☐ Have project cancellation points been identified that might result from changes in business objectives or direction?

The preceding list offers some typical questions that will be addressed throughout the book. One of the key reasons why projects do not achieve their desired objectives is the lack of attention to basic management principles by the project team. The basic management techniques (planning, organizing, implementing, and monitoring) must be understood by the project team, and these techniques should be practiced as an integral part of delivering the project objectives.

Project Definition

In a broad context, a project can be defined as a unit of work. This unit has clearly defined objectives, scope, expectations of results, and deliverables. To produce the deliverables, a project typically involves a project plan, project tasks, responsibilities necessary to achieve the tasks, resources to complete the tasks, and timeframes to complete them. A number of related tasks or a group of activities constitutes a project. A project is a way of organizing related components—a set of tasks, rules, practices, and processes—in order to achieve a defined objective. Projects are not ongoing—they have start and end dates for accomplishing the objectives set out by the project sponsor.

Project management deals with the process of managing the change created by a project. The project management function deals with the process of managing people and expectations within a project. It also

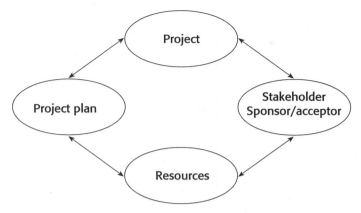

Figure 2.2 Project attributes.

means that the stakeholders and the project team want the new project and have a vested interest in ensuring its success. Figure 2.2 depicts the key project attributes.

A project can be applied to any business function of an organization—manufacturing, purchasing, marketing, sales, and so on. In each of these areas, there is an opportunity to benefit from initiating projects so that specific related tasks can be completed. Each project involves a project sponsor who has requested that the project be initiated and a project manager, who has the responsibility to ensure that tasks are completed and delivered to the project sponsor. The relationship between the project and the sponsor is depicted in Figure 2.3.

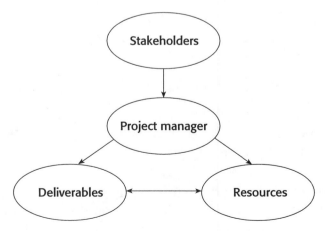

Figure 2.3 Relationship between a project and a sponsor.

Projects can be applied to various facets of business and family life. For instance, let us examine a project to purchase a new automobile for the Smith family. Let us assume that Mrs. Smith is the client because she needs the new automobile to replace the current seven-year-old car. She has asked Mr. Smith to be responsible for a project to acquire a new automobile. She has also specified the following parameters to help Mr. Smith to ensure that the project meets its objectives:

☐ **Project Objective.** Acquire a new and reliable automobile. (This is the reason for initiating a project.)

☐ **Project Scope.** The automobile should be new and must not be a first-time model; that is, it must have a proven track record covering a minimum of three years. (The project scope imposes constraints within which the project will operate.)

☐ **Project Sponsor.** This is Mrs. Smith. (The project sponsor has an ultimate stake in the outcome of the project and usually provides resources to complete the project.)

☐ **Project Costs.** Not to exceed $28,000, inclusive of all taxes and shipping. (Project costs are part of the resources required to complete the project. Cost is an important constraint—typically, a project ends when project funds have been expended.)

☐ **Project Completion.** The project should be completed in three months from the start date. (The time required to complete the project is another important constraint. If a project is not completed on time, it is conceivable that it has lost relevance and there is no longer the need to achieve the project objectives.)

To complete this project, Mr. Smith has decided to start with a project plan. His project plan is described in the next section.

Project Activities for the Smith Family

The key activities necessary to achieve the results set out in the business requirements for this short project are as follows:

☐ Determine the initial requirements that must be met by the features in a new automobile (i.e., a midsize four-door sedan from a North American manufacturer with air-conditioning, antilock braking system, dual air bags, and standard transmission that is within the designated price range).

☐ Review the requirements for a new automobile with Mrs. Smith, including features, cost, availability, and warranty.

☐ Document these requirements for initial acceptance by Mrs. Smith.

☐ Conduct research regarding different automobiles that meet Mrs. Smith's requirements; for example, review consumer reports and magazines regarding features, performance, reliability, and customer satisfaction data pertaining to new cars in the price range.

☐ Compile a short list of three automobiles that meet the requirements.

☐ Obtain comparative prices from three dealers.

☐ Take Mrs. Smith for test drives to experience car performance, handling, and other features.

☐ Narrow the selection to two cars based on a number of factors, including cost, comfort, performance, reliability, warranty and service levels, the number of "extras" provided at no additional cost that are perceived to be of value by Mrs. Smith, and track record of the automobile as determined by consumer reports.

☐ Recommend the most cost-effective automobile to Mrs. Smith.

The following additional parameters are also within scope of the project:

☐ **Project Deliverables.** Purchase or lease the new automobile.

☐ **Project Review.** Assess if the project deliverables meet the requirements identified by the project sponsor.

The preceding activities are one example of applying project management to the acquisition of a new automobile. Other personal or family-related project examples include buying a house, going on a vacation, renovating a kitchen, and preparing a retirement plan. These examples illustrate how project management concepts can be applied to get a job done in a timely manner, within budget, and with minimal or no surprises.

To complete the Smith family automobile acquisition project, no sophisticated tools were required. The project was completed using a piece of paper, a calculator, and a pen. As the number of activities and the size of the project team increases, project management becomes more complex and requires automated tools to monitor activities and resources. For instance, developing and implementing a computerized order-processing system for a large retailer servicing 200 locations in North America would require using a more sophisticated project management tool.

Project Stakeholders

A project stakeholder is a person or a group of people who have a stake in the outcome of the project. Depending on the size and complexity of the project, stakeholders could represent a number of players, including the project sponsor and/or the person funding the project, the ultimate user(s) of the project, and persons affected by the project. Stakeholders can provide helpful direction in the planning, development, testing, and implementation of projects.

The key stakeholders who are an integral part of this evolving process are the consumer, as a user of cost-effective computer technology; businesses, as users of technology to remain competitive; computer hardware and software vendors; and computer services vendors, who integrate the different components and make them work.

The project manager is a catalyst of change and is responsible for ensuring that results are achieved in a timely manner and within budget. Typically, the project manager's role begins when the project has been defined and its rationale understood by the stakeholders. The project manager is appointed to execute the project per the objectives set out by the stakeholders, as consistent with the objectives of the organization. The consumer as a project manager is responsible for determining requirements, exploring alternatives, and acquiring the appropriate technology to meet business objectives.

Project Management Methodology

Project management requires a methodology to successfully undertake and complete projects on time and within budget. The project management methodology is like a recipe—it provides a checklist of activities, a sequencing of these activities, roles and responsibilities of the project team, and designated resources. However, there is no guarantee that the project will be a success, even when a project management methodology is followed. Furthermore, by following a methodology too closely, there is a risk of being overwhelmed when unexpected problems arise.

What happens if you set out to deliver projects without following a project management methodology or using the associated tools? Typically, for smaller projects—less than three person-months in duration—chances are that there will be minimal impact on the outcome if a formal methodology is not followed. In such instances, the project manager has a plan of action, but the plan is not documented—it resides in the project manager's head.

As the project becomes more complex, it is increasingly difficult to deliver it successfully without a project methodology and the associated tools. For instance, buying an automobile for the Smith family could have been accomplished without following a project methodology, but using one helped the Smith family achieve their objectives.

The project management methodology can be supplemented by the use of a software tool that allows the project manager to document the tasks and their relationships and to understand the various constraints on a project. The software tool can be a spreadsheet showing activities and planned completion dates, or it can be project management software, such as Microsoft Project.

A project manager who is charged with the responsibility for delivering the project should have the set of skills necessary to increase the chances of success. As discussed in chapter 1, these skills include, but are not limited to, the following:

- ☐ Leadership skills to motivate and direct the project team and ensure that they remain focused on results
- ☐ Organizational skills to enable timely reporting of progress and delivery of project objectives
- ☐ Ability to select the right team with the required technical and interpersonal skills so that their efforts and project goals are in alignment
- ☐ The right level of technical skills to understand when the project team may be off course and direct them appropriately
- ☐ Delegation skills so that tasks are assigned to the most suitable team member

- Communication skills to report on project progress, including problems
- Political skills to manage the expectations of the stakeholders

Project Diversity

Project management can be applied to a variety of situations to achieve a valuable end result. As a simple example, we reviewed the Smith family's plan to purchase or lease a new automobile. Examples of projects that can benefit from understanding a methodology and using tools to help in monitoring its progress include:

- Setting up a recordkeeping system
- Developing an advertising strategy
- Developing a human resources plan for a department, including hiring staff, completing performance appraisals of staff, and other functions
- Building a house
- Planning a vacation
- Starting a business
- Acquiring a networked computer system for a 50-employee business
- Developing a computer application
- Planning a construction project, such as building an office tower or a road
- Planning an engineering project, such as building a factory or designing a power plant

The preceding projects are large in scope and therefore require different skill sets and resource requirements, but they have one thing in common—these projects follow a standard project management process to achieve the desired results, hopefully in a timely manner and within budget.

Information Technology Projects

A project is undertaken to address specific organizational goals, objectives, and business or technical requirements. It requires commitment from stakeholders to provide direction and the required resources to make it happen. It is important that the project team understands this stakeholder commitment and related project constraints in order to successfully complete the deliverables and meet stakeholder expectations. Figure 2.4 illustrates the relationship between the project manager and the expected deliverables.

An information technology project can be defined as the use of computer technology to automate the business processes and practices of an organization. An information technology project is initiated to respond to a set of demonstrated business needs. The solution to a business problem is driven by a set of objectives, including the need to lower costs, to provide faster turnaround for services, to restructure how a product or service is provided, or a combination of all of these reasons. The nature of a business problem might be as follows:

☐ The financial system is not current and does not produce reports that are readily usable for decision making.

☐ The payroll system is not flexible enough to allow for payments based on different staff classifications.

☐ Sales data is not helpful in launching new products and services.

☐ Billing information does not capture relevant information needed to keep the customers informed.

☐ It takes a long time to process customer orders.

Figure 2.4   Relationship between a project manager and expected deliverables.

☐ The business systems are not integrated.

☐ The business processes do not allow secure transactions over the Internet.

Information technology projects include a variety of initiatives, such as systems development and maintenance projects, infrastructure projects, information technology planning projects, hardware and software acquisition projects, and user support projects. Some examples of applying project management principles to information technology projects are:

☐ Acquiring a database management system

☐ Implementing a call center

☐ Developing a business-to-business e-commerce application

☐ Developing a new financial management system to replace the client/server system

☐ Outsourcing data center services

☐ Developing a wide area network and a wireless solution

☐ Establishing hardware, software, and communications standards

☐ Updating the company's information technology strategic plan

When a project is initiated, it generates expectations from the stakeholders. It is important to have a consistent understanding among stakeholders of project deliverables and the use of required resources.

In some organizations, project management is neither practiced nor accepted as essential. Typically, project management is taken seriously when problems arise—being behind schedule, being over budget, or experiencing difficulties between the project personnel and sponsors or with some of the project team members. Introducing the project management discipline only when a project is in trouble is usually indicative of throwing resources at a problem and magically expecting results, since intervention comes too late. Conducting project management by default is bound to fail.

A project management methodology is desirable because it can establish a consistent way of handling different projects in an organization. But how does a project management methodology help in delivering successful projects? A project management methodology helps a project manager and the project team to ensure that they are following the right

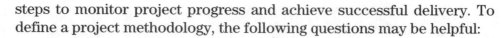

steps to monitor project progress and achieve successful delivery. To define a project methodology, the following questions may be helpful:

☐ Are the project goals and objectives clearly understood by the stakeholders?

☐ Who is responsible for approving the project deliverables?

☐ How frequently am I required to report on the status of the project?

☐ Are the expectations of the stakeholders clearly defined and understood by the project team?

☐ What is the culture of the project team (e.g., requiring minimal supervision)?

☐ Are all projects required to follow a project management methodology?

The concept of projects is well suited to the information technology disciplines because there is an expectation by the client that results will be provided within a fixed time period. Information technology groups are typically viewed as providing leadership in introducing new tools and techniques and as having the ability to translate business goals into practical solutions. When a project is undertaken, its aim is to bring about a change in a business process, and thus it becomes a catalyst.

A project manager sets the tempo of the project, provides direction to the team, and makes daily decisions based on prior experience in managing projects. The ultimate success of the project depends on how strongly the project management principles are practiced by the entire project team, how well the team delivers the results, and how well the change necessitated by the project affects the productivity of the business.

Project commitment is hard to define but relatively easy to spot in an organization. A committed project team works together to achieve results in a timely manner and is also synergistic and supportive of team members' efforts. A committed team looks for solutions. Without a committed project team the project is bound to fail, even though the individual team members have the required skills.

The Project Management Process

The project management process is about managing people and their tasks within a project. Project management tools facilitate planning, organizing, staffing, monitoring, reporting, and evaluating functions. In the Smith family example, the elements of a project were applied to produce the deliverables. Building on that example, the project management process in the planning cycle can be described as follows:

1. **Identify project objective.** Involves a clear definition of the project and the rationale for undertaking the project. Projects are established for a specific length of time and are not part of a normal ongoing operation in the organization. Projects have specific objectives to create end products and results.

2. **Define project scope.** Includes the areas affected by the project. Project scope can be as limited as a department in an organization or as broad as an international cartel; project size can be based on a certain dollar amount; project timeframe can be as short as weeks or months or as long as years; project type can be programs, processes, or systems that should be included.

3. **Introduce project sponsor.** This is the person responsible for identifying an opportunity, initiating the project, extending financial resources, and championing it inside the organization.

4. **Identify stakeholders.** Include all persons who have an investment in the development and outcome of the project. For instance, for a systems development project, stakeholders might include users, user managers, customers, and systems staff.

5. **Establish project costs.** Include the total lifecycle costs for the project, fixed and variable, as well as required resources. Project resources include staffing of project team with the required skill sets; financial resources for supplies, hardware, software, and travel; and administrative support personnel.

6. **Define project benefits.** Include the benefits derived from implementing the project—hard-dollar, soft-dollar, and value-added benefits.

7. **Outline key project activities.** Include the tasks required to complete the project, including known dependencies. This concept is discussed in greater detail in chapter 4.

8. **Specify project deliverables.** Include all the tangible results of completing a project in the project plan. A deliverable could be a report, a presentation, a business system, an information technology strategic or operational plan, or a feasibility study, for example.

9. **Set up a project schedule.** Include key activities on a project schedule or plan to build a roadmap for the project. This shows the relationship among activities over the life of the project.

10. **Define milestones.** Include important targets to be achieved during the life of a project on the project plan and as a separate list. A milestone can be the result of many subdeliverables being produced. For instance, a milestone could be to complete the design for a system in a series of steps.

Project management provides opportunities for stakeholders to focus on changes that deal with new ways of doing business that affect customers, business processes, practices, and procedures. The project management process implies that stakeholders want the project to succeed and want the benefits associated with the project.

The project management approach described in this book can be applied to a variety of projects—from large projects, which require a more comprehensive approach in planning and managing the project, to many small projects, for which the project structure proposed in this book can be compressed. In a large project, the activities and project milestones are established to reflect the skill differences of project team members, the complexities of the tasks, and the financial risks involved in project delay or failure. For shorter projects, it may be practical to assemble a small project team and give the mandate to complete it without a steering committee or formal reviews.

The Integrated Information Technology Plan

Planning is deciding what to do and why it needs to be done before you actually start work. It enables the right things to be done in the right order so that scarce resources are effectively utilized to achieve organizational objectives. The plan should include the overall business direction, the strategies to ensure that this direction will be achieved, and projects to realize the strategies. Planning provides an opportunity for senior management to discuss priorities at an organizational level instead of allocating resources to suboptimal projects that may benefit one part of the business to the detriment of another part.

Information technology plans are typically initiated to ensure that investments in information technology are coordinated and introduced in a cost-effective manner, consistent with the business plans of the organization. Business plans capture the priorities of the business. Both groups of plans must be consolidated and prioritized by the executive group.

The information technology plan is initiated at a senior management level. Normally, in large organizations the development of the information technology plan rests with the chief information officer. The information technology plan must be viewed from within the framework of the corporate vision, management's view of information systems, and the stage of information system maturity within the organization. The plan describes the current environment and framework used by an organization to direct information systems development, the current and planned business and information technology environments, and the strategies and policy directions governing the organization's development and management of its information technology for the future. The plan also describes the framework the organization will use to direct information systems development over the long term and the infrastructure for developing, maintaining, and supporting information systems in the organization, including new functions necessary to ensure that future systems development is, in fact, shaped and directed by the plan.

The information technology plan provides a framework to guide the organization's investment in and management of information over several years. The plan also outlines the specific initiatives required to translate the strategies into results and the cost and benefits of these initiatives.

The Strategic Planning Process

Projects are initiated because there is a specific business or technology need in an organization. For instance, a project may be initiated because the accounting department wants to keep track of all movable and fixed assets in the company. The controller may decide to initiate a project to automate the recordkeeping of all assets within the organization. It is conceivable that the controller may end up with an excellent assets management system, but the hardware and software used may not be compatible with other computer applications in the organization. How do you prevent an "islands of technology" syndrome?

The information technology planning process is one effective way to ensure that individual requirements are not considered in isolation. The planning process enables the organization to identify its "basket of requirements" over a three-to-five year planning period, and determine the most cost-effective and integrated ways of delivering those requirements.

Planning Practices

Strategic planning practices call for an appraisal of the current environment, identification of the issues and trends that must be addressed, and a depiction of the proposed future or target environment. From this picture, goals and objectives can be set out and broad strategies for accomplishing them can be developed.

Since information and technology are themselves becoming major resources used by more and more organizations to further their strategic objectives, it has become clear that planning for them must be done in the context of a strategic business plan. However, the interactions between business plans and information management plans are becoming increasingly complex.

The information technology strategic plan must serve the business strategy by defining the data, applications, and technology required to support the organization's products and services efficiently and effectively. It must set out the principles by which these elements can be developed, implemented, used, and maintained in a manner consistent with an organization's management culture and the rate of change for priorities. Finally, it must ensure adequate consideration of those areas in which technology itself may be an underlying change agent.

As a starting point, the strategies in the plan should be developed by reviewing trends and issues with the organization's managers and outlining several future business scenarios in which management of information technology will be an issue.

To ensure that strategic plans remain current and are representative of the realities of the business, they should be periodically reviewed. Typically, an annual review of a strategic plan is desirable because it enables an organization to review business and information technology objectives and update them where necessary.

In general, changes to the types and numbers of clients, products, and services provided and the types of new value-added services provided have an impact on how information technology is deployed in the organization.

Figure 2.5 shows the key elements of an information technology strategic plan and how they are interrelated.

The key objectives of developing an information technology strategic plan are:

- ☐ To provide a single focus of responsibility and authority for deploying information and systems strategically in the organization
- ☐ To provide an information technology structure that is responsive to client needs and provides a competitive weapon
- ☐ To provide an appropriate information technology platform for the delivery of applications in a timely, reliable, and cost-effective manner
- ☐ To develop flexible systems that can be quickly built and changed to meet the changing nature and requirements of the business
- ☐ To develop corporate or common applications in a coordinated manner to ensure better alignment of information technology with the organization's goals
- ☐ To develop an applications portfolio that is responsive to business needs and that has a demonstrated payback

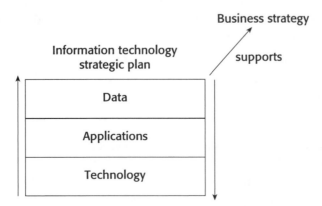

Figure 2.5   Elements of an information technology strategic plan.

Operational Plans

To translate the strategic plan, operational and tactical plans are developed for implementing a variety of projects over the planning period. The operational plan is a primary tool for highlighting projects planned for implementation, and the associated costs, benefits, and risks involved in achieving the objectives. Operational plans typically extend to one fiscal year, while the tactical plans cover about a three-year period.

Project team members should understand the background of the project, the overall goals, and the business and technical reasons for initiating a project. The operational plan provides an overview of different projects that should be undertaken and how they relate to organizational goals.

The operational plan should include a description of the project, the project scope, key stakeholders, and a broad assessment of costs and benefits. Figure 2.6 shows the relationship between strategic, tactical, and operational plans.

Figure 2.6 Relationship between strategic, tactical, and operational plans.

Elements

The following elements are essential in the development of a strategic plan:

1. **Establish the steering committee.** In many organizations, steering committees are set up to provide direction and guidance to the project. The steering committee also establishes project priorities, but not direct management control over individual projects. The steering committee's membership is typically five to seven members, chaired by the chief information officer, and representing departments affected by the project. Membership could be as follows: one representative from senior management, three representatives from departmental management, and two representatives from the systems department. The committee reviews the project progress and provides feedback regarding prioritization of various departmental and corporate initiatives.

2. The information technology plan should be developed within the context of the business plan of the organization. The information technology plan should be consistent with the goals and objectives of the organization as described in its business plan. Since information and technology are themselves becoming major resources, the interactions between the two should be understood to take advantage of new opportunities through emerging technology products and services.

3. **Initiate the project to develop a technology plan.** Define purpose and scope of the study, including deliverables to be produced. Review the planning schedule and ensure that the deliverables are realistic and attainable.

4. **Identify resources and skill sets required for the project team.** For most projects, the mix of technical and business skills varies depending on the project phase and the requirements of that project. As the project ownership ultimately belongs to the users, it is important that they be appropriately involved in the project in tasks such as developing an understanding of business practices and procedures, the design of screens and reports, system testing, and training.

5. **Assess the business and technology environment.** Include critical success factors, changes to the business environment, and new products and services.

6. Identify business needs and priorities. Include business processes, current problems, and proposed opportunities.

7. Formulate an information technology strategic direction.

8. Translate the strategies into concrete initiatives, such as a listing of applications that need to be developed and projects that need to be undertaken for the specific improvement of departments or processes.

9. Justify the overall portfolio of projects and prioritize these initiatives so that results are obtained over a four-to-five-year planning horizon.

10. Monitor and update the plan on an annual basis to reflect changes in priorities and business direction.

Each of the projects identified in the plan requires an effective project plan. The planning process provides a mechanism for translating project goals into detailed tasks, the resources required to complete those tasks, and the time parameters for producing the required results. The project plan should identify key tasks and the associated risks if those tasks are not completed in a timely manner.

Project-Planning Checklist

The project management approach enables the project team to function in a proactive manner throughout the project lifecycle, and provides a means to document tasks. The project plan can be used to document and communicate the project status, tasks completed, and issues that need to be resolved. The project plan is useful in interacting with the stakeholders and provides a sense of ownership—the feeling that the project ultimately belongs to the stakeholders. It is easy to lose sight of the original project goals when the current hot issues of the day surface. Although it is important to be sensitive to these issues, the project team should assess the issues' relevance, and stay focused on the project objectives and deliverables.

A project-planning checklist provides a standardized approach for describing and summarizing the initial components of a project plan for management's consideration. A project-planning checklist is provided below that ensures that the relevant project information is included.

☐ Project name

☐ Project description

- ☐ Project scope
- ☐ Project sponsor and stakeholders
- ☐ Project manager
- ☐ Frequency of communications for project status (e.g., weekly, monthly)
- ☐ Estimated project costs and benefits
- ☐ Project start and completion dates
- ☐ Key project risks and issues
- ☐ High-level project plan with milestones

Although the project-planning checklist provides an understanding of key project issues, it should be recognized that the actual project is developed and implemented in a dynamic organization where different business pressures may have a significant impact on the project at hand. Reasonable compromises between changes to the project and the subsequent impact on schedules and budgets should be handled as part of managing stakeholder expectations.

Summary

Project management deals with managing people and their expectations. The challenge for the project manager is to deliver a project in accordance with project goals, and with the resources and within the timeframe provided by the business. The project manager is expected to minimize the divergence between the realization of project objectives and the expectations of the stakeholders, and to ensure that projects are planned, coordinated, and successfully implemented.

This chapter reviewed the basic tenets of project management. It addressed some different types of projects that can be initiated and can benefit from a project management methodology. There is no guarantee that using a project management methodology will ensure project success. However, as depicted in Figure 2.7, the use of a methodology with appropriate software tools and an experienced project team can help in monitoring the progress of the project and in reducing the risk of project failure. The project management elements provide a framework for planning and implementing several projects in a coordinated and consistent manner.

Figure 2.7 Project management elements to enhance project status.

The project manager faces several competing pressures throughout the life of the project and must learn to juggle the conflicting priorities and interests of different stakeholders. Project management can entail compromises and changing expectations, which must be managed so that the project achieves its objectives.

The chapter also reviewed the strategic planning process as one way of introducing projects in an organization in an integrated, coordinated, and cost-effective manner. A project-planning checklist was provided to describe and summarize the initial components of a project plan. The planning checklist can also be used to show a number of projects on a consolidated basis. As shown in Figure 2.8, a collection of projects is

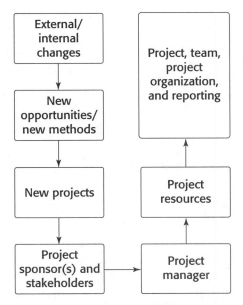

Figure 2.8 Project portfolio generation process.

derived for an organization from a set of internal and external pressures, new opportunities, and new business and technology requirements.

Project management is a discipline that requires a commitment from stakeholders, a results-oriented attitude to get the job done, a trained staff, effective tools to monitor the project, and a good understanding of the limits and potential of technology and its impact on the organization. Good project management requires proper planning and a commitment to implement the deliverables as outlined in the project plan.

The project manager is a key player in delivering projects on time and within budget. Like a quarterback on a football team, the project manager provides leadership, direction, delegation, and the support needed to enhance the chances of project success.

CHAPTER 3

Project Initiation and Justification

T his chapter deals with how projects are initiated and justified in organizations. As discussed in chapter 2, projects can be initiated for a variety of reasons. An immediate business problem can motivate a stakeholder to launch a project, or the strategic planning process can result in a prioritized list that allows project selections to be made in a coordinated and integrated manner. In this chapter the reader will learn about:

- Project initiation
- Project justification
- Project portfolio
- Business cases
- Project launching
- Benefits tracking
- Project risks
- Project control
- Project communication

Starting the Process

Project initiation and justification are initially addressed in the information technology plan where the project portfolio is developed, prioritized, and approved according to the goals and objectives of the organization. The project portfolio indicates which designated projects should be implemented, subject to the acceptance of a detailed business case.

Project justification is based on the value of the project to the organization. A project translates an idea or a concept into a performable result. The value of a project is assessed in terms of monetary and nonmonetary benefits to the organization versus the costs and potential risks.

Project justification is fundamental in ensuring continued investments in information technology. Information technology plays a significant role in ensuring that organizations have the necessary information to be competitive and participate effectively with a range of strategic partners, suppliers, and customers who share the organizations' values and goals. It also provides appropriate systems to support timely, efficient, and cost-effective delivery of products and services. Information technology has significantly changed how people work and communicate with each other. With newer applications, such as electronic commerce, organizations can expand their markets globally, and electronically link different business units for competitive advantage.

After completing this chapter, the reader will have a good understanding of how projects are initiated, how they are prioritized and justified, and the rationale behind the project approval process.

Reasons for Project Initiation

Projects can be initiated from any part of the organization where there is a demonstrated need to address a business problem. A project can be initiated by many different individuals in an organization—a plant manager, a director of marketing, a vice president of finance, a supervisor in the human resources department, or an individual staff member in an organization who believes that there is a better way of doing business. Projects are driven by the necessity of providing products or services more effectively. The project initiation process is depicted in Figure 3.1.

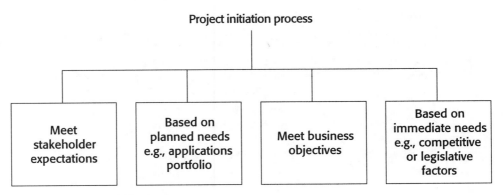

Figure 3.1 Project initiation process.

There are a variety of reasons for initiating projects, as shown in Table 3.1.

Project Initiation

The various projects in an organization require coordination so that the objectives are aligned and the project benefits provide a cumulative and synergistic effect instead of blocking each other. Typically, the project director is responsible for managing several related projects to ensure that different but related projects are coordinated and consistent with the overall goals of the organization.

There are two approaches for initiating a project—the project portfolio approach and the immediate needs approach. The project portfolio approach is based on a planning cycle of typically one to three years, is more coordinated, and is based on key business pressures that occur over that time horizon. The strategic and planning processes described in chapter 1 generate such a project portfolio. The immediate needs approach is more reactive and is undertaken to address specific concerns and immediate, often unanticipated, business opportunities in the marketplace.

Project Portfolio Approach

As described in chapter 2, projects can be initiated within the context of an information technology strategic plan to ensure that requirements are

Table 3.1   Reasons for Project Initiation

REASON	RATIONALE
Providing timely and more responsible service	Client service is an important business indicator—e.g., a retail store needs to provide prompt customer service regarding product availability, price, warranty, and service.
Marketing in-house computer applications to other businesses	This initiative is aimed at increasing the revenues of the organization by developing a market for their in-house applications.
Reducing the cost of a product or service	This is a typical reason to undertake an information technology project. Cost reduction includes streamlining a business process, thereby reducing the time and resources required; e.g., in the case of a bank, reducing the time required to process a loan application.
Providing newer products or services	Based on customer spending patterns, this initiative provides a more focused way of selling products and services to customers.
Building partnerships with suppliers	This initiative uses information technology to reduce inventory and carrying costs through "just-in-time" techniques.
Fostering better coordination between departments	This initiative will lower the overall cost of manufacturing a product or providing a service by ensuring that the information is better coordinated and more integrated between departments.
Providing improved decision support systems	This initiative provides managers and executives with information to support their decisions—e.g., information about competition, market share, and price sensitivity to their products.
Utilizing extra money in the budget	"Unspent" monies in the budget can be used to initiate projects.
Satisfying political considerations	This initiative responds to the need to justify, for instance, the reorganization of a department or influence a decision.
Complying with legislative factors	This initiative responds to the need to initiate or enhance an information system to provide reports that comply with or support legislative requirements (e.g., a new tax).

addressed in a cohesive and integrated manner. At a high level, this project portfolio describes a list of initiatives that should be undertaken over a one-to-three-year period. The project portfolio includes a brief description of each project, the resources required to complete the project, and the skill sets of the project team needed to complete the project.

The projects in the applications portfolio will be implemented over a one-to-three-year span, depending on the priorities established in the strategic plan. Subject to budgetary pressures and resource availability, it is likely that the higher-priority projects will be implemented first, while some may never be initiated.

Typically, before a project is implemented, there is a detailed assessment to ensure that the project is still relevant and addresses the defined business problems. However, for each project included in the applications portfolio, the following items should be included in an associated high-level project description:

☐ Project overview, briefly describing the project and the business objectives addressed by it

☐ Value of the proposition/benefit to the organization

☐ Key project stakeholders

☐ Project scope

☐ An overview of preliminary costs and benefits

☐ Timeframe for project completion

☐ Key dependencies

☐ Cost of not doing the project

It is interesting to note that not all organizations follow the formal process of developing an applications portfolio. In some organizations, projects are developed in a reactive manner, based on a designated need at a specific time.

Figure 3.2 illustrates how an applications portfolio is developed.

The Immediate-Needs Approach

Sometimes it is necessary to initiate a project to address sudden competitive needs or to address a business need necessitated by a change in legislation. These projects may fall outside the realm of the planning process and may not be included in the applications portfolio. Furthermore, some of these projects may require immediate attention to comply with deadlines. Typically, these projects have a sponsor with a direct stake in the outcome of the project. The project sponsor is also interested in ensuring that the project is carefully planned and executed by a competent project team.

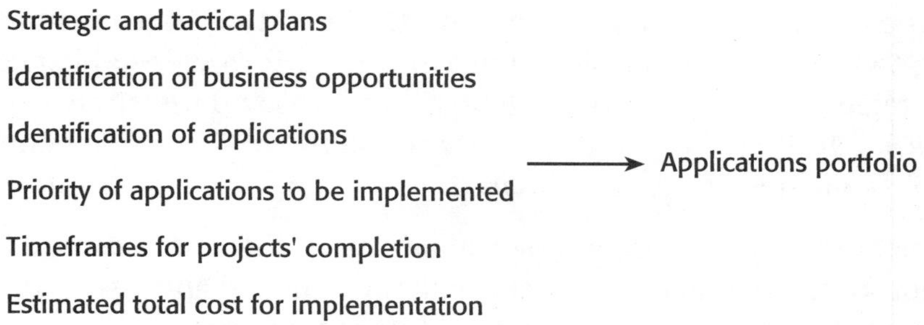

Strategic and tactical plans

Identification of business opportunities

Identification of applications

Priority of applications to be implemented ⟶ Applications portfolio

Timeframes for projects' completion

Estimated total cost for implementation

Figure 3.2   Applications portfolio.

Before starting a project, there will be a variety of ideas and opinions about the purpose and scope of the project, the final product of the project, and the way the project will be implemented. Stakeholders with a vested interest in the outcome of the project are typically the source of these ideas. It is quite likely that these ideas will be diverse and incongruent in many areas.

Young start-up companies backed by venture capital often rely on bringing a product to the market in a short time, typically in weeks. These companies are tightly focused on their products and how they can offer them to their customers before the competition does. These companies have to bring their products to the market in a short time to combat growing competitive pressures. Customer expectations drive their companies to manage the business processes more efficiently. The dot-com (.com) companies and their stakeholders have to operate under tight timelines, and they have a "must succeed" attitude for their projects. Examples of projects included in this category are:

☐ Developing a wireless application for transacting the buying and selling of stocks and bonds

☐ Developing Web sites for an online retailer for selling a variety of consumer products, from books and CDs to household appliances and furniture

☐ Developing enterprise-wide applications for integrating the ordering process with the financial and supply chain management systems

☐ Developing mobile devices to send and receive email, and receive customer orders and process them in a timely and cost-effective manner

☐ Developing applications for professionals, such as doctors and lawyers, that will allow them to provide value-added advisory services over the Internet for current and new clients

The project initiation phase deals with taking these diverse ideas and developing them into a more focused project with formal provisions for resources and timelines. Before a project is initiated, it must undergo a rigorous process to ensure that the investment in it is supported by demonstrable benefits and that it will provide value to the enterprise. The vehicle used to initiate and justify a project is referred to as a business case.

Given the speed with which new projects are developed for the Internet, the immediate-needs approach is gaining momentum because it allows organizations to be more competitive. The project implementation cycle can be in a matter of weeks! Consequently, all the elements, from project planning to project delivery, require speedy resolution and timely delivery if the company is to retain a competitive edge.

Project Justification

Specific projects are launched only after justifying their importance and value to the project sponsor and to executive management. A common method of doing this is through a business case.

Using a Business Case

The business case provides a mechanism for funding a project and securing resources for the project team. The business case identifies the benefits expected from the project, and balances these against the costs and risks associated with each benefit. The business case can be used to monitor the estimated benefits and compare them with the actual benefits obtained if the project is approved and implemented.

As indicated in Figure 3.3, business case analysis may actually reduce the number of projects being implemented, either because some of the projects may not be cost-effective or because they are not meeting the business objectives. Business case analysis also may alter project scope and the priority of projects to be implemented.

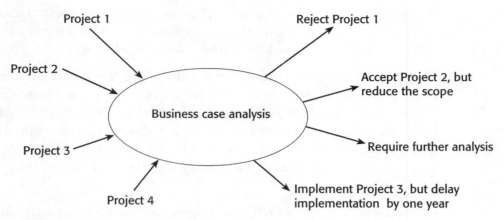

Figure 3.3 Project justification.

For consistent preparation and evaluation of business cases and when seeking approvals, the template of a business case described in this section should be used as a guideline. The details required in preparing a business case should be contingent on the actual size of the project and the type of business. For instance, a project estimated to cost $50,000 will require less supporting documentation than a project with a budget of $10 million.

The business case can also be used for auditing purposes—to compare projected results against actual results in order to assess the ultimate success of the project, and to apply successful experiences to other projects or to feed the best practices repository.

After it is completed, the business case should be reviewed and approved by the project sponsor, who is typically responsible for ensuring that resources are available to complete the project. The approval process is required to obtain financial commitment to the project, and also to affirm that the project will achieve the objectives and benefits identified in the business case.

Template for Preparing a Business Case

A business case can be an extensive document that takes many persons months to develop. We recommend a more streamlined approach with the major headings shown below:

1. Identifying Information
   a. Business case for the acquisition of a product or service
   b. Department
   c. Contact name
   d. Total cost of acquisition
   e. Account code to charge
2. Objectives

   The project should clearly define what the project is intended to achieve and the level of interest in the project. Explain business problems to be resolved or opportunities to be realized.

   The system objectives—such as improving response time, increasing throughput, providing a friendlier user interface, and migrating to a client/server processing environment—should also be addressed.
3. Project Scope

   The project scope deals with the boundaries within which the project will operate. It includes the specific business units and functions that will be affected (e.g., marketing and accounting departments), the key stakeholders who will be affected, and any constraints or limitations on the project. An example of a project scope is that the project will be implemented only in one geographical location, using a dedicated workstation.
4. Business Requirements Statement

   This section of the business case will assess the current business functions and processes and identify any weaknesses and potential opportunities for improvement. It will also describe the organization of work groups where the requirements exist, and the level of automation utilized.

   The business requirements should be documented by addressing the following items and providing a rationale for the proposed project:

   ☐ Business tasks and activities requiring automation

   ☐ Methods currently being used to accomplish or perform these activities

   ☐ Use of proposed information technology to accomplish or perform these activities

5. Alternatives

   Identify the alternatives that were considered for addressing the business requirements along with the costs, benefits, risks, and reasons for rejection. Alternatives include:

   ☐ Status quo

   ☐ Other technology solutions

6. Costs and Benefits

   a. Costs—provide the following costs:

      ☐ One-time costs of hardware, software, planning, and implementing the product or service

      ☐ Ongoing costs of operating, upgrading, and maintaining the product or service (e.g., service, training)

   b. Benefits

      (1) Provide quantifiable monetary benefits, which can include:

         ☐ One-time cost savings

         ☐ Annual cost savings such as eliminating the services provided on an annual basis by an external agency, reductions in staffing, and deferred hires

      (2) Quantifiable nonmonetary benefits that are improvements in performance directly attributable to the implementation of information technology. Quantifiable nonmonetary benefits can include:

         ☐ Measurable increases in the number of clients serviced

         ☐ Measurable increases in the number of requests serviced

         ☐ Measurable improvements in response to service requests

         ☐ Staff time savings redeployed to other quantifiable activities

         ☐ Increased confidence in the decision as a result of the availability of more relevant information

         ☐ Increased understanding of customer demographics

         ☐ Improved coordination between organizational units, thereby decreasing time needed to make decisions

   c. Summary of Costs and Benefits: Prepare a summary table of costs and benefits.

Wherever possible, value-added benefits should be quantified and shown under nonmonetary (quantifiable) benefits. When it is not possible to quantify benefits, a brief description of these benefits should also be provided (see Table 3.2 for an example).

7. Payback

   Payback is defined as the number of years it takes to recover an investment. Typically, the total monetary benefits should at least offset total estimated costs within a three-year period from the date of implementation.

8. Summary of the Business Case

   Include implications if the business case is not approved.

9. Risks

   Identify any risks that might arise as a consequence of the project and indicate ways for these risks to be minimized or avoided altogether.

10. Approvals

    Obtain approvals from the project sponsor. If the project sponsor is not authorized to allocate funds, obtain approval from the person

Table 3.2 Summary Table of Costs and Benefits for Project XYZ

COSTS	YEAR 1	YEAR 2	YEAR 3	TOTAL
One-time costs				
Ongoing costs				
Other costs				
Total costs				
BENEFITS	**YEAR 1**	**YEAR 2**	**YEAR 3**	**TOTAL**
One-time savings				
Annual savings				
Nonmonetary benefits (quantifiable)				
Other benefits				
Total benefits				
Net benefits				
Cumulative benefits				

authorized to allocate funds. After receiving approval, the project can be formally initiated and completed in accordance with the objectives set out in the business case.

Results of the Management Survey

Based on the results of the management survey we conducted for this book, the following list shows common activities and characteristics for the project justification and initiation phase observed by the responding project managers:

☐ Most respondents use a business case as a means to justify and initiate projects. The level of detail covered depends on the size and complexity of the project. The supporting documentation for a business case varied from a brief memorandum outlining the reasons for initiating a project with departmental management approval to comprehensive documentation requiring cost and benefit justification and risk assessment.

☐ Most respondents agreed that a business case provided an opportunity to document the business requirements, prioritize project requirements, and communicate them to the stakeholders.

☐ Most respondents agreed that project risks are better understood in the context of a business case, especially when alternatives are described and their implications are understood. Respondents also indicated that a benefit-tracking process would fine-tune the business case process and provide more accountability to the project management process.

☐ Most respondents also were in favor of developing a project portfolio, especially when larger projects were involved, because it encourages approval of higher-priority initiatives that maximize the value to the organization. The project portfolio also provided a picture of various initiatives over time, thereby enhancing the relationship between projects.

☐ The business case should become a document that is actively maintained throughout the project lifecycle. If this is too time-consuming, the benefits and risk portions should be extracted and maintained separately.

After the business case is prepared and approved by the project sponsor, the project can be formally launched.

Project Launching

After the project has been approved, the project manager is selected and assigned a series of tasks to start the project, including the following:

1. Prepare a project plan and obtain approval from the project sponsor and/or the steering committee. The project plan should include key tasks, milestones, responsibilities, deliverables, and corresponding completion dates for achieving them (see chapter 4).

2. Identify the staff resources and the skill sets of the project team.

3. Identify the funding requirements for the project, including hardware, software, office space, and administrative support.

4. Select the project team members. This could be a combination of in-house personnel and consultants, depending on the specific requirements of the project. Assign roles and responsibilities to the project team members.

5. Identify key project review points and timing with the project stakeholders.

6. Identify the project control function to ensure that there is minimal variance between planned and actual activities.

Time is of the essence in launching the project. As indicated earlier, depending on the project, the delivery time from the identification of business opportunities to the completion of project is weeks. Projects are launched to exploit opportunities and provide a competitive advantage to the organization. There is also the risk that another project may take resources away if there is too long a delay in getting started.

Tracking Benefits

When several competing projects require attention, project prioritization becomes important so that higher-priority projects with greater payback are initiated first, followed by other projects in a descending order of importance and value to the organization. However, projects necessitated by legislative requirements or projects that belong to the infrastructure category may be considered higher-priority projects by the senior management of an organization.

One of the primary reasons for justifying a project is the value of the benefits provided to the organization. Consequently, benefits tracking and reporting are essential to the project justification process. The benefits-tracking process should indicate how benefits will be reported and who will be accountable for realizing them after the project has been successfully implemented.

A key focus of tracking benefits is to ensure that managers are accountable for identifying, capturing, monitoring, and reporting on quantifiable benefits resulting from the proposed investment. The tracking and reporting of benefits is fundamental to ensuring that a rigorous process was followed in the acquisition process, with appropriate accountability for those acquisitions.

As part of the benefits measurement and reporting process, the following benefit management principles should be observed:

- ☐ Every investment in information technology must be clearly directed to meeting the business needs of the organization.
- ☐ Every investment in information technology must be justified by an approved business case prior to any acquisition.
- ☐ Benefits realized through the use of information technology will be captured and reported back to senior management of the organization.
- ☐ Wherever possible, information technology resources should be optimized to ensure that resources can be shared or otherwise redeployed to meet the organization's business needs.

Benefit tracking imposes discipline on information technology projects to ensure that the investment is rational and makes business sense. It also provides a mechanism to track planned benefits against actual benefits and, consequently, validates the justification process. To track benefits, a benefits-tracking form can be used for a better understanding of planned versus actual benefits and the reasons for variances, if appropriate. Table 3.3 shows a sample benefits tracking form to capture and monitor benefits and encourage management accountability.

Project Risks

All projects are exposed to varying degrees of risk, which can derail a project. Some of these risks are shown in the following list:

Table 3.3 Benefits-Tracking Form

NAME OF DEPARTMENT:			
PROJECT NAME	**YEAR 1**	**YEAR 2**	**YEAR 3**
	Planned Actual Variance	Planned Actual Variance	Planned Actual Variance
Project 1			
Project 2			
Project 3			
Project 4			
Project 5			
. . . .			
. . . .			
Totals			
Brief Explanation of Variances by Project:			

- ☐ Cost and time overruns
- ☐ Staff turnover due to burnouts and resignations
- ☐ Changing project specifications
- ☐ Changes in the company structure and ownership due to mergers and acquisitions
- ☐ Changes in the composition of stakeholders
- ☐ Bankruptcy of hardware and software vendors

For small projects, the importance of such risks may not be significant and can be usually managed without a serious impact on overall project performance. However, for large projects, the impact of such risks can be severe and can contribute to the ultimate success or failure.

It is useful to plan for potential project risks so that the consequences are minimal and manageable. The risk-management provision should include how the project risks will be addressed, who will be responsible for addressing them, and at what cost. A risk probability factor could be assigned to the project for a better understanding of the severity of the risk. To minimize risk, contingency cost factors should be included as part of the total project costs. Depending on the nature of the project and the experience of the project manager, contingency factors could range from 10 percent to 50 percent of the total project cost.

Project Control

While project planning deals with activities that should happen, project control deals with ensuring that the activities happen when they are expected to happen. Project control is an ongoing activity that forms an integral part of the project management function. It requires an understanding of the progress of actual project activities as compared to planned activities. Project control provides a mechanism for evaluating the project status, understanding problems about the project and their magnitude, and understanding risks associated with the project. It provides stakeholders with an opportunity to assess and influence the outcome of the project on the basis of current information available to them about the project. Depending on the reporting requirements, it is often desirable to provide a summary project control report for senior management and a more detailed project information report for middle management.

Project control is a reporting function and helps stakeholders to ask questions of the project manager about the condition of the project. The project control checklist indicated below can be used to gain a better understanding of the project.

□ Are there any changes to project objectives?

□ Is there a change in the scope of the project?

□ Are there any changes in the resource requirements?

□ Is there a change in the project delivery date?

□ Are there any issues that require resolution? What level of management needs to resolve them?

□ What actions were undertaken to resolve these issues?

The items in this list can be appended to a regular status report so that they are visible to the extended project team.

If there are changes to any or all of the elements in the above questions in the checklist, the project manager should provide a supporting explanation. The project control checklist enables the stakeholders to stay focused on issues and provides a means to resolve issues expeditiously. The project control checklist provides guidance to the project team and facilitates the resolution of smaller issues before they become big problems. An important consideration in project control for the stakeholders is not to be bogged down over trivial issues—give feedback to the project team and move the project forward.

Project Communication

A communication style should be discussed by the project manager with stakeholders so that both parties have an understanding of what information to expect and how it will be communicated. A daily or weekly project status report is an acceptable form of formal project reporting. Depending on stakeholder expectations, project reports can take place electronically over a network, and/or be communicated in a daily, weekly, or monthly time slot designated for project review. If the stakeholders are located in different geographical areas, project reviews can be handled by a videoconference or a teleconference.

For effective project communication, the project manager should establish an environment in which the project team members feel comfortable speaking up. At the same time, stakeholders should also promote a similar positive environment and encourage the project manager to speak out and clear the air. The key elements of project communication include listening to issues, reasoning about them, and then acting on them in the best interests of the project. Criticism should be viewed as an opportunity to fix problems in a timely and decisive manner.

Summary

This chapter dealt with how projects are justified and initiated in an organization. Projects can be initiated by addressing a business need identified by a stakeholder to resolve a business problem. Projects can also be initiated in a more coordinated and integrated manner as part of the corporation's strategic planning process. Since a project is an investment, it should be subjected to a review in terms of a cost-benefit valuation.

This chapter also discussed how projects are initiated and justified as part of the technology planning process and how they are prioritized and approved according to the goals and objectives of the organization. The technology planning process can be used to develop a project portfolio describing which projects should be undertaken and when they should be implemented. Another project initiation technique, based on immediate needs, was also described in the chapter. Sometimes, the immediate-needs approach is necessary to address sudden competitive requirements (for instance, the need to develop Web-based applications for competitive advantage) or to address a business need necessitated by a change in legislation. These projects may fall outside the realm of the planning process and may not be included in the application portfolio. These projects require a fast turnaround, often a matter of weeks from identification of opportunities to project delivery. A standardized template was provided as a way of preparing and evaluating a business case. The suggested business case analysis could be applied to a variety of projects and initiatives, such as developing new applications, acquiring hardware and software, implementing computer networks, and even outsourcing projects.

A benefits-tracking form was developed to study planned versus actual benefits and thereby encourage accountability of a project as part of the overall management process. Depending on the size of the project, the details of the business case may be adjusted—for instance, those for projects with lifecycle costs of less than $50,000 may not be as comprehensive as those for projects over $1,000,000.

This chapter also discussed the need to do a project risk assessment as part of developing the business case. It was determined that the risk-management provision should be included in the project initiation and justification process. The responsibility for addressing the risks and the associated costs should be included in the basic project plan. A risk probability factor could be assigned to the project to have a better understanding of the severity of the risks and to minimize any surprises.

A project control activity is an important part of understanding the progress of actual project activities as compared to planned activities. Project control provides a mechanism for evaluating the project status, understanding problems encountered in the project and their magnitude, and understanding the risks associated with the project. It provides stakeholders with an opportunity to assess and influence the outcome of the project, based on current information available to them. A checklist for stakeholders was provided to enable them to better grasp the issues and understand how they could be resolved.

Ongoing communications to the stakeholders about the state of a project is an important project management function. For effective project communications, the project manager should establish an environment in which the project team members feel comfortable in speaking about issues when things are not right. At the same time, stakeholders should also promote a similar positive environment and encourage the project manager to speak out and clear the air.

CHAPTER 4

Project Planning and Scheduling

This chapter describes the project planning process that must be performed for every project by the project manager. It positions this process in the context of the overall project development lifecycle. The planning phase requires the attention and abilities of the project manager more than any other phase. Decisions made at this time ripple through the other phases and have a magnified impact on the final result. In this chapter the reader will learn about:

- Project initiation
- Project planning and scheduling
- Milestone dates
- Resource identification
- Project plans
- Workshops and meetings
- Planning tools
- Project management office (PMO)
- Planning pitfalls
- Project planning terms

- Project estimating
- Risk analysis
- Quality control

Starting the Project

The strategic and tactical processes discussed in chapter 3 generate multiple lists of projects that are prioritized in terms of importance to the organization. An initiative is officially launched when a manager or an interim champion is identified to take the project to the next level. During the initiation activities, a project manager must:

☐ Examine the high-level business case that should exist for the project

☐ Complete some basic due diligence around the project objectives, goals, support levels, and background

☐ Maintain its relative priority against other initiatives and the level of support it enjoys within the organization

☐ Identify the criteria that will be used to evaluate whether the project is successful

If not positively addressed by the executive, issues identified at this stage of the project lifecycle may be a signal of enormous problems ahead. Project managers should be wary of accepting further responsibilities on the project until the executive accepts the responsibility for resolving these critical issues. Project managers who proceed into the project without this commitment implicitly accept the responsibility for resolving these issues and will be accountable for any problems that result. At a minimum, the project manager should document each issue along with a mitigation strategy that is supported by the executive.

Aside from being assigned to a project at initiation, a project manager can also be parachuted in after it has started. The former situation is preferable because it provides a better opportunity to position the project for success. This is done through a properly conducted planning phase that includes selecting skilled resources for the project team, lining up business support, and selling the project's business case within the organization. Projects can be lined up for success or failure in the planning phase. Based on our experience, this single phase requires more energy and focus on the part of the project manager than any other phase in the project development lifecycle—although testing comes close. The work done at this time will pay dividends over the life of the project. Likewise, poor decisions, laziness, or oversights on the part of management will be magnified in subsequent phases of the project.

Project managers are parachuted into projects for a variety of reasons, including: replacing a project manager who is leaving for another pursuit, replacing a project manager who was counseled out, and replacing an interim champion. The basic mandate usually involves assuming responsibilities on a project that is experiencing difficulties or a spike in workload. In any of these situations, the incoming manager does not have an opportunity to conduct a planning phase, as tactical demands on the project require immediate attention. The project manager is then faced by two challenges. The first of these is the need to jump in and get the work done. The second is to pick the right time to accept responsibility for the project's success and its prior history. Fortunately, these two roles are not mutually exclusive. The timing of the latter role is critical to the project manager's own career goals, and will also contribute to the success of the project. An approach that has a proven track record involves conducting an audit of the original planning phase. This is done by using a checklist to review each planning deliverable, backfilling missing information, and questioning any decisions and assumptions that were made. This review can be done in parallel with the tactical activities on the project. While this approach may double the manager's workload for a period of time, it satisfies both challenges and may uncover reasons for the project's current difficulties.

The planning process is the first official phase in a project's lifecycle. It commences immediately after a project business case is accepted (with a clear project mission statement), but before the requirement-gathering activities are started. Figure 4.1 illustrates a basic linear project lifecycle without features such as iteration. The project planning process generates a formal project plan (or schedule) that identifies the major activities needed to satisfy the project's business requirements by a specified delivery date and with specific resource constraints. This allows the resource availability to be scheduled per the project plan. The planning process can also generate a list of issues that need to be tracked going forward. An acceptance process that describes how the project results will be accepted within the organization and ultimately implemented should also be defined in draft form at this stage.

Strategic and Tactical Planning
Project Justification
Project Initiation
Project Planning
Requirements Gathering
Analysis and Modeling
Architecture and Design
Development
Testing
Signoff
Implementation
Project Review

You are here

Manager is selected

Figure 4.1 Placement of the project-planning process.

The Project-Planning Process

Once assigned to a project, the manager must assemble an interim team to conduct the planning activities. A small team, consisting of three to six resources, works well. There should be representation from the business and technology areas in this group. Since there will be a significant amount of contact with senior stakeholders within the organization at this time, the planning team should be seasoned and preferably have prior experience working together. To ensure continuity, the manager should ensure that some members of the interim team are dedicated to the project on an ongoing basis.

Figure 4.2 shows the stages of the project-planning process. The objectives of the planning team include establishing the groundwork needed to support the project, building support at the grassroot level, and extending the high-level business case that was created earlier. The key relationships that need to be established at this time, along with the expectations that need to be communicated to other groups, are shown in the following list:

☐ **Executive management.** Identify key executives with an interest in the project and communicate about mutual expectations with them for the rest of the project lifecycle. You should establish regular touch points with the executive group.

Confirm executive approval

Understand project requirements

Reflect on issues

Identify milestones

Identify phases

Identify activities within phases

Identify tasks within activities

Figure 4.2   Breaking down the planning process.

☐ **Stakeholders.** Identify all groups and resources that have a material interest in the outcome of the project. You should communicate about expectations with them and establish regular touch points.

☐ **Users.** Identify key users who will determine business requirements and who can resolve contradictions. Communicate about user-testing expectations with this group. Negotiate full-time user involvement for the duration of the project. Users typically involve those groups that operate the production systems.

☐ **Technology.** Identify resources required to support the project's technology infrastructure needs. This includes reserving time with database administrators, network administrators, architecture specialists, and capacity planners. Also identify resources who will purchase equipment and set it up for the project.

☐ **Functional groups.** Identify resources from any other areas in the organization who will have input into the project. This can include accounting, legal, and marketing personnel.

☐ **Other project groups.** Identify other project teams that may compete for resources with your project. Communicate about key project dates with their project managers and build a process to avoid future conflicts.

☐ **External groups.** Identify any external groups that will affect the project. For example, this could include banks that need to set up a process to interface with the system(s) being built (e.g., a lockbox to accept checks). Identify a key contact in every external group and establish regular touch points.

☐ **Vendors.** Identify all vendors that will supply material to the project. Ensure that a service level agreement in writing or in principle is in place with each vendor. Also ensure that your project is a priority for the vendor and clearly communicate ongoing expectations.

The following section reviews the activities that are part of the planning phase, including securing approvals, gathering business requirements, issuing identification and resolution, and updating the overall business case.

Confirm Executive Approval

Managers must identify all sources of power and influence that can affect their projects. It is important to verify that a prospective project has executive support and an executive sponsor, who in turn has the full support of the executive team. A steering committee should be established as soon as possible to resolve the inevitable issues that will arise during the project lifecycle. This information can be used to build a standard escalation process that removes obstacles encountered on the project.

It is also important to identify key users and to agree on acceptance criteria that document how the final results will be accepted or rejected. It may be necessary to form more than one steering committee and resource each one differently. A common practice is to build a tactical steering committee staffed with business and technical users for dealing with day-to-day issues on the project. A second, executive-level steering committee is staffed with senior management and focuses more on budgeting and strategic issues.

A manager should also understand the nature and importance of a prospective project. Are the project results mission-critical to the organization? What is the relative priority of the project as compared to others? What is the level of risk in the project? How much risk is the organization willing to tolerate? What are the project drivers? Answers to these questions will allow a manager to understand the pecking order of active projects within the organization. The more important the project, the more visible it will be within the organization. This will make it easier to get and keep resources. On the other hand, the increased visibility also places a manager under greater pressure to deliver.

Understand Project Requirements

A manager cannot create a complete project plan without understanding the business requirements at a detailed level. However, requirements are generally not well understood anywhere in the organization at this point in the planning cycle. In practical terms, the known requirements tend to be simplified vision statements or a description of a strategic direction. Both options are open to different interpretations and clarity must be provided in later phases of the project. Detailed business requirements are developed in the requirements gathering phase shown in Figure 4.1. Managers are thus faced with the challenge of building a project plan without having the benefit of fully understanding the business requirements. This situation can lead to other difficulties because the project plan is also used to estimate project costs and deadlines. Many managers are able to balance this collection of problems and plan successfully through a combination of experience, intellect, hard work, and intuition. Another helpful personality trait is the ability to accept a lack of precision and the unknown.

However, by balancing several factors, it is possible to build a plan that will evolve into a more complete view at some later point in the lifecycle. An iterative planning approach provides a solution that compensates for the lack of available details this early in the project. This approach involves doing detailed planning in a short time horizon and doing increasingly high-level planning as you go further out in time. The overall project plan and any estimates are then presented with a specific degree of uncertainty at any given point. The further out the point in time, the more uncertain the known figures. A contingency bucket should be built with the knowledge of the project executive and the business users to compensate for the uncertainty in dates and funding. This approach also involves continuous refinement of the project plan and estimates. Constraints, such as fixed implementation dates and budgets, must be accommodated during these periods of refinement.

Design meetings and workshops can be used to great advantage in trying to understand business requirements. A manager can either run the meetings personally, or appoint a facilitator to do most of the work. Prior to calling design meetings, a manager should learn as much as possible about the project's objectives and requirements. These should be documented in easy-to-follow dataflow diagrams, data models, flowcharts, and entity relationship diagrams (see chapter 7 for details). These should

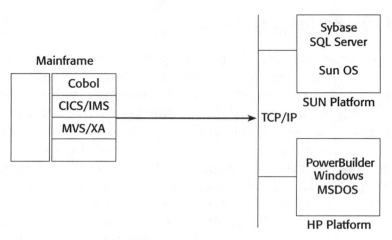

Figure 4.3   Payroll project.

be presented in the design meetings with the words: "This is what I think we're doing—correct me where I'm wrong." Attendance at the design meetings should be open to anyone the manager feels can assist in getting a better understanding of what a project is trying to achieve. The only obligation here is that key users must be in attendance.

As an example, consider the requirements for a payroll system for contract staff at a medium-sized business. These are described in the following paragraphs and shown in Figure 4.3.

Migrate a mainframe-based COBOL application supported by a CICS interface and IMS files to an n-tier Web-based architecture using Microsoft SQL Server, Visual Basic, MTS, and IIS on a LAN/WAN, with wireless support, by January 4 of the following year.

The contract staff payroll system must interface with the payroll system for the rest of the company. There are some differences, especially in the approval process. The total payroll system feeds the corporate general ledger.

The contract staff payroll application consists of a series of user screens, some of which are identified in Table 4.1.

Identify and Resolve Issues

The project manager is, by definition, the central figure and authority on the project. As the person who is ultimately responsible for the fate of

Table 4.1 Payroll Project User Screens

SCREEN NAME	PURPOSE	USER GROUP
Timesheet	All company staff use this screen to enter the hours they worked during the week into a computer system.	Employees
TimeApproval	Timesheets entered by staff are examined and approved online by their immediate managers.	Administration
PayApproval	Payroll staff accept invoices from contract staff and do a line item consolidation with the hours reported on the timesheets and those approved on the system. Payroll staff also access daily rates and any other pertinent information to approve the invoice. The invoice is accepted or rejected online.	Payroll
Corrections	The system allows corrections to items according to a security table. Staff members are allocated clearance to specific items and functions. Values that are not posted to production can be modified by staff with the appropriate clearance. After posting, the items are protected against changes, but can still be browsed.	Employees
History	Browse paychecks for up to one year after generation.	Payroll

the project, the manager is empowered to interview any resource, ask any question, and challenge every assumption. Indeed, the manager is obligated to exhaust all possibilities before committing to a project plan and business requirements. By dividing the issues into several categories, the project manager can determine the likelihood of project success before investing a lot of time and resources on the ground. This section contains examples of the types of questions that should be asked at this stage of the project.

Planning Questions

Planning questions focus on the long-term viability of a project in the context of other initiatives within the organization and against competitive pressures. These items will determine if the project is going to succeed in the context of organizational support. Some questions that should be considered in this category are:

- ☐ Does the project have a true measurable purpose?
- ☐ Does the project have an executive mandate?
- ☐ Does the project have middle-management backing?
- ☐ Does the project have an adequate budget and a reasonable contingency fund?
- ☐ Does the project have adequate time for delivery?
- ☐ Who is championing the project?
- ☐ Who is the sponsor of the project?
- ☐ Is the technology infrastructure in place, or will it be considered as part of the project?
- ☐ What is the relative pecking order of the project in the resource pool?
- ☐ Who will ensure that the results (e.g., systems) are implemented and used within the organization after they pass the acceptance criteria?
- ☐ Does the project require custom development? How much? Who is paying for it?
- ☐ Does the project require a commercial software package(s)? Does the project require a combination of a packaged solution and development (e.g., interfacing to legacy systems)?
- ☐ What benefits does the project offer to the organization?
- ☐ What factors can cause the project to fail?

Status Questions

Capturing the status reporting needs of the project team ensures that all relevant resources are aware of the expectations. Some of the questions to consider in this category are:

- ☐ How will resources report their status?
- ☐ How should information be shared on the project?
- ☐ Who should attend status meetings?
- ☐ How often should status meetings be held?
- ☐ What are the organizational status requirements?
- ☐ What are the status standards of the organization?
- ☐ How often will a status report be released?

- ☐ How will issues be escalated?
- ☐ Who should issues be escalated to?

Resource Questions

Resource-related questions focus on human, technology, work space, and other physical materials. The questions are intended to understand which resources are needed for the project, the amount, and the timing. Some of the questions to consider are the following:

- ☐ Is there a dedicated project team?
- ☐ How many key resources are also committed to production duties? In the event of a conflict, who will support the project needs?
- ☐ Which users will help drive business requirements?
- ☐ Which users will resolve business requirement conflicts?
- ☐ Which users can test the results?
- ☐ Are staff resources adequate to deliver the project?
- ☐ Should one or more components of the project be outsourced to consultants or third parties?
- ☐ Is outside (i.e., agency) assistance required to recruit adequate resources for the project?
- ☐ What is the technology architecture (hardware and software)?
- ☐ Managers should ask themselves the following candid question: "Am I able to properly manage the project, or should another architect or manager be involved?" If the answer is yes, the manager can either resign from the project (not suggested) or plan to hire the required expertise on a contractual basis to augment the necessary skill sets. This will also provide the manager with an opportunity to develop skills for the next project.
- ☐ How much working space is needed for the project team?

Background Information

Background information refers to anything that is already known about the project. Finding this information is rarely straightforward, and requires examining many different sources. This can begin with a review of corporate document repositories (e.g., Web site, intranet, Lotus Notes). There could have been previous attempts at the project, so there might be useful project documentation stored on an intranet somewhere. Users and technology resources may also have hard or soft copies that may not be loaded anywhere. Sending a request through a company mailing list will potentially draw this information out. In other circumstances, it is worth building a leads list and personally following up with all the names to uncover information. Some questions to explore are:

☐ Who's been involved with this type of problem in the past?

☐ Is there a data model? Process model? Object model?

☐ Are there other written requirements or documents?

☐ Were there previous attempts to do this project? What happened?

☐ Were any feasibility studies or benchmarking tests done?

Acceptance Criteria

As functionality becomes available, it is important to have documented evaluation criteria to assess the value and quality of the deliverables being produced. This criteria should be established at the start of the project to ensure its objectivity. Examples of some questions that should be asked at this stage are:

☐ What are the key requirements?

☐ Has the acceptance criteria been documented?

☐ Who will ultimately make the decision to accept the project?

☐ What are the acceptance metrics for the various deliverables on the project?

☐ Who can develop test plans for the various types of testing?

Managers must be able to articulate substantial details in their answers to these questions. For example, if the budget is adequate, there are still more questions to answer. What is the total amount allocated for the project? Who is paying for the project? How does the budget break down by phase or activity? How closely should the budget be monitored? Is it possible to get an increase in the budget? How long will this take?

Risk Analysis

The planning phase should be used as an opportunity to identify and mitigate project risks. The project manager should actively gather information about risks to the project through interviews and questionnaires. After finalizing and prioritizing the known risks, a mitigation strategy and deadline should be developed for each one. Resources should also be assigned to execute the individual strategies. For example, some common categories for project risk include the following:

☐ **Technology.** This includes the capabilities of the technology infrastructure in terms of capacity, scalability, and performance.

☐ **Team.** This includes the capabilities of the team, too much information being concentrated in too few resources, and resource turnover.

☐ **Requirements.** This includes such items as clarity, consistency, and requirements creep.

☐ **Environment.** This includes the impact of the physical environment on the development effort. For example, what happens if there are too many snowstorms?

☐ **Availability of resources.** This includes the ability of the project to reserve other resources in the organization in the face of competing priorities. This can include work space, test regions, key users, and funding.

☐ **Contingency.** This includes the development environment's ability to support the effort, despite problems such as a database crash.

Quality Planning

The objective of a quality process is to ensure the integrity of the project solutions and an ability to justify the results that are achieved. This process should be initiated in the planning phase as part of the overall project plan. It is common to appoint senior resources outside the regular project team to monitor quality on an ongoing basis. A quality process includes the following: a statement of quality, quality expectations, a statement of responsibilities, deliverable standards, and a quality plan.

Identify Milestones

Every project can have clearly defined events or milestones that mark important dates along the project lifecycle. By definition, a milestone should be a significant event that leads toward the direct success of a project. A milestone is typically accompanied by something called a deliverable, which can be defined, measured, and demonstrated. A deliverable is not always a milestone—it may just be the measurable product of expended effort on a project. By tracking milestones, it is possible to have a high-level view of the project status. This view is easy to explain at the steering committee level. Missing a milestone is a significantly negative event that must be explained at this level.

For the payroll system, possible milestones include the following: a pilot project, mapping of the legacy data and functions to an n-tier system, development of the Web screens, physical database development, data conversion from the legacy system, and report development.

Identify Phases

Project phases allow large projects to be divided into manageable pieces based on a prioritized list of user requirements. Phases are generally constructed to implement project deliverables in an order that provides users with important functions first, with a minimum of risk to a business unit. A project phase can produce multiple deliverables.

Another benefit of dividing a project into phases is to facilitate control over the budgeting process. This means that a project need not be funded in its entirety. This allows continuous refinement of a project plan and its budget as issues develop in the project lifecycle. Since important functions can be completed in earlier phases, it becomes possible to delay subsequent phases (that have less important functionality) without affecting an application's core functionality.

A consensus among managers who were surveyed for this book is that large projects should be divided into phases of six to eight months' duration, as a standard. For reasons discussed in chapter 7 this appears to optimize application development, testing, and implementation activities. Each phase can then be divided into a set of subphases that collectively contribute to the construction of that phase's deliverables.

The payroll system can be divided into two basic phases. Phase 1 involves mapping, user interface design and development, physical database, and data conversion activities. Phase 2 involves building control reports and administrative functions (that previously required batch scripts and operational support to satisfy).

Each phase can be divided into start and end dates, resource requirements, budget allocation, and deliverables.

Identify Activities within Phases

A phase should be divided into activities so that each produces a single deliverable or leads to the production of a deliverable. An activity is defined by a start date–time, an end date–time, allocated resources, and dependencies. If an activity can be divided into several additional hierarchical levels, a common approach is to introduce a subphase level between the phases and activities.

Both phases of the payroll application can be further divided into a small collection of activities. The following list shows deliverables at the phase level. It also shows a list of activities for each phase and the deliverable produced by the activity.

Phase 1 (Deliverables: mapping, user interface, physical database, data conversions)

☐ Conduct mapping activity (Deliverable: map)

☐ Build user interface (Deliverable: user interface)

☐ Build physical database (Deliverable: database schema, scripts)

☐ Convert data (Deliverable: data conversion scripts)

☐ Gather test results and get user sign-offs (Deliverable: test scripts, test results, testing sign-offs)

Phase 2 (Deliverables: control reports, administrative function list)

☐ Build control reports (Deliverable: control reports)

☐ Build administrative functions (Deliverable: administrative function list)

Identify Tasks within Activities

Complex activities can be divided into a series of tasks. A task has a definition similar to an activity, namely a start date–time, an end date–time, allocated resources, and dependencies.

The following list provides an example in which some of the activities in the payroll system have been expanded to include their detailed tasks. Deliverables can be identified at the task level; however, for practical readability they continue to be identified at the task level. Notice the volume of information that is generated by the simple act of moving down another level in the phase hierarchy. Magnifying this task-based list on a project with a dozen or so phases and a few hundred activities in each phase will produce a project plan that becomes quite difficult to maintain and update. Some trade-offs need to be made in terms of documented detail versus the time required to maintain the information.

Phase 1

Activity 1 (Mapping)

- ☐ Gather existing documentation and programs.
- ☐ Develop data dictionary list for existing system.
- ☐ Develop data dictionary list for new system.

Activity 2 (Build user interface)

- ☐ Gather all forms and reports.
- ☐ Gather CICS screen prints: enter employee hours, maintain employee history, browse checks, support corrections, reprint checks, consolidate, feed general ledger, initiate batch program.
- ☐ Develop prototype of Powerbuilder user interface.
- ☐ Demonstrate prototype to users.
- ☐ Fix prototype based on user comments.
- ☐ Analyze "enter employee hours" function.
- ☐ Build "enter employee hours."
- ☐ Test "enter employee hours."
- ☐ Analyze "maintain employee history."
- ☐ Build "maintain employee history."
- ☐ Test "maintain employee history."
- ☐ Analyze "browse checks."
- ☐ Build "browse checks."
- ☐ Test "browse checks."
- ☐ Analyze "support corrections."
- ☐ Build "support corrections."
- ☐ Test "support corrections."
- ☐ Analyze "reprint checks."
- ☐ Build "reprint checks."
- ☐ Test "reprint checks."

- ☐ Analyze "consolidate."
- ☐ Build "consolidate."
- ☐ Test "consolidate."
- ☐ Analyze "feed general ledger."
- ☐ Build "feed general ledger."
- ☐ Test "feed general ledger."
- ☐ Analyze "initiate batch program."
- ☐ Build "initiate batch program."
- ☐ Test "initiate batch program."

Activity 3 (and so on)

These names, of course, are not cast in stone. A phase could be called a process, which means that activities could be referred to as phases, and so on. Further levels of breakdown are also possible, in that tasks can be divided into subtasks, and so on. The important element being presented here is the division of a project into several implementation schedules, each of which satisfies one or more project requirements. These relationships are illustrated in Figure 4.4, which shows that a collection of subtasks makes up a task; a collection of tasks makes up an activity; a collection of activities makes up a phase; a collection of phases makes up a project.

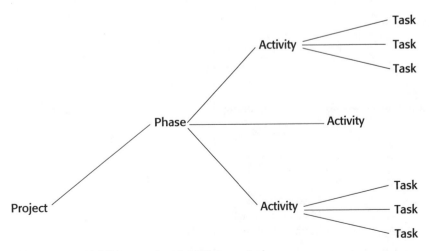

Figure 4.4 Dividing a project into time periods.

At the planning stage of the project, it is recommended that you place a focus at the activity level for the most part. Many details of the plan will continue to evolve over the project lifecycle. Operating at a more detailed level may distract you from other important issues. There are some supporters of the more detailed approach, and it may have its advantages in some situations. It is hard to argue in the early stages of the planning phase that resources, requirements, and situations will not change during a multimonth project lifecycle. From our survey results, and past experience, it seems that detailed plans created upfront are generally thrown out when a project starts, to be replaced by higher-level plans that are easier to maintain and present.

Project-Planning Constraints

Constraints are applied at various stages in the life of a project. A constraint is a limiting factor on a project (e.g., budget, delivery date). A collection of constraints applicable to most projects is shown in Figure 4.5, and discussed in more detail in this section.

Budget

An overall budget is usually assigned to a project during the project justification stage. Depending on the sophistication and frequency of mea-

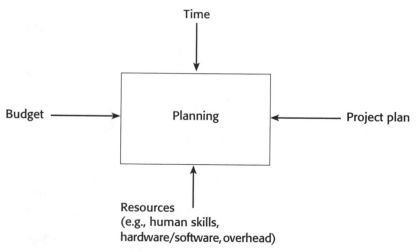

Figure 4.5 Project constraints.

surement, the budget can include human skills, equipment, space, time-sharing, fixed costs (e.g., telephone, stationery), and even food costs. Budgetary limitations are also applied at other levels of a project: They are fairly common at the phase level, but not so common for activities or tasks. Shifting budget amounts proportionately between phases is commonly done to shift project priorities.

Budget expenditures are tracked on an ongoing basis for management reporting. A common approach to tracking frequency is to consolidate budget expenditure reports monthly for senior management meetings.

Time

A project starts and ends on specific target dates. The duration of the project is iteratively divided into shorter periods, often called phases, activities, tasks, and subtasks. Dates for the phase and activity levels are usually related to measurable deliverables.

Sometimes start and end target dates for the project are flexible. In such instances, a manager can use the sum of the individual lower levels to determine the total duration of the project, and thus the start and end dates.

The day-to-day progress of a project is usually tracked in terms of time spent on activities or tasks. This can also be expressed as a percentage of the total time that was reserved for the activity or task.

Resources

Until the mid-1980s, project teams tended to be quite large, with many layers of supervision and management. Individuals focused their efforts on a few specific activities inside fairly long project delivery cycles. The mainframe-based technology infrastructure generally supported this type of resource organization. The '90s saw a dramatic reduction in the length of time that the business community was willing to wait before seeing a return on their IT investment. This has been addressed by a general reduction in the length of project phases, as well as the number of resources allocated to each phase in a project. Individual resources have multiple roles on a project, which requires them to develop multiple skill sets. In general, project phases of four-to-eight-month durations work well, with team sizes of six to eight professionals. In the new century, the trend towards smaller work teams continues; however, Web-based architecture tends to use a collection of these teams working in different parts of the overall picture. The IT environments of 2000+ are actually seeing a merger of the team structures of the 1980s and the 1990s.

Multiple types of resources are required on projects. A project manager generally tracks these at various times during a project. Some types of resources are required only at specific times (e.g., those with the skills to build a network), while other resources are required on an ongoing basis (e.g., the services of a developer). Project resources are divided into the following categories.

Human Skills

Human skills are often the only project resource that many managers consider when planning their projects. Managers should determine which skill sets are required on a project at an aggregate level and then divide them across a task or activity level. Required skills can sometimes be provided by the same human resource. For the purpose of allocation on the project plan, each resource should be identified as follows: *resource title, resource name, percentage of time on project, rate, start date, end date*

Suppose that Neil Sector is an architect on the project. He can be used half time; his hourly rate is $200. He is only available between January 3 and July 20 of any given year. This information translates into the following example: *Architect, Neil Sector, 50%, $200/hr, January 3, 20xx, July 20, 20xx*

IT Hardware and Software

In *n*-tier, Web-based environments, it is increasingly important to plan to have technology available at the time it is needed on a project. For example, in most applications, many different hardware and software components are required, but not always at the same time. Development can begin on a small UNIX-based machine with limited capacity, but testing of the application must be done on a larger machine. This means that the larger machine should be budgeted for and delivered in time for testing to begin. Getting the machine too soon may result in needless expenditures; getting the machine too late will delay the project.

The authors have seen examples of projects with tight deadlines where the development software was available, the hardware platforms were leased and available, the development team was hired and trained, the business requirements were signed off, but meaningful work could not begin because the operating system on the hardware platform was inconsistent with the database server. This stopped meaningful development from beginning for several weeks on a 12-week project. Although other work could be done in the meantime, there is no question that this sort of delay was costly and harmful to the success of the project.

Managers must be careful to ensure that the correct hardware and software combinations (with the proper add-ons) have been selected for the project and ordered so that they arrive when they are required. Project managers must also ensure that it is technically possible to meet the business requirements. Administrative issues, such as ensuring that the technical environment contains licensed products, are also within the scope of this phase.

Overhead Requirements

This involves planning for resources such as office space, telephone lines, and furniture. Demand for these resources can fluctuate dramatically (e.g., hiring 12 testers during testing). Optimization of these resources can save significant amounts of money on the project. For example, office space can be shared with other departments. Other methods include short-term leasing of office space, flexible working hours, and work-at-home strategies.

Pitfalls in Planning

Project planning is not an exact science, thus it is rare that the plans of any two projects are the same. Every project has unique aspects that make the planning process unique and problematic. For managers who are looking to duplicate the same management approach from one project to another, this results in significant jeopardy to their success. Following a generic recipe is not possible and should not be done.

Furthermore, the problems this approach causes may not become visible until it is too late to save the project.

Human nature is another key pitfall in the planning process. Given difficult and easy tasks, many managers (who, of course, are human beings) have the tendency to do the easy ones instead of focusing on the new challenges of the current project. Add to this that bad planning does not become evident for many months, or years, and it becomes apparent that lazy or sloppy planning is easy to get away with. This is not to say that managers want to follow this route deliberately, just that they may be doing so without realizing it.

Chapter 5 describes many factors that contribute to project failure. Some of these are particularly applicable during the planning process, and include the following:

- Lack of a project plan
- Requirements not understood by the project team
- Insufficient funding
- Unrealistic expectations of stakeholders
- Lack of project management and leadership skills

Managers who do not have the ability to plan effectively should be prepared to hire resources to assist them in avoiding the pitfalls mentioned in this section. This can be done painlessly by hiring contract architects or project leaders for assistance, with the clear mandate for skills transfer. These contractors do not become permanent expense items, nor do they compete with the project manager.

Another insidious pitfall in the planning process occurs when managers, uncomfortable with their ability to deliver the project successfully, resist putting a proper project plan together to avoid being held to a particular schedule. Managers sometimes use this technique to delay a project until they can get themselves safely out of the picture. In other cases, the manager is comfortable with the technique with no plans to change. Completion dates of such projects usually slide and slide until executive management either cancels the project or motivates the manager to commit to a plan and deliver the product—or else.

Project managers can improve their management ability by learning the objectives and tools of planning, understanding the guidelines, and attending management courses.

Planning Tools

This chapter has discussed project planning at a conceptual level—generally a weak area for many managers, who tend to spend more time at the execution and administrative levels. Effective planning requires the ability to analyze a project and build a series of steps that allows its successful completion with incomplete information. Creating the proper plan is a mental exercise, while putting it into a format that can be communicated and monitored requires physical tools.

A project plan can be started by simply writing it down on a piece of paper or typing it into a word-processing file. In fact, this is a useful method of beginning the planning process, because the manager is free to reflect and plan without the distraction of using the complex editing facilities that are offered by most planning tools. At this stage, speed of thought and typing is important, since the plan is constantly changing. Once the skeleton of the project plan is in a reasonable state, it can be imported or entered into a project management tool and subsequently refined.

To gain an understanding of a project and to be able to communicate it to others, a manager can start investigating at either the activity or the task level. This requires an understanding of the following information:

- Activity number and name or task number and name
- Title
- Resources
- Start date
- Target date
- Deliverables
- Dependency
- Duration
- Person days
- Description

We have found it convenient to use a word-processing package, such as WordPerfect or Microsoft Word, to enter this information for each activity into a file. The file is then printed and iteratively validated until a good understanding of the project activities and deliverables is attained. This is shown in the following example:

Filename: payplan.1 Summary of Findings for Phase 1

Activity No: 1   Mapping

Title: Gather existing documentation and programs

Resources: Neil Sector, Rohit Jaiswal

Start Date: Jan 5, 2000

Target Date: Jan 20

Deliverables: data dictionary, function list

Depends on: nothing

Duration: 10 Days

Person Days: 20

Description: Use current documentation and application as a source. Technology is CICS, IMS, VSAM, COBOL, and PL/1.

Activity No: 2   Build User Interface

Title: Develop user interface in Powerbuilder

Resources: Darryl Coombs

Start Date: Jan 5

Target Date: Feb 1

Deliverables: The following screens: Timesheet, TimeApproval, Pay-Approval, Corrections, History.

Depends on: nothing

Duration: 10 days

Person Days: 10

Description: Migrate current CICS screens.

Activity No: 3   Build Physical Database

Title: Build an optimized physical database for the payroll application for Sybase SQL Server

Resources: Amarjit Singh

Start Date: Jan 22

Target Date: Feb 15

Deliverables: database creation script, data script.

Depends on: Activity 1

Duration: 8 days

Person Days: 20

Description: Build a logical data model and convert it to a physical data model for optimized implementation under Sybase SQL Server.

The preceding file should be expanded for the remaining activities previously defined in this chapter. After receiving confirmation for the activities, the file can be modified to include details for the tasks. During the process of seeking confirmation, a manager should be open to making changes to the plan. Clearly, this is a time-consuming and complex process. But this is the nature of planning. Time spent doing this properly will benefit the project greatly.

Several iterative cycles later, when the file has been fixed and validated, it can be typed into a project management tool and archived (it probably will not be required again). The version of the plan in the project management tool is subsequently used. Some popular tools on the market for this purpose are Microsoft Project and Project Workbench. Project plans are commonly built in, the form of Gantt charts. A sample Gantt chart is shown in Figure 4.6. A Gantt chart is a pictorial representation of a project plan with the following elements:

☐ **Task name.** This is the user-defined name of a phase, activity, task, subtask, or other line item.

☐ **Duration.** This is the length of time required for the line item defined under task name (generally in days).

☐ **Start date**. This is the start date of the line item defined under task name.

☐ **End date.** This is the expected end date of the line item defined under task name.

☐ **Resources.** One or more resources can be allocated to the line item under task name. These resources can be selected from a pool of resources that are allocated either to the project or to a group of projects.

The reader is referred to chapter 10 of this book for a tutorial on Microsoft Project, which is the selected tool in this book for use in implementing project-planning concepts.

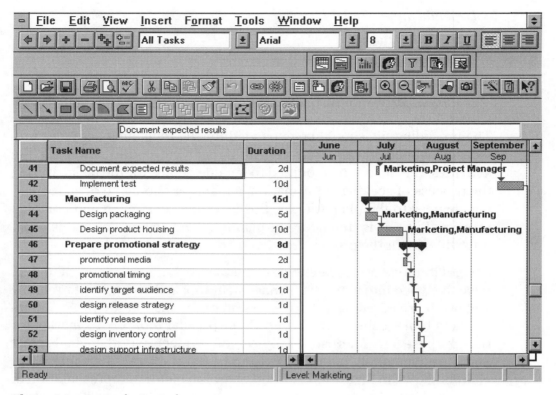

Figure 4.6   A sample Gantt chart.

Other Pictorial Tools and Views

In addition to Gantt charts, several other graphic tools are available to assist managers in the project-planning effort. Although the Gantt chart is arguably the most useful, the following tools can serve a useful purpose in planning efforts as well.

Critical Path Method (CPM)

This graphical technique identifies critical tasks in a project plan. A CPM network shows the minimum amount of time required to deliver the project. Changing any of the tasks on the critical path will change the time required to complete the project. CPM also shows dependencies between tasks and priorities among tasks. A sample CPM network is shown in Figure 4.7.

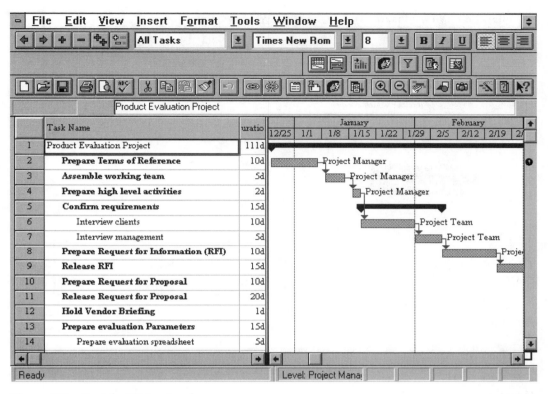

Figure 4.7 Sample CPM network.

Program Evaluation and Review Technique (PERT)

This is a scenario-based approach that uses a graphical tool to identify dependencies between tasks, durations, start dates, and/or end dates. The scenarios consist of examining cases that are *best*, *expected*, or *worst*. A sample PERT screen is shown in Figure 4.8.

Project Development Methodologies and the Project Lifecycle

Project development methodologies have become common in most organizations, where the question is not "Is there a development methodology in this organization?" but rather, "How many methodologies does this

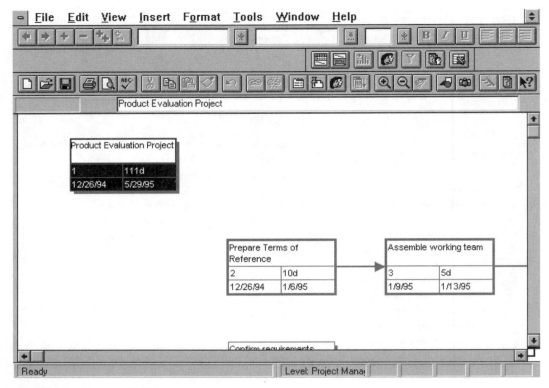

Figure 4.8 Sample PERT screen.

organization have, and which one is being used in this department at the current time?" Methodologies have become a selling feature for many consulting organizations who offer their services, along with a proprietary methodology that was developed with the support of several large clients. All of these methodologies have some success stories.

The planning stages discussed in this chapter are standard in a broad range of methodologies. A project manager can designate the remaining unused processes defined in the methodology as activities in the project plan. The specific details, such as the duration or cost for a process, depend on several factors, beginning with the methodology being used and, of course, the specifics of the project. Chapter 7 of this book defines a methodology called the Iterative Project Development Methodology, which has been used successfully in projects ranging in size from $25,000 to several million dollars. This methodology is a refinement on Rapid Application Development (RAD), which has been popular for the last couple of years.

Role of Facilitating

Many project managers are sincere in wanting to develop a meaningful project plan by conducting a comprehensive planning process. The difficulty is knowing how to get the information that is needed to do this, and also how to reach consensus among future team members. Documentation will only get you so far, and in most organizations this is either absent, out of date, or only a starting place.

Properly conducted joint application design (JAD) sessions, consisting of two or more members, can serve a dual purpose. A manager should do a fair bit of learning in private and endeavor to build a series of graphic views of a project, including a data model, a process model, a flow of the application, and a rudimentary project plan at a minimum. This information should be checked with key users in a series of one-on-one meetings (call them JADs, but they are just effective meetings). This information should be used to improve the documentation. When the manager is satisfied with the quality of the information obtained about the project, JADs should be organized to bring key people within the organization together to review the documented information.

JAD attendees should include key business users, architects, designers, project leaders, and anyone else who has an interest in or influence on the project. The manager should be careful to limit attendance to a dozen people at most. When numbers go beyond this limit, different groups of JADs should be organized to maintain the effectiveness of the process.

The JAD sessions will allow key members of the organization to become involved in the process, provide input, confirm the proposed solution, and get to know each other. The importance of these factors on the success of the project cannot be underestimated. In most cases, the JAD sessions will also generate changes to a manager's documentation. This is good, because the end product will be a better plan than at the start of the process.

There are several potential pitfalls to the JAD process. Some people in the organization may not see value in attending them, or may object to the amount of time they consume. The manager should attempt to overcome these objections by drawing on success stories. If this does not work, a manager can promise to limit the amount of time a particular member needs to actually spend in the meeting, or provide a written summary if attendance is impossible. As a final resort, it may be necessary to force an invitation and cooperation by involving a higher authority in the company. This has also been known to work.

Another potential pitfall in the JAD process is insufficient planning on the part of the manager. The manager should have developed a good understanding of the project, given the available information. It is perfectly acceptable to be wrong in an opinion, or to say, "I could not reach a conclusion with the information I had." It is not acceptable to look embarrassed when someone in the meeting holds up a purchase order (PO) and you did not even consider that POs were an issue. In other words, the manager should be in a position to propose—and admit to being totally wrong, if necessary—a complete solution or to ask questions that lead to a complete solution. Furthermore, a manager should prepare sufficient documentation of suitable quality to be able to walk the attendees through the discussion.

The final pitfall that will be discussed here is the choice of a facilitator. Not everyone can facilitate a JAD session—this requires unique skills that many managers simply do not have. Sometimes it is better to hire a contract facilitator to lead the JAD sessions. This allows an expert to handle extremely delicate discussions, and it may also allow the members in attendance to speak more freely to an outsider, who is not a direct threat or a superior.

Estimating

Project plans are also used for estimating or confirming resource requirements for a project, with a focus on the following three components: time, cost, and resources. The accuracy of the estimates depends on the detail level and accuracy of a project plan. There are several estimating approaches, including bottom-up, top-down, and by-aggression, that are examined in this book.

Estimates are used for many purposes in project planning, with an emphasis on the following situations:

1. To determine fixed price bids on projects. This is especially important for consulting companies, including outsourcing firms, systems integrators, and contracting firms. These firms survive on

project billings, making accuracy a paramount concern. The risk associated with an estimate is offset by a buffer amount to protect the company. Manager compensation is often tied to how closely the estimates and actuals comply.

2. To request budget and staffing support. Estimates are used to forecast a future internal budget for a company. This can cause management to make decisions on which projects are supported and which are canceled.

The Effective Project Plan

When can a project plan be described as being poorly put together? This is determined by how well the project manager completes his or her homework. There are some clearly objective conditions that can be identified. For example, the activities in the following project plan are not well thought out. In fact, the project manager who designed this plan has not really built a plan at all, but rather a list of "to do" items that is being passed off as a plan (see Table 4.2).

The key weakness in this plan is that it is too generic. The project manager has clearly not understood the scope of the project. In fact, how would one estimate the scope, cost, or timeline of this project based on this ambiguous information? Each activity is left wide open. To improve the plan and add value to it, the following questions need to be answered:

☐ What are the main functions?

☐ What are the input screens?

Table 4.2 Project Plan: Invoicing Application

ACTIVITY	DESCRIPTION
1	Kickoff meeting
2	Determine main functions for the invoicing system
3	Design input screens
4	Meet with users to confirm screens and functions
5	Develop programs
6	Test
7	Implement

☐ Which users will be involved in meetings? What will be done with each of them?

☐ What programs need to be written?

☐ What is the approach for testing? Who is involved in the testing?

☐ What are the dependencies between tasks?

Someone needs to investigate these activities at a more detailed level.

Summary

The project management survey conducted for this book identified a lack of effective project planning as a serious contributor to the failure of projects (as discussed in chapter 5). This planning process involves a series of stages leading to the development of a project plan. A key component of the project plan is the ability to describe a project in terms of building blocks—namely, phases, activities, and tasks. This allows a manageable view of a project to occur. Each task can be described in terms of a start and end date, deliverables, and resources. Deliverables are important because they provide a measurable method of evaluating a task. A project was also described in terms of milestones (major events).

Pitfalls in planning were described in this chapter. The common pitfalls include lack of a project plan, requirements not being understood by the project team, and insufficient funding. The use of JAD techniques for developing and communicating project plans was also described. JAD techniques can be applied to the team as well as used to seek consensus with client management.

Three graphical representations of a project plan were introduced, Gantt charts, PERT, and CPM. Gantt charts are the most common graphical representation to show task description, resources, task and overall project duration, and important dates on a project plan. The CPM method identifies the critical project tasks and shows the minimum amount of time required to deliver the project. PERT is a graphical tool to identify dependencies between tasks. The use of project plans for estimating and confirming resource requirements was described. The key components of estimating are time, cost, and resources.

Why Projects Fail

T his chapter identifies five broad categories of project failure and describes proven approaches for minimizing their impact on projects. A working definition of project failure is also provided and examined in the context of several case studies. This leads into chapter 6, which focuses on techniques a project manager can employ to improve the opportunities for achieving project success. In this chapter the reader will learn about:

- Negative project events and outcomes
- Project failure categories
- The human element
- Technological limitations
- Power politics
- Funding limitations
- Methodology limitations
- Case studies
- Rules of failure

Defining Project Failure

Project managers offer leadership to others in the organization, including their teams, senior management, steering committees, and business users in building a solution to a set of business problems. Project managers must provide the vision to resolve these potential areas of project failure. As temporary owners of the project, it is their responsibility to maintain the commitment of senior management, use the project steering committee to remove obstacles, deal with factors that can harm the project's success, actively manage the project team, involve key users during the project lifecycle, and communicate with other project teams.

Project failure can rarely be described in absolute terms and is better described in terms of degrees of failure. Some projects fail so badly that companies go out of business. Other projects fail, but their impact is hardly felt by the organization or the people affected. In many cases, projects are successful in some areas, while failing badly in others. Project failure is clearly dependent on many variables. Project managers are usually in a position to weigh the available options and determine which variables they should protect and which they can compromise.

Table 5.1 identifies a set of events that are generally indicative of some degree of project failure. The second column in the table identifies the severity of the effect of the project event on the success of the immediate project. The severity value for a project event in this table is presented in a vacuum and is abstracted from real life. The severities will accumulate over projects and will ultimately affect the health of an organization. Table 5.2 and its legend explain the impact of the event on the careers of the manager and members of the project team. The legend also identifies the corresponding effects on the organization.

The events in Tables 5.1 and 5.2 can also be described in terms of degree. For example, a project can be a few dollars or a few billion dollars over budget. Projects can also suffer more than one event, such as late delivery and being over budget. Depending on the circumstances, some events may be more acceptable than others. For example, some projects are so important that a manager is free to go over budget and will still be congratulated for running a successful project. Other projects can be considered to be successful even if they are delivered late.

Table 5.1 Events Indicative of Project Failure

PROJECT EVENT	SEVERITY
Cancellation	High
Late delivery	Medium to High
Over budget	Medium to High
Low quality	Medium to High
High employee turnover	Low to Medium

Table 5.2 Impact Associated with Project Failure

SEVERITY CODE	DESCRIPTION	PRIMARY IMPACT
High	Worst event	Organization + Manager + Team
Medium	Career damaging	Manager
Low	Embarrassing	Manager

Legend The Severity Code corresponds to the Severity column in Table 5.1. The Primary Impact column identifies the parties directly affected by the related severity code. Events that have a high severity code affect everyone involved, including the organization, the manager, and the team members. Events that have a medium severity affect the same parties, but to a lesser extent. In this case, companies are not expected to go out of business. Team members are rarely fired or disciplined, but do receive tarnished reputations; however, they can point the blame at someone else—the project manager. Consequently, the primary impact of the medium severity code is on the project manager's career and reputation. The embarrassment factor can be a nightmare to a project manager and will ultimately be career limiting.

Why do so many IT projects fail? If projects in other industries had the same failure rate as IT projects, there would be widespread public outrage. Imagine the reaction you would have if an architect's response to a public inquiry into why a newly constructed building toppled over was: "The municipal building codes kept changing." In defense of the information systems industry, municipal building codes do not change nearly as frequently as IT specifications do; furthermore, people have been constructing buildings much longer than they have been programming applications.

There are also the additional issues of magnitude and exposure to potential points of failure to consider. Many construction projects, though visually large, do not have a high degree of inherent complexity that varies dramatically from one project to another. This makes a comparison of a construction project to a typical corporate IT project unfair. However, when comparing megasize construction projects to large IT projects, more overlap becomes visible, and many of the same problems emerge.

IT projects have the additional distinction of being unlike projects in other industries in many key areas. For example, the IT industry is faced with a chronic shortage of staff, an ever-evolving and changing set of development tools, a relatively high rate of employee turnover, and a very large number of working components. In fact, every line in a program, every data element in a database, every development product, and every network link is a potential point of failure. Rapid technology changes, and the accompanying changes to methodologies and approaches, add to this burden.

Some standard problems arise from the high complexity seen on most IT projects. The first problem occurs because of a general inability to recognize that a given solution is correct (e.g., defining metrics to evaluate a solution against industry standards). Because of the large number of components and combinations in any application, it is a real challenge to describe what a successful solution should look like. For example, consider evaluating a software package like Microsoft Project in terms of functionality. Defining metrics for all possible test conditions would be a colossal task.

A second problem occurs because phases in a project receive deliverables or products from other phases, and then go on to create some of their own. As the number of phase levels increases, so too does the overall complexity in the project. This is shown in Figure 5.1. Increasing complexity increases the potential points of failure dramatically. This creates an added challenge in maintaining the integrity of an IT project.

A final consideration in understanding project complexity is the feedback loop. This occurs when phase A builds a deliverable that feeds into phase B. If something new is learned in phase B, a change must be made to the product from phase A, which could result in a further change in phase B, and so on. This creates a moving target that can keep both phases from being completed successfully. The classic example of this is

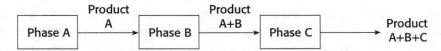

Figure 5.1 Phases and their products.

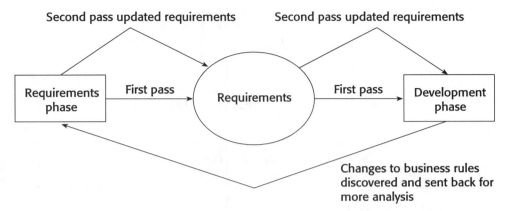

Figure 5.2 The feedback loop.

the case in which requirements are produced in one phase and passed into the development phase, where an enhancement or a correction is identified. The impact of this is shown in Figure 5.2.

On large projects, the complexity of the work that needs to be done to complete a project can be staggering. Typically, many individuals share discrete pools of knowledge that must be combined for the project to succeed. Several factors thus come into play: As project size increases (in terms of functionality, technology, and difficulty), there is pressure to increase the size of the project team and the pool of stakeholders. As these groups increase, so too does interpersonal complexity.

Complexity leads to chaos. Someone is needed to tie all this together. That responsibility falls on the project manager, who must somehow manage the project and navigate it toward success. One way to start this process is by understanding the common reasons for project failure. Some actions and structures will always cause a project to fail. Learning and avoiding these will at least reduce the level of the severity codes on your projects and allow you to focus on the factors discussed in chapter 6 to make your projects successful.

This chapter identifies five broad categories, as shown in Figure 5.3, that commonly contribute to project failure. At times, a particular issue may fall into more than one category. For example, insufficient funding to hire testing resources can be viewed as a human issue as well as a funding issue. This does not affect the discussion, since the issue itself is a contributor to project failure, and its precise categorization is unimpor-

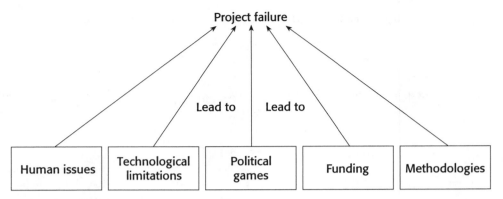

Figure 5.3   Categories of project failure.

tant. This chapter also suggests methods to avoid the factors that lead to project failure.

Human Resource Issues

Despite the continued rapid evolution of technology, project success or failure is still determined by the human element. An understanding of this dimension allows project managers the ability to bridge problems by building compromises with the business units, project teams, stakeholders, and other parts of the organization. It is rare that a solution can be built that will be 100 percent compliant with the business requirements. It is also rare that business requirements will be 100 percent accurate, precise, and clear. Project managers who have built strong relationships and expectations are better positioned to navigate vague waters.

This broad category includes factors such as employee turnover, soundness of the business requirements, understanding of the business requirements, and technical skills. Each of these factors can destroy a project, so a project manager must become intimately aware of what these factors are, what the exposures are, and how to avoid them.

Technological Limitations

Technical limitations can also cause a project to fail. These include factors such as inadequate response time, insufficient bandwidth for data transfer, and an inability to host certain types of software on a hardware platform. The authors' experience has been that good project management can often find a way around a technical limitation. Technological limitations will always exist, since there are some things that simply cannot be done with available technology. In such instances, manual processes can be used to integrate manual processes with an automated solution until appropriate technology becomes available. This is illustrated in the following example.

PhysCorp International provides medical services to patients in a metropolitan area. Company drivers receive a clipboard in the morning containing paper copies of service orders identifying the patients requiring service that day. The drivers sort the service orders to determine the best route for the day. At the end of the day, the drivers return to the head office to drop off their clipboards. The data entry organization updates the corporate database by rekeying everything (including comments and notes) that the drivers scribbled on the service orders. Another set of service orders is printed for the next morning.

There are several ways to automate PhysCorp International. An effective method would be to recognize situations in which current technological limitations are expected to be resolved by leading-edge technology in the near future. The paper service orders will ultimately be phased out as mobile technology becomes more reliable and affordable—and when the organization is ready to implement the technical solution. But until that happens (in one year, ten years, or more), an optimized alternative solution can be designed. The bottom line is that the business of the corporation must be serviced, and solutions that jeopardize this should not be tolerated. This may mean the acceptance of an old-fashioned manual procedure.

An effective project manager knows what is needed, what is possible, when it is possible, and when an organization is ready to implement a specific solution.

Political Games

Political games are played by individuals within an organization to gain rewards for themselves, or, at the very least, to take them away from someone else. In this context, their existence is hardly surprising, since most humans work for money, personal fulfillment, or to gain membership into a group. However, political games, as inevitable as they may be, have a tendency to become highly destructive to projects and even organizations. If left unchallenged, political games can cause irreparable damage to both.

Many years ago, one of the authors was working on a project in a large organization. A 25-year veteran of the company, noticing that roadblocks were hampering the success of the project, offered a pearl of wisdom that is just as true on many other IT projects today. He said, "Nobody wants the project to be implemented because it will highlight their weaknesses. They're also afraid to maintain the application on an ongoing basis because they don't have the skills required to do so." As it turned out, it was easier to keep the project going until the technology changed. When that happened, the project was quietly terminated.

To the question, "Why was the project started in the first place," the veteran replied: "As an insurance policy, and because there was money in the budget. Everyone has an agenda, sometimes it just isn't the same as yours."

The veteran also made another remarkable prediction. He pointed out who was going to be promoted, who was going to be transferred, and who would be tarnished as a result of the project's eventual failure. These rewards and punishments were not based on merit, but on how different individuals presented themselves to others in the organization. He turned out to be 100 percent accurate, less than a year later.

Political games are played on at least four levels in most organizations, as follows:

□ Organizational politics

□ Team politics

□ Individual politics

□ Business versus IS competition

Each of these levels will be discussed later in this chapter in the context of their team dynamics, impact on the project/organization, ways to recognize them, and ways to avoid them.

Funding

A project that is not adequately funded is bound to fail. This is no secret, yet many projects are still started with the futile hope that somehow things will work out. This only frustrates project team members and causes them to cut corners, ignore details, and build project plans that are incomplete and sloppy. The costs of underfunding a project will also be felt after the project is completed as the business is forced to spend a lot more money to maintain the system and fix errors. Employee turnover will also increase as resources leave the organization to avoid a similar type of project in the future.

In some cases, project funding may be adequate, but project managers create their own crisis by creative accounting. They build a funding contingency by slashing their original budgets and then use the smaller amount as a basis for planning the project. The contingency fund is then used as a backup when the project begins to derail. This approach can lead to the same problems described above. Furthermore, team members eventually catch on to this tactic and begin to mistrust estimates and deadlines. It is difficult to build constructive relationships when this happens.

Paradoxically, an overfunded project is also likely to fail, for a different set of reasons. Overfunding creates a set of behaviors that result in inefficiencies and redundancies that detract from an ability to deliver a project successfully. If money is no object, it is useful to build incentives for a project team to deliver under budget.

Methodologies

Methodologies are important in enabling project success. However, many organizations either depend on them too much, or avoid them altogether. A balance needs to be struck by leveraging a streamlined, customized methodology that is available across an organization. It should be accompanied by training, templates, and standards. The methodology must also be easily accessible and current.

One mistake that is commonly made across organizations using project development methodologies is to view them as recipes (following the fancy process boxes without an understanding of the problem). It is easy to depend on a methodology for success, or perhaps more accurately, to place blame on a methodology when a project fails.

The Human Element

It can be argued that the human element, in one form or another, is a dominant contributor toward project failure. As President Harry Truman once said: "The buck stops here." This is true of systems projects as well. The buck stops with the project manager.

Some typical human problems that can cause projects to fail are explained in this section.

Inability of Users to Agree on Business Requirements

This is like having General Motors paint a car red, then repaint it blue, then yellow, then red again. General Motors handles this problem by producing cars in different colors because there is a market for them. IT project managers can make similar concessions by supporting multiple sets of requirements, but this usually requires trade-offs in time, cost, and complexity.

As another example, consider the situation in which users agree that a merchandising system is required, but cannot agree on the functionality it should support (e.g., multiple languages, multiple currency types, multiple product types). This is primarily a problem in the early project phases and again in testing and implementation.

Suggested Solution

Recognize that indecision is a part of life and plan for it. Plan regular JAD sessions using an impartial facilitator who draws users and IT staff into constructive discussions. Document all communications and interpretations so that it is clear when decisions are being made or avoided. Public, friendly discussion gets people involved and encourages them to make decisions. The project manager should insist that experienced users, designers, and architects build an initial design that is iteratively modified until stakeholders agree on the proposals. It is important to have an escalation procedure that allows someone to ultimately make a decision if compromise is not reached within a project team. The manager can also use various techniques, such as prototyping, to allow users to see the impact of their decisions early in the process.

Inability of Users to Communicate Business Requirements

Another problem encountered on IT projects is a general lack of communication between users, managers, and the development teams. This also includes the accuracy, timeliness, and content of the communication.

Suggested Solution

A manager should insist that communication channels be open within a project team, no matter the size of the project. Effective methods of doing this include regular JAD sessions, status meetings, good documentation, and centrally located logs of issues, recommendations, and conclusions. It should be mandated that team members share information openly.

Inability of Users to Understand the Implications of Business Requirements

This is similar to the inability of users to agree on business requirements; however, this problem arises when users agree on a solution without fully understanding its ramifications. In other words, everyone may agree that a purchase order is required, but they may not understand that it is needed in French, English, and Spanish. This is commonly a weak area on projects, for the following reasons:

- ☐ Failure of users to understand the implications and totality of their business requirements
- ☐ Failure of the IT team to internalize and fully understand the business requirements
- ☐ Failure of users and the IS team to understand and agree on the same business requirements
- ☐ Incomplete business specifications

Suggested Solution

There is no easy solution for this problem. Again, well-facilitated JAD sessions that carefully take a project team (e.g., users, IT, management, and architects) through various levels of the system, from strategic planning to system design, will allow understanding to be gained. Patience and a willingness to share details with all parties concerned will enhance an understanding of the requirements. The manager should insist that this JAD approach be followed.

Inability to Accommodate Changes to Business Requirements

Business requirements are subject to change for a variety of reasons, even after they have been agreed to by stakeholders and formally signed off. After all, how many people can walk into a department store and buy a suit without changing their minds at least a few times? It is not surprising that users change some of the requirements, even in the development phases or during implementation.

Managing changes to business requirements is a complex part of a development project, and requires understanding, cooperation, and commitment from all stakeholders. The authors were involved on a project where a consulting firm was brought onsite to complete a fixed-price piece of work that involved migrating a standard A/R legacy application to an Oracle environment. Executive management agreed that because the migration was pretty standard, there was no need to have what was believed to be a costly and time-consuming formal requirements sign-off process. It was agreed that the project would be finished when the migrated application had the same functionality as the original legacy system. The executives withdrew from day-to-day involvement and left the managers and team members from a variety of departments to interpret what this actually meant in terms of sign-off criteria.

A lot of political pressure was exerted in many directions, from the business users, the client development staff, and the consulting team. This made development especially difficult and open to interpretation because it was impossible to have the legacy application work exactly like the newly migrated application.

The user community was responsible for accepting functions of the migrated application during a series of testing phases. As they continued to test, the testers started asking for changes to the application. Initially, these requests came over the phone or by short memos. The development team complied and maintained a quick turnaround time for problem verification. Within a few weeks, several observations were made that could have seriously affected delivery of the product:

1. A change was requested one week, and reversed within a few weeks after the testers had a better chance to understand its implications. In some instances, other mutually exclusive changes were requested (e.g., move the date to position 3 and row 3, position 5 and row 4, position 65).

2. Some changes were clearly outside the scope of the release. They may have been important, but they were not part of the original contract, and could not be done by the consulting team without incurring financial losses.

3. All changes were being treated with equal priority. This meant that simple display changes (e.g., print commas inside large numbers) were being given the same priority as more serious errors that were showstoppers (e.g., a product code accounting for 25 percent of the business was not processed correctly).

4. The developers had misunderstood some of the business requirements.

Suggested Solution

A simple process mechanism solved all of these problems. As the testing team discovered a bug or a change, they put the information into a central ASCII file. Each change was numbered, assigned a priority, and carefully described with examples. Members of the development team began to browse and update the file on a routine basis. Problems were selected on the basis of the priority assigned by the testers—thus urgent problems were selected first. Enhancements to the scope of the release were identified, estimated, and saved for future releases. The central file allowed duplicate or contradictory requests to be quickly discovered, and this saved the project team a great deal of time and aggravation.

This simple file allowed the entire change-management process to become more civilized and easier to manage. The file itself was used as one of the reports passed to the steering committee; consequently, there was a clear audit trail of what was happening and all participants became accountable, sometimes despite themselves. It is far easier to ask for a contradictory change over the phone, with no paper trail, than to record such a request in a file that will be scrutinized several weeks later.

The application was implemented successfully.

Insufficient Technical Skills

Insufficient technical skills can result from a variety of situations—for example, hiring resources with mainframe backgrounds for Web-based projects, or vice versa, and hiring inexperienced people. Another cause of insufficient technical skills is high turnover. Depending on the length of a project, it is inevitable that some team members leave, get promoted, or are transferred to another area. A final cause could be a lack of technical ability. This problem can occur in all phases of a project lifecycle.

Suggested Solution

Depending on the timeframe available for the project, technical skills can be learned through in-house courses, self-training, university and college continuing education courses, mentoring and centers of excellence, and textbooks. Provide training for people who have demonstrated ability and commitment. Hire competent technical resources with demonstrated successful track records. Ensure that development standards are in place, so team members have something to emulate. Try to have access to technical gurus, as needed, and provide orientation for new team members.

Failure to Effectively Manage One or More Phases of the Development Effort

Failure in any of the project lifecycle phases as described in chapter 7 can cause the whole project effort to fail.

Suggested Solution

A project manager should develop a comprehensive plan showing clear deliverables, as well as clear criteria for measuring success at each step. The manager should track aspects of the project against these carefully and take corrective action as soon as a problem is encountered. Quick fixes, such as expanding a timeline or just throwing another resource into a project to keep the per person time allocation under a threshold, should be avoided, because these approaches do not help the bottom line, which is a project's success. By developing an intrinsic understanding of a project's issues, a manager is able to react to problems when they are identified. This is what project management is all about.

Insufficient Testing

Applications that do not go through a cycle of thorough testing will probably fail in production or during acceptance testing. This phase requires preparation of test cases, advance notice, and adequate staffing in terms of numbers and knowledge. This should be viewed as a separate activity, not as a subcomponent of the development activity.

Suggested Solution

Invest the time and money for iterative testing phases. Allow time for fixes and retesting. Impress all team members and associated teams with the need for thorough testing. Consider the implementation of total quality management (TQM) programs. The following tests should be included in the project plan: unit, system, functional, integration, regression, performance, and acceptance.

Weak Implementation Strategy

Implementation requires careful planning, including a method to back out an application if something goes wrong. A carefully planned, phased approach is used by some organizations instead of an all-or-nothing effort that has a significant downside if something goes wrong.

Suggested Solution

Implementation involves risk management. Project plans, no matter how well thought out, cannot anticipate or handle all eventualities. Develop an implementation strategy that protects the whole organization against failure. Conversely, plan for success by using a phased strategy that implements low-volume, low-risk, and low-priority components first. Consider things such as response time and capacity issues with realistic data volumes and user demand during benchmarking activities and capacity planning, far in advance of the implementation phase.

Insufficient Resources

Projects require a specific amount of effort and materials—computers, telecommunications equipment, people, and other items. A project plan should identify what is required, when it is required, and the quantity required. Since this number cannot, by its very nature, be 100 percent accurate, a project manager must draw on experience and consultation to budget resources throughout the project. The following events should be considered and planned for:

☐ Architecture/design skills to get started

☐ Normal turnover of key resources

☐ Skills transfer

☐ High-intensity deadlines

☐ Short-term skills requirements (e.g., facilitator, auditor, GUI standards expert, technical guru)

Suggested Solution

Build a pool of resources, with members who have more than one skill-set to offer. Plan for short-term and long-term needs. Do not fill positions with bodies, but rather with individuals who have attitudes, abilities, and skill-sets appropriate to the project.

Inability to Deal with Contractors and Vendors

Managers must learn to deal with vendors and contractors—who have almost become a permanent fixture on projects. Contractors, or consultants, as some prefer to be called, generally augment organizational staff by providing specialized skills or, bluntly, additional bodies. Contractors can also build an entire project team through outsourcing, but they are still responsible to the client manager.

Vendors generally support a product that is required by an organization. This could be hardware, software, services (communication), or packages.

In dealing with contractors and vendors, managers are faced with two main challenges. The first is to ensure that their organization is properly dealt with by the vendor or contractor. The second is to create an environment in which the vendor or contractor can succeed and will want to succeed.

Suggested Solution

Develop a cooperative effort with vendors and contractors. Make it clear that you want regular, open, honest communication. Develop a service agreement or at least an unofficial expectations agreement. Establish key contacts to maintain ongoing information flow. Understand that vendors and contractors have their own businesses to run. Give them enough notice to react to expectations, and treat them as human beings.

Bad Planning

Bad planning is caused by many factors. Projects require a certain amount of effort, measured in person-hours, and a wide variety of skill-sets to succeed. These are also required on a specific schedule. Planning means to make sure that resources are available when they are needed, and that the project plan is feasible and well tracked. This is a good measure of a manager's effectiveness.

Suggested Solution

The manager should develop a realistic plan, not unduly pessimistic or overly optimistic. Be prepared to aggressively change the plan to meet the present situation. Planning issues were discussed in chapter 4.

Unrealistic Expectations

This type of failure occurs when managers are not concerned with facts, but insist that some dream be fulfilled at some particular point in time of their choosing. This does not refer to the ambitious manager who is trying to get people to give their best. This refers to those trying to accomplish blatantly impossible undertakings (such as working 2.5 full-time jobs at the same time—this does happen in some consulting firms). Some employees attempt to fulfill this mandate, either because they have bought into what is being asked or because they are too timid to contradict someone in authority. The result is that managers will find out at the worst possible time—when the deadline is imminent—that what they are asking for is impossible to deliver.

Suggested Solution

Do not expect someone with a COBOL background to learn C and UNIX overnight, or vice versa. This is not to say that employees cannot be taught new skills, but sometimes there is not enough time to do so within a project's timeframe. Other unrealistic expectations include having new requirements incorporated into a project at any time, having no time allocation for training, building an application without support from stakeholders, and building an application without signed-off specifications.

Some managers also think of a workday as consisting of twenty hours and a workweek as having seven days. The reality is people need a life outside the office to be complete and productive in the long term. A workday is really only about eight hours, and a workweek is five days. There are also various statutory holidays and celebrations during the year. Another accepted practice in many companies is to budget a two-to-four week vacation during the year.

Working with Poor Performers

Some people may have noble intentions, but sadly, lack the experience or ability to perform well on some projects. A manager may have to deal with workers who have made significant errors on previous projects or who have no relevant experience.

Suggested Solution

Look for opportunities to train and mentor such employees, either through your efforts or those of other members of the project team. Judge people on past performance, but understand that they can improve (or devolve) over time. Be prepared to give people opportunities in situations that you are able to control. In other words, if your trust is not met, this error in judgment should not derail a project.

Technical Limitations

Many years ago one author was working on a development project to build a shrinkwrapped piece of software for the greenhouse industry. The analysis and design of the application went strictly by the book. Standards were meticulously set and followed. Walk-throughs of the application revealed the presence of structured code, meaningful variable names, and easy maintainability. The application ran on top of an xbase database.

Presentation of the initial prototype to the business users was well received. This was in the early 1980s, and it was easy to impress users with a dash of color, specific message and errors lines, and an intuitive menu. The prototype was robust and had some functionality already completed. Additional funding was provided for the project and full-scale development began. The design of this application was innovative and exciting.

Several iterations of the product continued to improve its functionality. Several optimization and performance improvements were realized by building specific indexes, tokenizing the code, and using a RAM disk for faster access to data. However, no matter how many clever improvements were made by the development team, the PCs horsepower came from an Intel 8088 chip, and there were consequential performance limitations imposed by this bottleneck. Adding functionality to the package made it noticeably slower.

Hard disks were not yet readily available and disk drives were reading 5½-inch floppy disks with 360 KB capacity. The application quickly exceeded this space and grew to fill several diskettes. Eventually the application had to be divided into physical partitions that required a user to swap the floppy disks while navigating through certain features.

The application was clearly limited by the available technology. Fortunately, the use of hard disks became more popular, and a version of the application was built to run off a hard disk. A significant performance improvement was noticed; however, the underlying chip was still an 8088. The application was beta tested at greenhouse sites, but due to performance limitations was not actively marketed. Under 286+ technology and with SCSI disk drives, the same application runs with subsecond response time for the most heavily used transactions, but the marketing opportunity was missed. Technical limitations proved to be a showstopper for this application.

Technical limitations can become showstoppers under the following conditions:

□ Overambitious development

□ Insufficient benchmarking

□ Lack of capacity planning

☐ Migration from a development to a production environment (sometimes requires changes to hardware or software)

☐ Inability to identify functionality that cannot be automated with current technology

Before selecting a technology architecture, careful benchmarking with a high volume of data should be conducted. It is important to avoid conducting limited benchmarking with only a few thousand records and then multiplying the results by a hundred or a thousand to calculate the application performance at a few million records. Performance degradation is rarely linear, which can strangle production systems. A full benchmark test will also reveal other exposures such as disk capacity, throughput considerations, and backup and recovery rates.

Independent reference checks with the same type of business for a technology infrastructure are also highly recommended. Do not accept a vendor's claim without independent verification. For example, if running a financial application on a database server xxx under operating system yyy, with a network protocol zzz, take the time to visit a similar configuration, or at least send a questionnaire to the organization using the product and critically examine their responses.

Political Issues

Political issues, more often than many people want to admit, can cause projects to fail. Political issues fall into four categories, namely: organizational politics, team politics, individual politics, and business versus IS politics.

Organizational Politics

Project managers are sometimes frustrated to find a general lack of commitment within an organization to implement a project. Such situations are difficult to resolve completely. When confronted with this situation, a project manager should undertake the following activities, in the order shown:

1. Try to understand why there is a lack of commitment.

2. Try to get commitment for the project with sound reasoning and judgment. Demonstrate personal commitment to the project.

3. Limit the scope of the project until it receives commitment and does not offend anybody.

4. Document issues and concerns. Turn the project into a study with recommendations. If an application can be completed, table it with an implementation strategy. Allow executive management to make the decision to deploy or shelve the application.

5. Identify lessons learned and present them to other managers in the company.

6. Do not appear frustrated or difficult to work with. This only back-fires.

An inability to function in such a difficult situation can stagnate a career and produce unnecessary stress for those involved. This is an example of politics at the organizational level. A project manager generally has no choice but to participate successfully in this type of politics. As a final resort, a manager can always make a career more, either internally or externally.

An example of this type of problem occurred on a project with a seven-figure budget. This project was started by an IS director to guarantee the integrity of the corporate database—just in case. Executive management funded the project, not understanding the technical consequences, but accepting that a database exposure existed and wanting to make sure the project director had no excuses—just in case.

Development progressed along nicely; however, cooperation across departments was rare. For example, whenever a CICS region was required for testing or the database needed to be frozen, the project was given a lower priority relative to other projects within the organization, and consequently its deadlines kept getting pushed back. Meanwhile, pressure increased on the project manager to implement the application according to a schedule that assumed all resources would be available instantly. At some point, after many missed deadlines, the political will to implement the project disappeared. After all, a year had passed and the database had exhibited no integrity problems, so why implement a system that offered soft advantages, but could cause widespread disruption if it did not work? Furthermore, the daily work routine of the users would be changed, when they acquired additional responsibilities, after implementation of the system. The users could see no reason to buy into the system for the soft tangibles that were being offered. There was pressure on the manager to implement it, but no desire within the organization to do so.

A situation such as this one is extremely frustrating for everyone concerned, and usually the project manager is left holding the bag. Incidentally, this system was not implemented, and the entire team was reassigned. The project manager ended up having a reputation as trying too hard and being a bit moody and was skipped over for a promotion.

The bottom line is that a lone project manager can rarely beat the system, and quite frankly, the value of a project must be measured in terms of the whole organization. Some projects are initiated as insurance policies against a potentially cataclysmic event. A project manager must have the political astuteness to recognize such a situation and take appropriate steps to satisfy the expectations of senior management while protecting his or her job.

Senior management should also recognize that some projects exist as insurance policies and may never be implemented. If this is the case, senior management should be honest and not set anyone up for blame. The project manager should be providing status reports and other documentation to promote this idea so that there are no surprises if the application is not implemented. This should be clearly communicated to the steering committee (e.g., a typical person spends $x on insurance. If the IS budget is $xxx, then $yy is not a bad insurance investment). As a final resort, the manager can always find another project or another job.

Generally, managers who are frustrated by organizational politics can follow some or all of the following steps:

☐ Document ideas, information, and observations. Keep a paper trail going with senior management, other departments, and team members.

☐ Do not become impatient or difficult to deal with.

☐ Start changing the visibility of the project from a tactical one to an investigative one.

☐ Write memos to members of the steering committee, politely detailing all issues and concerns.

☐ Publicize the purpose and nature of the project. Try to build internal momentum.

☐ Do not hide problems.

Team Politics

Politics can also be played within teams, with the objective of gaining the following rewards:

1. **Tangible rewards.** Just like birds chirping in a nest to draw their parents' attention in the hope of getting the worm, members of a team compete for the manager's attention to get a better position, pay raise, window office, faster computer, or some other perk. Managers who support this competition should not be surprised at the increased political games that result when team members learn that this attitude gets positive rewards.

2. **Power and influence.** Human beings love to tell others what to do. This is seen everywhere in society. Actors who are paid $8 million per picture will settle for a fraction of this salary in order to direct a movie. It should come as no surprise, then, that team members will play the political game if it helps them get the power to tell other team members what to do. For example, some managers promote spying within a team. This is done by having frequent informal, one-on-one meetings with team members to gossip about what other people are doing. If a manager wants to know what Bruce is doing, why not ask Bruce, instead of going to Terry? Terry may relish the idea of having power over Bruce or influencing the way Bruce works (e.g., Bruce comes in late or talks on the phone a lot). If this has not come to the manager's attention, why is it important to hear it from Terry? And why is Terry noticing what someone else is doing, and not doing his own work? Managers who participate in this sort of management style should not be surprised at the negative results and the lack of team building.

3. **Protection against organizational politics.** Many potentially good project teams are subverted by organizational politics. When it is known that this is happening, team members begin to protect their jobs instead of trying to deliver the product. Symptoms that show a growing level of politics are a surge in self-protecting memos, constant questions about responsibility, and a lack of quantifiable results.

At best, politics at the team level can encourage team members to attain peak performance, while competing with each other. In the worst and more common case, team politics degenerates into backbiting and infighting that severely undermine the project schedule. Projects can be undermined so as to fail, go well over budget, or be severely late.

Certain types of projects are more likely to exhibit this problem than others. Projects that do not delineate responsibility clearly, and those with poor project management and too many prima donnas, among other factors, are likely candidates. Other causes include failure to recognize loyalty and hard work, poor project management, and a high degree of workplace stress.

In the very worst situations, some team members will actively sabotage the project unless they get their way. Their message is simple: "We benefit or the project does not succeed."

Individual Politics

Individuals play politics against other individuals anywhere within an organization. This was observed on one project, where a senior manager, who was waiting for early retirement, was primarily interested in risk avoidance. Anyone who was aggressive enough to want something done was removed from the project unceremoniously. This form of politics becomes a significant problem if the individual playing politics has a high rank within the organization or is left unchallenged by higher management. Like a radioactive isotope with a fleeting half-life, this form of politics quickly degenerates into team politics (thus becoming a more complex problem) as individuals learn that a certain behavior is rewarded, that another is punished, and that the reaction is not based on value to the company.

Business versus IT Politics

Business is taking a much more active interest in projects previously managed by IT. There are many reasons for this. Powerful, easy-to-use desktop technology (e.g., SQL tools, screen painters, xbase, decentralized computing, CASE) allows nontechnical users to build a lot of product without help from technical staff. Another reason for this trend is that projects run by IT suffer from the problem of differences between business priorities (e.g., month-end report consolidation) and IS's need to test a system. In such a situation, business typically wins, and IT cannot acceptance-test a system until business users can devote time to this activity. By giving control of a project to business, IT, in fact, gives the responsibility of juggling deadlines to the department that can control it anyway.

This works well in some environments; however, this situation allows political games to be played very easily. In reality, both groups need each other. IT offers skills in system development, planning, and design that cannot be replaced by fancy screen painters on a PC. Similarly, business users have a day-to-day understanding of the business that IT cannot learn through a few weeks of intensive JAD sessions. Success or failure is clearly a shared responsibility between the groups.

Funding

Two project managers were discussing a sticky problem. They had a solid team working on one project, but they had just won another project. Each project offered a slim profit margin. They decided to improve the profit picture by using essentially the same team on both projects at the same time, with a few additional players. Furthermore, they determined that the project plan could be designed to fit the available budget (e.g., $100 was available, so the project would have to cost $100— whether it did or not). Items such as learning new products and client training were left out of the plan entirely. Also missing from the plan was the amount of time taken by vendors to deliver products and expertise to the project site. This meant that a product (a database server) was expected by a certain date. Late delivery would affect the rest of the schedule. Accommodating these items would have meant less profit, so they felt it was better to ignore the issues and hope they went away.

This planning scenario could have been catastrophic. In the end, the ability and dedication of the project team and the managers themselves pulled it off (perhaps that is what the managers were banking on). Both applications were implemented, but the stress level on the team members, especially the project leaders, was very high. Add to the picture twelve-hour days and many summer weekends in the office, and one has to ask if the limited funding was reasonable. In the end, the actual profit margin was about what it would have been had both project teams been staffed properly. Perhaps coincidentally, several key team players left the company after implementation.

A funding crunch is a serious concern in 2000+. Organizations seemed to be much more liberal with their IT budgets during the last part of the 1990s and when dot.coms were the rage of Wall Street. In the more bottom-line-oriented marketplace, IT budgets have been slashed and trimmed significantly. This has forced organizations to reevaluate their computer solutions by examining broad-based technology solutions and the like. Staff expenses have also been targeted because they are usually a significant portion of the budget. The problem with this is that projects are often dramatically underfunded. The resulting pressure and stress are put on the project manager, who often has no choice but to accept the mandate and guidelines of a project as laid out by senior management.

Some organizations exercise the option to pass the funding crunch pressures on to consulting firms (as discussed in chapter 9). This only begs the question, in that managers with the consulting firm are faced with the same problems. Some would argue that consulting firms should be "experts" in the assignments they undertake, and so should be capable of completing the project within a smaller budget. While this is true, any competitive advantage derived from being an expert is soon lost when more than one consulting firm is bidding on an assignment. Since the firms are both experts, their respective bids will be cut appropriately.

Failure to Successfully Apply Project Development Methodologies

There is certainly no shortage of development methodologies available. Each of them undoubtedly offers implementation success stories. However, can anyone recall a project in which a methodology was followed, but success was not attained? The authors can.

Development methodologies are often used as cooking recipes or connect-the-dot puzzles. Without a complete picture of a project's issues, development methodologies are exposed to failure. Development methodologies are not magic, and they do not operate in a vacuum. There are many activities taking place inside the boxes that require experience, analysis, and ability to complete. If a manager does not have a handle on a project at every stage of the development cycle, meticulously following a methodology only postpones the inevitable realization that a project is not on track. The sooner a manager realizes this and takes corrective action, the better it will be for the success of the project.

Chapter 7 describes a new methodology, called the Iterative Project Development Methodology (IPDM), which has successfully delivered a broad range of projects. This methodology differs from many other commonly used development methodologies in terms of its flexibility and also in its attention to deliverables, rather than processes. IPDM depends on four factors:

☐ Extensive utilization of JADs

☐ Reusable, functional prototype(s)

☐ Meaningful dialogue between stakeholders

☐ Professional facilitation

Some basic strengths of IPDM are that it supports communication among all players involved on a project, it builds a broad base of commitment, and it shortens the time for deliverables to be implemented (early payback).

Project Properties

This chapter has presented a group of factors that can cause a project to fail. The existence and applicability of these factors depends on the type of project being managed. Any given project can be described in terms of four properties: functionality, duration, scope, and size. Tables 5.3, 5.4, 5.5, and 5.6 identify expectations in terms of human reaction, technical impact (on the project), and the management challenge for each of these properties. These tables can be combined to generate a combination of properties for any given project. For example, a project that has medium functionality, a short duration, limited scope, and medium size has the possibility of failing, because a stressed-out project team builds a low-quality product to meet a schedule. A project manager can avoid this problem by recognizing that the relevant architecture must be available at the appropriate time and by communicating this requirement to the vendors. The project team should also be freed from unnecessary tasks (e.g., do not waste their time by having them fill in countless timesheets or follow bureaucratic procedures that do not add value to the delivery of the product). The team should be encouraged to work without distractions, with clearly defined rewards for a successful delivery.

The medium category in each factor offers a better chance for success than the other two categories. This is consistent with the results of the management survey, which suggests dividing large projects into consecutive medium-sized projects of six-month durations each.

Table 5.3 Functionality. Project functionality refers to the business requirements that are incorporated into an application.

FUNCTIONALITY	HUMAN REACTION	TECHNICAL IMPACT	MANAGEMENT CHALLENGE
Simple (a few screens, applications, and business rules)	Overconfidence. Sloppiness with details.	Buy only the architecture that is needed (no need to overspend).	Make the team understand the importance of the project despite its apparent simplicity. You need to hire appropriate resources for the project despite an organizational attempt to cut back on a supposedly straightforward project (there is not such thing).
Medium (a few dozen screens, applications, and business rules)	Reasonable opportunity to study the problem and develop a good solution.	Limited impact on architecture selection. Develop a scalable solution in case the project requirements expand rapidly.	This project offers a good balance in terms of simplicity and complexity. It is an opportunity to implement sound management practices and a development methodology. If these already exist, this project can be used to further validate these and build another success story.

Table 5.3 *(Continued)*

FUNCTIONALITY	HUMAN REACTION	TECHNICAL IMPACT	MANAGEMENT CHALLENGE
Complex (no limit on the number of screens, applications, and business rules)	Overwhelmed by information overflow. Team members concentrate on overviews instead of important details. No one has a complete understanding of the total problem or solution. Team members may begin to request that more staff be assigned. Team will continue to focus on the easily achievable activities, while avoiding the complex issues.	Performance, scalability, and stability problems may result as complex business requirements are implemented. Complexity will also result in a high number of application bugs that will need to be fixed. Plan for contingencies.	Understand the details of the business requirements and ensure that the team is not always avoiding the difficult parts of the application. Conduct a detailed planning phase. Use risk analysis to identify bottlenecks. Use limited pilots and proof of concepts to validate the key parts of the solution. Implement a consistent management process. Keep on top of what the team really knows. Ensure good documentation is created from the beginning of the project.

Table 5.4 Duration. Project duration refers to the length of the project. While this is often expressed in terms of months or years, any time period can be used.

DURATION	HUMAN REACTION	TECHNICAL IMPACT	MANAGEMENT CHALLENGE
Short (less than five months)	High level of stress. Quality principles are ignored while the team focuses on just getting the job done.	Opportunity to acquire proper architecture may not be available. No opportunity to shop for best prices. Risk that architecture cannot be established in so short a timeframe.	Ensure that all hardware, software, and other resources are exclusively available to meet the deadline. Protect team from unnecessary inevitable stress. Try to keep the whole team intact for the duration of the project. Avoid non-value-added activities.
Medium (between five months and one year)	Ability to plan. Competition for promotions.	Ability to shop for the best deal.	Ensure that staff is concentrating on deliverables. Have a short-term plan to accommodate occasional turnover.
Long (more than one year)	Procrastination. False starts. Duplication of planning efforts. No pressure to get started. Politics to avoid blame.	Architecture could become obsolete before the project is completed.	Divide the long project plan into manageable phases to deliver usable functionality every six months or so. Measure success at frequent intervals. Need to handle staff turnover.

Table 5.5 Scope. Project scope refers to the number of business areas touched by a project. This is one level higher than functionality.

SCOPE	HUMAN REACTION	TECHNICAL IMPACT	MANAGEMENT CHALLENGE
Limited (one department or area)	Internal competition for turf.	Ability to use architecture of choice.	(See simple functionality.)
Broad (many departments or areas)	Competition for the control of the project between departments or areas. Who's really in charge and responsible?	Requirement for architecture standards or open systems.	Maintain regular communication with management in the other departments.
External (broad, includes areas outside the company)	Possibility of chaos, as scope of a project may get out of control. Disturbances to a project team.	Possibility of multiple architectural standards and incompatibilities.	Understand external influences to ensure they do not hinder the project. Protect the project team from the unnecessary stress of a large scope.

Table 5.6 Size. Size refers to the physical size of the application (number of screens, programs) and data volumes.

SIZE	HUMAN REACTION	TECHNICAL IMPACT	MANAGEMENT CHALLENGE
Small (measured in megabytes)	Efficiency of design and code ignored.	Simple low-capacity architecture.	Invest in a solution that can be reused if size increases.
Medium (measured in a few gigabytes)	Focus on design and code.	Low response time. Not enough capacity. Constant equipment upgrades.	Invest in a scalable solution. Insist on true benchmarks of performance and capacity early in the project.
Large (measured in many gigabytes)	Too much time spent on optimizing design and code.	Low response time. Not enough capacity. Constant equipment upgrades.	Invest in a scalable solution. Insist on true benchmarks of performance and capacity early in the project.

Ten Ways for a Manager to Spot a Project That Will Fail

1. Your team only gives you good news at every status meeting.

2. The implementation date is only a few weeks away but you, the manager, have never seen a hands-on demonstration of the application.

3. Most of the memos your team sends to you complain about the lack of skills in the other team members.

4. Team members continue to engage in the fine art of protecting themselves at every opportunity.

5. Team members are resigning on a regular basis.

6. Team members are either frustrated and constantly on edge or, conversely, feel no pressure to get the job done.

7. The project has already missed several deadlines and is well over budget.

8. There have been no detailed walk-throughs of the application design and code by independent reviewers.

9. When you think of your project, there is no thought of a team, but only of separate individuals.

10. The user community is not even aware of the project.

Case Studies: Ingredients of Failed Projects

This section contains a list of case studies that can be used to learn from projects that failed in one or more dimensions. These examples are drawn from discussions with project managers.

Case Study A

The objective of the project was to build an application for removing certain types of data from an online relational database that contained tens of millions of records. Some of the removed records were to be archived and reinserted into the database upon request (within a 24-hour period). Other types of records were to be purged from the system forever.

This project was initiated as a response to the rapid growth of data in the database, whose volume was projected to exceed the upper bound recommended by the software vendor. No clients of the database had ever exceeded this limit; consequently, the software vendor could not guarantee that the application would continue to run successfully, in terms of response time, utility support, data access, and overall integrity of the data, after this limit was reached. Because the application was highly visible and mission-critical, supporting millions of users, this uncertainty was unacceptable to the organization's executive management. They determined to offset the growth in data volume by removing data that was no longer needed by systems or users within the organization.

The project mandate had several intrinsic factors that led to the failure of this project. These were the following:

1. **Aligning IT and business concerns.** Business units were happy with the current application and were slow to buy into the project. These business units were not offered immediate benefits for their participation in the project—except to be told that the application would continue to run in the future. Since it was currently running successfully, the risk of inaction could not be adequately conveyed to them. In the meantime, they had other priorities, such as statutory requirements.

   Business units were forced to support the project, but they consistently focused most of their resources on other projects. Projects that were deemed to be more important (e.g., those that satisfied the public or statutory requirements) had a higher priority in getting resources. This was important because the project was affected several times by failure to get testers, business analysts, and physical space in the computer system. On one occasion, business analysts were removed from the project and reassigned to a more visible one with higher priority. The project was clearly seen as an IS project.

2. **Inherent project complexity.** This was a challenging project that required an understanding of a multitude of factors to design an effective solution. Business rules that needed to be incorporated into the system represented the most complex part of the product. This part required full input and support from the business community, which was never forthcoming. Since they were happy with the

current system, they were reluctant to consider changing it in any way.

3. **Risk aversion.** Finding end users to define data that was no longer needed by applications proved to be an impossible task. Furthermore, they had to determine if such data would ever be required in the future. If this was so, the data could be archived on tape (meaning it could be brought back into the database within a day), otherwise it would be purged forever. The complexity of the business rules also frightened the business community away from participating fully. No one wanted to take responsibility for removing data that could be needed by someone, at some time in the future. This potential risk destroyed whatever interest there was in the business community to actively support a project that could protect their investment in an application by removing the risk of physical database problems.

An examination of this project in hindsight also shows many other problems that foreshadowed its eventual failure. The project started with an artificially tight schedule in the hope of saving money. This forced the application architects to propose a solution that was not investigated fully, because there was no time to do so. The business requirements were also loosely defined. Although the executive sponsor was identified, key users were not. This forced the business analysts to build requirements and conditions that were not confirmed with authorized users. The first release of the application was developed in two months. Unfortunately, with no key users, it was not clear whether the application satisfied business requirements. Furthermore, without key users, it was not clear that the defined business requirements were valid. Consequently, most of the organization had not bought into the application. There was some ensuing discussion to determine how to proceed. The executive sponsor made the strategic decision to allocate physical and user resources to the project. Before this happened, another project with a more defined mandate took the users away, with the result that the project stayed in limbo for three months. While development continued during this time, other key groups (e.g., database services) became uncomfortable with the idea of taking responsibility for the project's implementation. Quite simply, they were happy with the status quo, and they did not want to assume responsibility for new risks.

During the three-month delay, the project team had time to review the basic architecture of the system and several weaknesses were discovered as a result. The original concept of saving money by rushing the application through the design process had two weaknesses: The rest of the company was not ready for the project, and the design was substandard. A redesign was initiated with good results, requiring a rewrite process that lasted six weeks.

Organizational politics led to team politics. Several key members of the team adopted a siege mentality, as did members from other departments of the organization who were loaned to the project. This made every major decision slow, as everyone covered himself or herself and refused to make decisions.

The project dragged on for an additional six months. During this time, user teams were brought into the project, and yanked off it, without warning, to attend to other projects. The application was developed according to the specifications that were drawn up and signed off by the business community, and it passed unit testing. Executive and senior management reluctantly agreed to consider implementation. Unfortunately, they could find no users who were willing to validate the written business requirements, nor supply any of their own. After several weeks of posturing, management decided to make a decision. In a single day, they determined that since the database had not failed during the year of development, perhaps the answer was simply to purchase additional disk drives. This allowed everyone to avoid assuming responsibility for implementation. The project was basically shelved until a future date.

The major errors made in this project are summarized in the following list.

☐ Key users were not mandated to describe requirements and conditions for the project on a full-time basis. IS was responsible for the project, so the user community never bought into it. Perhaps it would have been better to have given responsibility to the user community.

☐ Users who were assigned to the project were moved to tactical projects without warning. Other users were allowed to procrastinate until they too were transferred to other projects.

☐ Two business analysts were alienated during the requirement definition phase by management, so they both quit at the end of the first phase. Their business requirements were left without any takers or defenders.

- ☐ All possibilities, such as true database limitations, benchmarking with high data volume, and additional hardware, were not exhaustively considered before a design and approach were finalized.

- ☐ Benefits of the application were not clearly investigated and defined for subsequent measurement.

- ☐ Constantly changing business users resulted in changing business requirements (e.g., conditions under which records were archived).

- ☐ The pilot project duration was too long. It should have been shorter, with less detailed functionality.

- ☐ A pilot should have been used to excite the user community. This offered the best opportunity to make this project a success, because users would have been able to see what the application would look like, with a minimum of effort. This would have given them more time to buy into the process.

- ☐ The project team consisted of contractors and in-house resources. Some confrontation occurred between the groups, because in-house resources were concerned that they would be held responsible if the project did not succeed. The loose mandate made this a likely event.

- ☐ Some of the team members were ineffective (but not disruptive).

- ☐ The project plan left out key steps.

- ☐ Milestones could not be met due to lack of support within the organization.

This project failed due to the following factors: organizational politics, project team politics, lack of communication, requirements that were not clearly understood, and insufficient commitment to project.

The project manager could have taken the following initiatives to save the project:

- ☐ Build a downsized version of the system that only removed terminated records that would never be required again. This would have allowed the business community to accept the application because of reduced risk. More management support would have resulted for implementation. After a period of time, management may have approved an expanded version of the application and staffed it appropriately.

- ☐ Sponsor additional feasibility studies.

- ☐ Benchmark high data volumes.

Case Study B

The objective of this project was to build an n-tier sales analysis system for a software house that was building a retail package. The overall project was managed by a marketing director who had contracted a beta site to partially pay for the development effort. The sales analysis project was managed by a partner in a consulting firm. The project team consisted of a project leader and four programmers, all alumni from other highly successful n-tier implementations. Due to budget restrictions, the project plan was compressed to make a profit. The first phase was defined, while the second phase would remain ambiguous until beta implementation of the first phase.

Phase 1: Sales Analysis System

Activity 1:   Build specifications (1 week)

Activity 2:   Get specification approval from clients (1 week)

Activity 3:   Build client/server infrastructure (1 week)

Activity 4:   Develop code (5 weeks)

Activity 5:   Unit test (1 week)

Activity 6:   System test (1 week)

Activity 7:   Acceptance test (1 week)

Phase 2: Integration with Retail Package

No details available.

The schedule was clearly ambitious. The sales analysis system consisted of four major processes with about a dozen screens developed under the C programming language and SQL Server. Program specifications were written and quickly approved on schedule. The first problem occurred when the client/server infrastructure deployment was delayed because the hardware and software were not available when promised by the vendors. This delayed Activity 4, Develop code, by a week or so. The project team developed a prototype that was demonstrated to the clients. It became clear that the approved specifications did not fully represent expectations. In particular, there seemed to be shifting requirements, in that the client wanted a generic user interface such as that supported by Excel, Lotus 1-2-3, and dBase4, with the flexibility to adapt to specific requirements. Furthermore, they wanted an application for resale. This was a new requirement. The trouble was that such an interface would take far longer than two months to build, and a team that was considerably larger than five.

The program specifications were revised to satisfy the new requirements, and the project team iteratively developed the application. It should be mentioned that the development team worked with great dedication, through head colds and fevers, and with 60- to 70-hour weeks. Unit testing was completed on schedule. As system testing started, it became clear that a retail package was not going to be developed. With no retail package, there was no need for a sales analysis system. The project was quietly canceled, resources were reassigned, and only part of the bill was paid.

This project failed due to a number of factors that were mentioned earlier in this chapter: insufficient funding, insufficient time to complete the project, lack of a project plan, requirements that were not clearly understood, unrealistic expectations from stakeholders, and not learning from past experience.

Case Study C

The objective of this project was to manage the IT facilities of a client in the insurance industry. The client expected the service bureau to handle all day-to-day operations, including support of online report generation, backup and recovery, and other facility management concerns. The client also maintained a project portfolio that contained enhancements, modifications, and fixes to the mainframe application software.

The service bureau allocated one project manager, a project leader, and seven developers to satisfy the client. The service bureau staff selected projects from the project portfolio and implemented them on a schedule that was agreed upon by the two companies. This is a typical service bureau/client relationship.

The client continually complained about the lack of employees in the service bureau who fully understood the client's systems. This issue threatened their continued relationship. The cause of this problem was straightforward. The service bureau, as a whole, had a very high turnover (50 percent within six months). The project team had a rate worse than this. This meant that no one stayed on the project team long enough to become an expert on the client's systems.

The service bureau management was directly responsible for the high turnover rate for the following reasons:

☐ Employees were not treated as professionals (e.g., no flexibility in working hours, dress code)

☐ No employee training

☐ Ineffective management techniques (e.g., management could not be reached for help, even in a crisis)

☐ Low pay

The sum of these factors discouraged many employees from working with the service bureau for an extended period of time. Once staff started to leave, a bandwagon effect started that was difficult to curtail.

The project manager was an active contributor to the high employee turnover. The manager's style alienated many employees. He was authoritative to the point where staff members resented being watched so closely in terms of when they arrived for work, what they talked about, and when they left. The project manager was not a problem solver, either. He did not encourage the project team to approach him with problems.

This project manager could have prevented the high turnover quite easily. A good place to start would have been by developing his own management skills through courses and seminars. He should have also concentrated on developing his staff, finding out their concerns, adding value when they approached him with problems, delegating more responsibility to those who were capable of shouldering it (some definitely were), and encouraging team building. A clear career path for his team would also have encouraged many to stay.

Case Study D

The objective of this project was to reengineer financial services in a large company. The project team consisted of a project manager, six business analysts, and some administrative staff.

The following project plan was identified, with a duration of six months for the first phase.

Phase 1: Business Analysis

Activity 1:   Select key users

Activity 2:   Interview key users

Activity 3:   Design new processes

Activity 4:   Identify IS projects

Activity 5:   Publish recommendations

Activity 6:   Present recommendations to steering committee

Phase 2: IT Projects

Activity 1:   Identify projects to initiate

Activity 2:   Select project managers

Activity 3:   Scope projects

Activity 4:   Present design documentation to steering committee

The project was successful in producing recommendations; however, it was unsuccessful in gaining steering committee approval to initiate them. The project was initially started to address a tactical problem. Within the space of a few months, responsibility to resolve the tactical problem was given to another department. This happened through no fault of the project team, which was suddenly left with only a vague mandate.

There is almost nothing the project manager could have done differently to make this project successful in its original mandate. The project manager instead focused on changing and reducing the project scope. The project team was diverted into another useful activity that would provide value to the organization—to study architectural alternatives. The manager lobbied the steering committee to accept the change in scope, which they did. Future problems were avoided by keeping them informed about the project on a weekly basis.

The project team took the initiative and actively interviewed key individuals within the organization and managed to build a strong set of recommendations that were presented to the steering committee on the original schedule. Unfortunately, none of the recommendations were accepted, so the project team was disbanded and moved to other projects.

This project provides an example of a project manager salvaging the careers of a project team by making the best of a bad situation. By most project criteria, this project did not succeed, as none of the recommendations were accepted. However, the result could have been far worse had the project manager not taken the correct steps.

Summary

Five categories of project failure were defined in this chapter: human issues, technological limitations, political games, funding, and methodologies. Factors that can cause project failure and suggestions on how to avoid these problems were also discussed. Empirical evidence for the arguments provided in this chapter was drawn from a comprehensive survey that was completed by managers and executives in the IS industry, and it is included in Appendix C.

Several case studies of failed projects were provided in this chapter. The first case study was described in terms of a business scope and involved mainframe architecture. Errors in each of the basic project phases were described to give the reader a broader perspective of why this project—representative of many others—was not successful. Most of these errors could have been avoided, given the appropriate foresight.

This project involved client/server technology and a very short duration. Although the project began with several advantages, such as a winning project team that had worked on previous successful assignments, these were not enough to make the partner software house fulfill its mandate. Quite simply, the project was unsuccessful because the project manager could not affect the larger software house and its ability to deliver the parent retail system. In such an instance, a project manager must take appropriate steps to respond to an anticipated failure to avoid personal career shock and also protect the careers of the project team. This is, in fact, what the project manager was able to do by following steps that were discussed in this chapter.

The second case study clearly showed that some projects cannot succeed no matter what a manager does. In such instances, the project manager is faced with many choices, not the least of which is to protect his or her own career.

This chapter also provided a list of ten ways for a manager to know that a project is going to fail. The chapter concluded by describing projects in terms of four properties: functionality, duration, scope, and size. Management responses to these properties were also provided for a variety of attributes.

CHAPTER 6

Why Projects Succeed

This chapter establishes a definition for project success—one that is commonly difficult to attain in reality. Usually, a gray area measured in terms of functionality, customer satisfaction, budget, and timeliness is usually acceptable to executive management. This chapter provides project managers with an expanded toolkit—including leadership and interpersonal skills—that allows them to recognize the level of success that they can achieve on a specific project and then attain it. Several case studies of real-life projects are also described in this chapter in terms of their challenges and the key management decisions that allowed them to succeed. In this chapter the reader will learn about:

- The project manager's toolkit
- Project practices and techniques
- Project case studies
- Project standards
- Rules for project success

Why Projects Succeed

Projects are believed to be successful when a combination of project objectives are met within budget and on time. Achieving this state is the focus of this chapter. This is not the same as doing the opposite of the behaviors described in chapter 5 pertaining to the factors that make projects fail. Defining project success is often as elusive as defining project failure. The two concepts are not mirror images of each other. There is project failure, there is project success, and there is a gray area in between where many projects end up. The gray area is attained by achieving some critical results, while missing others. This area can be described as a combination of weighted objectives, conditions, factors, perceptions, and results. Some of the conditions that can be used to describe the gray area include budget, requirements, timeliness, quality, and customer satisfaction. These terms are described in the following list and are shown in Figure 6.1.

- ☐ **Budget.** Measured in units (e.g., dollars), budget can be defined according to a fixed price, a ceiling, or time and materials. It is allocated to a project or its components.

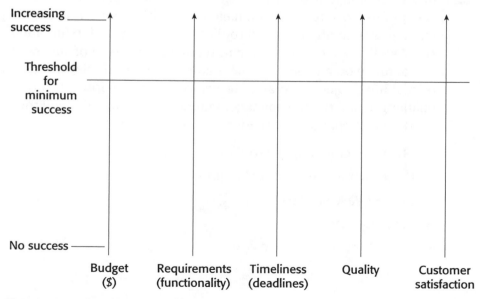

Figure 6.1   Measuring project success.

- **Requirements.** Project requirements are identified and captured in some form. Historically this has been done in a set of paper documents and electronic forms that include descriptions, data models, ER diagrams, flowcharts, dataflow diagrams, pseudocode, decision tables, and data dictionaries. A trend in the 1990s is to use a working prototype to capture the look and feel of the functionality that a project is expected to support.

- **Timeliness.** This refers to the deadlines for the project, milestones, and phases. Deadlines are expressed in terms of a fixed day of the calendar, and can also refer to duration and total hours of effort.

- **Quality.** Quality measures many dimensions of the final product. One common measure includes the reliability of the finished product. Reliability in turn can be measured in terms of a minimum bug or problem count and the frequency of product failure. It can also be described in terms of availability, performance, and flexibility.

- **Customer satisfaction.** The customer satisfaction factor is simple: "Is the customer happy with the delivered product?" This is arguably the most important consideration and can be ascertained with three simple questions: "Are you happy with the results?" "Would you recommend the project team unconditionally?" and "Can we do more work for you?"

Getting a project into the gray area is usually based on a few factors that project managers can identify in the planning phase of the project and confirm with the executive. Projects that end up in the gray area can be described as successful if the alternative is clear project failure and if the project sponsors clearly identify what conditions are important to them. In other words, sometimes gray is all you can be expected to achieve.

For example, on one large project that involved a package implementation and a system conversion, the key success factor was the conversion of a meaningful block of financial business. This project was being closely observed by third parties, so the executive team wanted specific conversion milestone dates to be met. Budget, functionality, manual workarounds, and other factors were less important because the third parties watching the results had the power to affect the company's stock price. The answer acceptable to the executive was to reduce functionality and risk, but deliver project milestones on their established dates. If the organization was able to conduct its business on the new systems on those dates, the results were acceptable. This project was an example where gray meant project success.

The following steps define a practical roadmap for understanding why some projects succeed and for helping to define a framework that can be repeated across projects:

1. Understand and avoid the reasons for project failure.

2. Understand and implement project success factors.

3. Learn from other people's experience.

4. Learn from personal experience.

More Elements of the Project Manager's Toolkit

The project manager's toolkit contains tools that are easy to touch, feel, and define, such as estimating tools, management software, and project templates. These may be enough for short, straightforward projects. However, most IT projects require a broader range of tools that are softer and less easily defined. These are discussed in this section.

Interpersonal Skills

The success of the project manager is entirely dependent on other resources in the organization. IT managers must have solid interpersonal skills to do their jobs effectively. They are typically involved in the following relationships:

☐ **Team relationships.** This includes working in a variety of roles and with various individuals on the team. These relationships can be developed using a combination of management styles.

☐ **The client/sponsor relationship.** This involves reporting information to the project sponsors, ensuring their cooperation in removing obstacles blocking the project's success, and ensuring their commitment to see the project through to implementation.

☐ **Vendor relationships.** In distributed computing environments, multiple vendor relationships are the rule, not the exception. It is necessary to manage these relationships closely in order to enjoy good support and pricing. It is also important to ensure that the vendors communicate with each other in order to resolve connectivity issues among their products.

- **User community relationships.** The user community provides expert information, process information, standards, and testing support, and ultimately accepts the product. They must be managed to provide vital support to the project on a timely basis. The user community is also the lifeblood of the project. Their support for a project can keep it going, while their reluctance can turn strong sponsors away from a project.

- **Relationships to other projects.** The manager must develop relationships with other project managers and teams to ensure that requirements and solutions are shared. These relationships also offer an opportunity to market the importance of the project and maintain a sense of excitement within the organization. Failure to do this can result in redundancy, a competition for vital resources, or conflicting solutions.

Knowledge-Based Management

Solution-specific knowledge has become a key enabler for effective project management. The good news is that knowledge can be acquired through discipline, hard work, and experience. The challenge for the project manager is to determine the level of detail and the breadth and depth of the knowledge that needs to be acquired to complete an assignment. The trend toward knowledge-based management in its current form is relatively recent. Managers traditionally have been able to focus their efforts on the operational aspects of project management, such as budget tracking, time tracking, status reporting, and other reporting functions. The need to build a solution-oriented knowledge base and experience was limited to rare occasions. The knowledge base of the manager in the current job market needs to be diverse, including aspects of management theory, marketing, quality control, human resources, employment law, accounting, commerce, and information technology.

Status Meetings and Reporting

Status meetings and reports are often maligned in terms of their effectiveness in managing projects. Much of this is because of their inappropriate application on projects. In too many cases, status meetings are called too often and run for far too long. Furthermore, status reports are often used to capture redundant or unnecessary information. The result of this is a distraction to team members who end up viewing both tools as necessary overhead to educate management as opposed to vehicles that add value to their own efforts. This is unfortunate because these can be powerful structural tools that can keep both a project and resources on track. The key is to get team members to accept these tools as described in the following sections

Status Meetings

Always have a regular weekly status meeting with an open invitation to a wide audience. After initial hesitation and some push-back, team members and sponsors will get used to it and will eventually use it as a forum to raise and discuss important issues. This can easily become an important lifeline to the project members and will become their regular forum for discussion. Be prepared to listen and act on their feedback to make the meetings more effective. For example, there will be requests to shift topics and limit discussions.

A couple of administrative instruments are important for effective status meetings. It is useful to have a dial-in number so that members can conference into the meeting if they cannot attend in person. An agenda should always be distributed before the meeting. The project manager should facilitate the meeting and ensure that everyone gets an equal chance to express opinions. Meetings with little to discuss should still be held, but kept short. An issues log should be reviewed at each meeting to ensure that the team members know that their concerns are being resolved.

Status Reports

Status reports are another tool that can be positioned so that the team sees the benefits they offer to them and the project as opposed to simply being another method for educating the project manager. This can be achieved by removing administrative complexity from filing status reports. A useful approach is to have resources fill out a simple template on a weekly or biweekly basis and email it to the project manager or a designate. This person can then assemble a formal status report for the project. This should be distributed to the expanded project team, by email or by a hyperlink to a Web page. The value of doing this will become evident when team members recognize that their work is being recorded, issues are being followed, and a common body of knowledge is being built up. This will eliminate eventual contradictions and misunderstandings during the project lifecycle.

Project Management Office (PMO)

Managers should get their projects onto the regular PMO agenda. This will provide several benefits to the project, including a higher level of visibility, a chance to understand the needs of other projects, and gaining an opportunity to affect corporate priorities. This will also reassure team members that the broader management of the organization is paying attention to the project.

Successful Practices and Techniques

Understanding which practices and techniques to leverage on projects is a problematic task for the project manager because of the changes brought on by the emergence of new technologies. Every manager is sooner or later confronted with the concern that they are missing the new and best way of doing things. Other managers, of course, cling to their tried and true methods, no matter how outdated they may appear to be to others. Some of the techniques that have survived several technology shifts and are worth adding to your permanent toolkit are as follows:

☐ **Rapid Application Development (RAD).** RAD is a technique for developing applications rapidly in an iterative approach. In business terms, RAD provides a fast response to business needs and a quick payback on their investment. The basic approach for RAD can be described as "build as you go." The idea is to gather enough business requirements to build something tangible and then to let users review, test, and modify it until they are satisfied with the result.

☐ **Enhanced RAD.** This combines the traditional waterfall-based development methodologies with RAD to provide the best of both worlds. RAD is not effective when developing large, multiyear application systems, generally because of a failure to accurately capture business requirements. Conversely, the traditional development methodologies, in isolation, are slow to provide results to users. Enhanced RAD divides the overall project lifecycle into a number of distinct phases that proceed in a waterfall approach. RAD is used within each phase. This approach allows systems to be developed with extensive input from business users. Applications are repeatedly enhanced and evaluated until they are complete.

☐ **Prototyping.** This technique allows a small portion of a system's functionality to be developed and shown to users before a larger investment is made. The manager must decide the parameters of a prototype, for example, whether it should be reused or thrown away after users sign off on it. Prototyping can be used to gather business requirements or to support a RAD type of development approach.

☐ **Build versus buy.** Package solutions are a strong alternative to custom development. Many organizations are more likely to succeed in transforming their business processes to match an existing package than the other way around. A common approach is to select a package that offers a good portion of the functionality required by an organization and to customize the package to obtain what is left. Project managers should consider a package solution before committing to a custom solution.

☐ **Reusability.** Code reuse is a popular goal intended to provide development savings, lower risk, and higher quality. This approach is sometimes considered as a limited version of the "buy" approach. Common methods for achieving reuse include Object Orientation (OO), components, frameworks, and package solutions. Business objects and components can be purchased from third-party vendors to save development time. When using this approach, it is important to realize that buying this type of commodity is like buying a wheel for a car or a transistor for a radio. It is important to have a quality assessment process in place, payment expectations and a schedule, access to component source code if it is needed, and confidence in the long-term viability and survival of the supplying vendor.

Standards and Templates

A common element among successful projects is the use of consistent standards within the project lifecycle and across the organization. Standards specify a common way to format and communicate information. Just about any portion of a project can be standardized. Too much of this will create significant overhead that will negatively affect the project. Too few standards will create communication difficulties and discrepancies. An approach that works well is to start with a minimum number of standards around the following:

- ☐ **Status.** Specify the contents of status reports, the agenda of status meetings, and timing issues.

- ☐ **Workshops and meetings.** Specify how these should be conducted and documented.

- ☐ **Documentation.** Specify the minimum amount of documentation that is required in the project and provide a format for each document. This must include a business case, business requirements, an architecture diagram, test cases, and a communication plan.

- ☐ **Technical.** Specify formats for coding, screen layouts, and walk-throughs.

- ☐ **Issues.** Specify the format for reporting an issue, the way issues are tracked, and the way issued are resolved.

The contents of this list can be modified as the need arises. Project standards should be based on corporate standards wherever possible. Standards specified for a project should be easily accessible by the team. Standards should be enforced as part of an overall project quality plan.

Templates can be provided to a project team as a way to standardize some parts of the reporting function. These provide project teams with a quick-start to their documentation efforts. The appendices contain templates for the following reports: Project plan (both an executive level project plan and a detailed project plan), tables for tracking milestones, status report, status page, issues log, final report, final presentation, memos, contact list, and an email list.

Rules for Achieving Project Success

Ten rules for achieving, or at a minimum, enhancing the chances of attaining project success are described in this section.

1. Document each team member's goals and objectives for the project and their career. Get team members to serve as coaches for each other.

2. Lay the foundation for team communication by holding regular status meetings.

3. Get the project teams, users, and sponsors to work off a short list of documented milestone dates. Track intermediate results and

share them with project sponsors. Keep this information up to date along with the issues log.

4. Always create a regular status report and maintain an issues log.

5. Do not opt for an elegant solution at the expense of risking delivery.

6. Assemble and nurture several project teams that you work well with and can use on successive projects.

7. Use a methodology or framework to build the project plan.

8. Rely on a testing cycle to find problems earlier in the lifecycle.

9. Insist on documented business requirements and use the status reporting function to escalate a lack of these to the executive.

10. Keep an open door policy with your resources.

Case Studies: Successful IT Projects

The case studies included in this chapter have been generalized to protect the privacy of organizations. Individual names, where provided, identify real people who have agreed to have their names included in this book.

These case studies were selected on the basis of technology, budget, project length, complexity, and team size. Four of the projects have multiple phases, totaling several years of effort with multimillion dollar budgets and teams with several dozen staff members. The remaining projects have durations of less than six months from initiation to implementation, with project teams of less than a dozen people.

Case Study E

This project with a multimillion dollar budget serves as a good example of how to run a successful IT project. The client, the consulting company, and the individuals on the development team found the experience to be both profitable and fulfilling. The application is currently serving tens of millions of customers each year. Customers of the client who have seen the system serving the public have commented on the high satisfaction level it has achieved.

The project's mandate was to develop a mission-critical, online ticketing application for an overseas client. This was a pioneer client/server project that had Sybase SQL Server supporting 100 PC client machines running an application developed using JAM from JYACC and functions coded in C language. The clients were connected in a LAN/WAN environment through Ethernet boards and a TCP/IP interface. Each PC was connected to a thermal ticket printer and an optional ticket scanner.

An experienced two-person management team led the project from the start. The project director had the ability to understand the business requirements and the foresight to hire an effective technical architect to pull the pieces together. Using a rapid development tool to quickly build a usable prototype of the application, the architect quickly gained the confidence of the client. The client and the consulting group selected the hardware and software products on the basis of established criteria (e.g., vendor support capability, price of the products, functionality of the products, reliability, and fault tolerance, among other criteria). After gaining the client's approval to proceed, a project team was quickly assembled. An organization chart for this project is shown in Figure 6.2.

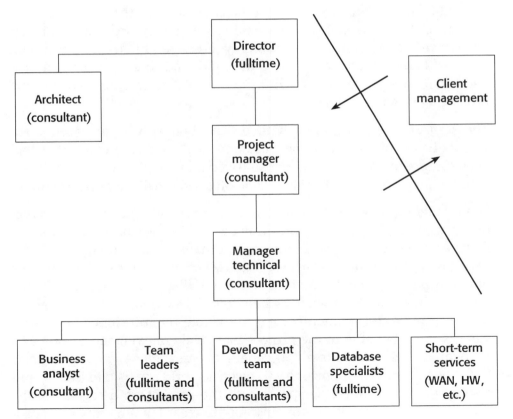

Figure 6.2 Organization chart—Case Study E.

A project plan was developed on the basis of the prototype and parameters received from the client. Implementation of the product was separated into three phases, or releases. The first release was mandated to implement a small portion of the client's business portfolio. A mistake at this level would not be devastating (but would be extremely embarrassing and inconvenient). Specific screens were selected for full functionality development.

A development platform was leased and placed at the consulting site. The client also set up a testing environment for its staff. At the start of the project, the team consisted of generalists. Original team members were sent on Sybase SQL Server training courses. Developers focused on selected areas and within a short period of time built up a substantial level of expertise. There was a Sybase specialist, a C specialist, a DBA, a hardware specialist, and so on. Cross-training was encouraged among the team.

The ability of the team to work together was perhaps the strongest component of this project. There were no visible destructive politics being played, yet many members were highly interested in attaining personal success. Management was results oriented, and there was no time for delay in the project deadlines. Information was actively shared and turf protecting was not visible.

The project was adequately funded. The budget was analyzed on a weekly basis for time and materials and explained to a client that had been disappointed by another consulting company. Team members were paid for all hours worked or given time off (at some distant point in time).

Team building was also encouraged on this project. Team members regularly went to lunch together. (Having lunch does not automatically make a project successful. In fact, teams that socialize too much can be harmful to project success. However, lunches and other social activities that are used in the context of team building and opportunities for reflection have been shown to be beneficial.) One of the senior members of the team would frequently take the whole team to lunch. This provided several benefits to the project that easily outweighed the $300 to $500 lunch tab. First, team members became closer and friendlier. Lunches became an opportunity to discuss world topics and issues, and also to look at another perspective of the project on a regular basis. These lunches were also an opportunity to treat team members as professionals, and thus all started acting as professionals. Lunches appear to be a better team-building method than weekend ballgames or dinners.

An important factor in the success of this project was the development of a solid relationship with the client's management. This was done by building trust, delivering products, and providing functionality as promised. Weaknesses in the functionality were clearly described in the release notes. Functions within each release were delivered to the client on a regular basis to allow management to see what they were getting, to become comfortable with the product, and to begin testing. The project team also respected the feedback provided by the users, prioritized requests, and made relevant modifications to the product.

The project architect focused the team on building the significant functionality first and left routine functions (such as table updates and maintenance screens) for later releases. This allowed the client to build confidence at the outset of the project. After all, if the difficult functions are basically working in the first three months of a project, the client can lay infrastructure, train staff, and make the other investments necessary for a future implementation date. Without this confidence, a client may not make the commitment necessary for a successful implementation.

The project team also tended to be proactive rather than reactive. This was seen in many instances. A user guide was started at the outset to force good documentation and to give the client something to evaluate. Problems were anticipated as far in advance as possible. Benchmarking was done early because it was known that response time would be a critical issue. This process taught the team several techniques that reduced online transaction response time for frequently used functions from 10 seconds to 2 seconds.

The management team was experienced and willing to play many roles. The technical manager routinely walked around and spoke to each team member. This allowed him to offer advice, while also learning firsthand what was being done and the actual capabilities of each team member.

The team also established standards early during development. This involved screen layout, navigation, change control, code style, messages, report layouts, and other areas.

For personal or other reasons, several key members left the project. This did not cause a major disruption because other team members rose to the challenge of replacing the skills that were lost, and management had had the foresight to cross-train team members from the beginning.

Release 1 was implemented successfully. Release 2 was implemented and required optimization and fine-tuning. Release 3 was implemented successfully.

Interestingly, this project also demonstrated the use of several philosophies that are popular at the time of writing, namely, reengineering, team empowerment, and rapid prototyping.

Reengineering

The original system had dozens of core screens to support the human process of selling tickets to the public. The new application was built around improved processes, and consisted of about six core user screens with enhanced functionality.

Team Empowerment

The members of the team were empowered on many levels. Most team members were process owners. They completed the analysis and specifications, sought approval, coded, and tested their process. Development was done in parallel.

Rapid Prototyping

This played a big part in the project. To allow the client to touch and feel the completed application before developing anything, the project architect initially completed a data model and prototyped all the screens in the application. These were presented to the client, who made useful suggestions that were incorporated into the prototype. This process was iterative, until consensus was reached with the users. The client found this exercise reassuring, especially since a previous consulting company had attempted the project without using this technique and had achieved no measurable success.

Rapid prototyping was used throughout the remainder of the project. All screens and reports were prototyped and demonstrated to the client, iteratively enhanced, then developed. This provided several benefits, as discussed in chapter 7.

Summary of the Reasons for the Project's Success

This project was successful for the following reasons:

☐ A clear mandate was articulated.

☐ There were talented resources on all levels—client, development, and management.

☐ Appropriate funding was provided.

☐ Requirements were understood clearly and were flexible enough to accommodate modifications.

☐ A minimum amount of politics existed.

☐ The project plan was effective.

☐ Project management was excellent.

Case Study F

This project involved an outsourcing company (the "vendor") that was serving a property and auto insurance company (the "client"). The relationship had become progressively more strained for several reasons, most of which started innocently enough. The outsourcing contract specified that the vendor was responsible for running the client's mission-critical applications on the vendor's IBM mainframe. The vendor was responsible for all operations, including backups and the generation of daily reports. Frequent enhancements to the application were required and completed by the vendor on a contractual basis. The client was responsible for acceptance testing. The vendor was paid for computer time, overhead costs, and hourly rates for all vendor employees on the project.

The client asked for some major enhancements to the system with a three-month deadline. This date and it could not be readily shifted because of plans according to this date. The technology JCL XA, Cobol, CICS, and VSAM.

The project team consisted of three business side. The vendor provided a senior consultant These were responsible to an account manager senior consultant to build a good relationship with the client. The project plan was built to satisfy a three-month schedule, with a comfortable margin for unforeseen circumstances.

The senior consultant became the project champion and the acting project leader. Initially, the client mandated an approach they felt should be followed. The senior consultant evaluated the approach, and at once felt uncomfortable with it because it involved populating rate tables without going through the standard edits in the front-end CICS screens. After some investigation, with the tight timeframe in mind, the consultant raised this issue with the account manager, citing the danger of trying to change within a three-month timeframe procedures that had taken a decade to develop. The account manager sided with the client's approach simply because they were the client. At this point the senior consultant had a crucial decision to make. Feeling that the suggested approach was not viable and realizing that the client, in the final analysis, was interested in a successful implementation, the senior consultant decided to defend his position. Again the account manager acquiesced to the client, basically brushing the consultant aside with some veiled comments about exceeding his authority.

The consultant, analyzing his career, and realizing that the marketplace offered other opportunities, took a risk and continued defending his position, because the alternative would have resulted in a failed project. Approaching the account manager, the consultant essentially said: "If you are ordering me to follow the suggested approach, I will. But first, I will document my misgivings and copy them to your boss, the director, the client director, and the president of this company. Then in three months, when the system is implemented and the online system crashes, I can point to my memo when people point at me. The memo will point them to you." The account manager agreed to a feasibility study of the two approaches.

The consultant spent two days completing the feasibility studies and emailed them to the client director, who approved the new suggested approach within a day. It seems that the client was, in fact, more interested in a successful implementation than in a particular approach.

The consultant then led the team through standard development phases, namely analysis, specifications, approval, coding, and testing. These were completed, after consistent hard work, one week shy of the deadline. Although 60-to-70-hour weeks were standard during this project, overtime was not requested because of the existing strained relationship between the client and the vendor. Implementation of the application proceeded smoothly—with the exception of one disk file that overflowed because more than double the data volume identified for conversion was placed into the file, without communication to the development team. This was a harmless problem and was fixed painlessly. The enhancements went live with no further problems on the designated implementation date.

The client was very pleased with the results of the project. A reference letter was emailed to the consultant, the account manager, the director, and various other senior members of management in both companies. The account manager's reaction? After taking a holiday during the week of implementation, the account manager only commented on the disk file overflowing.

Summary of the Reasons for the Project's Success

This project was successful for the following reasons:

☐ Commitment of the development team

☐ A good project plan

☐ A talented project champion

☐ Support from executive management that overrode bad decisions made by middle management

Case Study G

This project involved a consulting company (the "vendor") that was contracted to build a property and automobile insurance application from the ground up, using new hardware and software technology, for the "client." This was a large multimillion dollar venture with some unique challenges.

The vendor management team consisted of a senior manager and two technical managers. The rest of the team consisted of a few dozen business and technical people at various levels, from entry level to project leader. The client also provided about 18 staff who were divided into several key areas. The first area consisted of overall project management, where one client manager was in charge of technical management and another was in charge of business management. Several junior client managers reported to these two. The second area consisted of an extensive client testing organization that reported to the business manager. This group was responsible for ongoing testing of the application, acceptance of new modules, tracking of bugs and problems, and enhancements to the application. Client technical staff were included on the development team to facilitate skills transfer from the vendor to the clients.

This technical and human organization posed two challenges. First, the vendor staff had to reside onsite at the client building. The vendor staff had built a lifestyle around flexible hours, relaxed clothing, eating at their computer terminals, and reading hex dumps for fun (no kidding). The client staff started work every day at 8:30 A.M., took a 10-minute coffee break at 10:00, lunch at noon, and another coffee break at 2:30 P.M. The workday ended at 5:00. There was an immediate culture clash between the two groups. The client insisted that the vendor adopt its work ethic. The vendor management, looking at the importance of the client, reluctantly agreed to the terms. Key players of the vendor development staff immediately threatened to resign. The trouble was that some of these folks were brilliant and incredibly dedicated workers. They were also serious about quitting. The vendor went back to the client and explained the situation. The client acquiesced.

The second challenge faced by the project team consisted of deploying a fairly sophisticated application on new technology under a tight development schedule. Several client references existed with the same technology, but these were much smaller versions of the system. This challenge was handled by studious prototyping and extensive benchmarking. Consultants with excellent track records were involved in determining the feasibility of the solution. With their determination that the system was possible, the project proceeded.

Development was achieved in two phases. Phase 1 implemented the automobile insurance component of the application; phase 2 implemented the property insurance component of the application.

Summary of the Reasons for the Project's Success

This project was successful for the following reasons:

☐ Commitment of the development team
☐ Good project plan
☐ Excellent project management

☐ Effective understanding of the business requirements

☐ Thorough testing

Case Study H

This project was intended to accommodate several hundred store locations nationwide for a large retail store. The business requirement was to support price changes to products carried by the retail chain on a weekly basis. Pricing had to be approved by several departments in the organization.

The technical architecture consisted of an IBM 3090 running MVS XA, Cobol, CICS, IMS, VSAM, and a 4GL. The 4GL was new to the organization, and had no internal experts to support it. The new application was intended to accept input from a nightly batch job, produce various results, and then feed other systems in the company.

The project team consisted of a project director, a project leader, a business analyst, a systems analyst, a user director, and several users and developers. The team was small, but the mandated project was highly visible within the organization and important.

The project length was a comfortable six months. The systems analyst effectively led the development and built the project plan to have a duration of four months, leaving a margin of two months to handle unexpected circumstances.

The business analyst completed some paper specifications and left the company. The systems analyst set up a series of JAD sessions with the user director to discuss the project requirements. Other technical staff and users were also invited to participate in these sessions. The result was a set of paper specifications and a prototype using the 4GL product. These were approved by the user director.

Development proceeded smoothly. The user director was regularly informed of progress. Hands-on demonstration of the application was also provided to the users. New requirements were incorporated when possible, without impact on the project plan. During system testing, the user director requested that the project be implemented six weeks early, asking if this would be a problem. As the project was proceeding on schedule, it would be ready at least a few weeks prior to this. The request was easily accommodated.

The application was implemented with a plan to back it out if problems were encountered. The development team was onsite to address any difficulties. Not a single problem or bug was detected when the application went live.

Summary of the Reasons for the Project's Success

This project was successful for the following reasons:

- □ Commitment of the development team
- □ Good project plan
- □ A talented project champion

Case Study I

This project was intended to satisfy legislative requirements for a large government department. Geographically separated offices required a common application-processing system for the health industry. There were literally hundreds of online users with extensive batch reporting requirements.

The technical architecture of the system consisted of a DEC VAX running Ingres and a 4GL forms tool in each of the dozens of offices. Faxing requirements were handled through Intel-based processors running Windows, Winfax, and Microsoft Access.

The project team consisted of a project director, several managers, several DBAs, a pool of developers, and occasional contract staff. The overall team size would have to be classified as large.

The project duration spanned several years. Because of its length, an iterative approach was used to deliver functionality in phases. Rollout was initially limited to a few pilot sites that were able to test the full application under real business conditions.

The application was developed using an iterative approach. The 4GL tool was used to prototype the basic screens after a data and process model were developed. Regular JAD sessions were scheduled to iteratively develop the prototype into a working application, complete with reports and interfaces to other applications.

Summary of the Reasons for the Project's Success

This project was successful for the following reasons:

☐ Commitment of the development team

☐ A talented project champion

Case Study J

This limited project was intended to perform a massive conversion of claims and policy data from an IBM mainframe to a GEAC mainframe at a medium-sized property and casualty insurance company.

The project team consisted of a project manager, a project leader, several users, and junior developers. The project leader was responsible for the planning and execution of the conversions.

The project duration was a comfortable six months. Two basic deliverables were defined: policy conversion and claims conversion. Due to the heavy volume of data and the consequential impact on the online application, the actual conversions were done on the weekends when the online system was not active.

The basic operation of this application was to accept an input tape in IBM EPCDIC format with a tape header and tens of thousands of corresponding records. A relatively small number of policies, about 60,000, were available for conversion. In addition to this, several hundred thousand claims were available for conversion. The header record indicated whether the subsequent records were to be policies or claims. This value selected a C-like program that mapped each record into a new format for a relational database. Control reports were produced for the audit department.

After the programs and batch procedures were developed, a substantial testing procedure was completed to ensure that each mapping step was correct. The conversions were planned over a period of successive weekends, beginning with the policies. The actual process ran smoothly and the control reports proved that what went in came out. The following weekend, about 20,000 policies were copied to tape for the conversion. Unfortunately, the actual conversion crashed. The project leader was called at home, and trying to be helpful, suggested a solution without properly thinking things through. On Monday morning, it was discovered that the entire weekend conversion was botched. In fact, the advice offered over the phone by the project leader had made things far worse than they were because of the first crash. At this time, everyone in the user and IS community became involved looking at the control reports. Executives and auditors who had never been seen before entered the picture. This was an online disaster, and everyone wanted to know what went wrong. Duplicate copies of several claims had been created. One claim was copied 57 times in the production database!

The problem was quickly traced to bad sectors on a defective input tape. This was a physical problem that had never been tested. The testing process used two tapes, one for policies, the other for claims. In both cases, the actual tape medium was not defective, so logic to handle this possibility was never considered. Having discovered this, the problems caused by the weekend conversion were reversed within two days. Although it was a remote possibility that another defective tape would turn up, the conversion programs were changed to protect against this. Conversion of the claims on the next weekend went smoothly, much to everyone's relief. The remaining claims were successfully converted over the next month without incident.

The project became a success and several people learned valuable lessons. The first of these was to test for even remote, ridiculous conditions. The second lesson was to refrain from offering quick, off-the-cuff advice over the telephone. The final lesson was not to underestimate the risks in any production-level implementation.

Summary of the Reasons for the Project's Success

This project was successful for the following reasons:

- ☐ Commitment of the development team
- ☐ Ability to react to unexpected problems
- ☐ A talented project champion

Case Study K

The objective of this project was to select a corporate technology infrastructure for a midsized life insurance company with offices across the country. The engagement letter for this project was signed by a team that was not directly involved with delivery. The first showstopper with this project was that the letter was drafted by non-IT resources who overcommitted to the client by several magnitudes. The agreed-upon scope included reviewing best-of-breed products in every solution category and building a production-ready application in two of the toolsets that were short-listed. This included setting up a test lab, coordinating vendors, gathering business requirements, and winning buy-in from the client. The timeline for this project was a short six weeks, and the budget was fixed. A project manager was assigned to the engagement and given the letter as the contract for delivery. The project team consisted of a project manager, several consultants, and technical support from the vendors that were part of the selection process.

This was a project designed to fail from the beginning in terms of budget, functionality, client satisfaction, and the well-being of the project team. The project manager recognized this exposure before deploying the project team. This allowed him an opportunity to change some of the basic principles of the project without becoming personally exposed. By putting the scope problems in front of the team who had drafted the original proposal, the manager was able to get them to understand the impossibility of delivery under the defined scope. Getting their support, the manager was able to communicate with the client sponsors to show them that what they really needed out of the engagement was not what was originally agreed to in the letter. There was no point in building the same application under two different product suites for a production environment. Not only would one of them be thrown away, but business requirements for anything meaningful could not be gathered during the specified timeframe because of other production pressures. From a technology perspective, there was little point in evaluating every possible tool combination in the world. It was better to build a shortlist that could quickly be dropped down to two or three basic end-to-end suites in line with the client's preferences, constraints, and requirements. The tight deadline was driven by the need for the client management to take a vacation. This allowed the manager to argue for an extension by offering a preliminary presentation of the results before the vacation and a final presentation after client management returned to work. This added two weeks to the project timeline.

There really was no alternative to these changes. The project manager, without saying it, would need to withdraw if they were not made. Another concession made to the client was to retail the original fixed-price budget. Some of the additional cost attributed to the expanded timeline was absorbed by hiring external contractors at a more competitive price. Another method was to offload some of the integration effort to the vendors, who were offering their products with their clear knowledge that this was being done.

The new project scope was accepted, and the engagement letter was revised. Client management agreed to free up resources to support the expanded but still very aggressive timeframes. Achieving the new results still required enormous effort from the project team, tight coordination of the vendors, tracking of the project plan on a daily basis, and strong communication with client management. The approach to reduce the number of tool options under consideration was critical to completing the engagement.

The project ended "successfully" as the recommendations were accepted by client management, the bills were paid, and a strong relationship between the organizations was established. This engagement led to several million dollars of development work over several years.

Summary of the Reasons for the Project's Success

This project was successful for the following reasons:

☐ A project manager who recognized and changed a project scope

☐ A client who understood what they really needed instead of what they wanted

☐ Vendors that understood the meaning of and implemented client service

☐ Strong communication between the project teams

Case Study L

The objective of this project was to manage a legacy conversion and a package implementation for a large financial organization. The scope of the project crossed functional boundaries, including operations, sales, accounting, and marketing. The organization had offices throughout the world, with a heavy concentration in the northeast United States. The project involved over $500 million in sales. The project team exceeded 150 resources, which included permanent staff and several consulting companies. The project had an aggressive timetable that was partly driven by Wall Street analysts and an impending merger.

This project faced many challenges that threatened the success of the project. The project team members were highly distributed geographically. This created cultural differences and communication difficulties. These were exacerbated by the history of the development organization, which was the result of several corporate mergers. This resulted in local loyalties, but none to the larger team. Each of the development organizations had their own management team, mostly at the vice presidential level. A lack of success on the project for the past year had jaded much of the team and created a highly politicized and defensive extended team. The business groups had also lost a lot of confidence in the process and felt alienated.

Aside from the personalities, there were other problems as well. The business requirements were complex and undocumented. There were many interfaces to external vendor applications, most of which were undefined. The financial nature of the applications required extensive validation, which had not yet started. Some of the application components had never been tested together. Others components needed to be built, but were not staffed. The production environment had not been defined and, consequently, had not been ordered.

A lack of progress forced the executive to step in and appoint a hands-on project manager to help deliver the project. The reporting relationship went to the EVP of the organization. A lack of success also resulted in a warm welcome from the business leaders who were becoming desperate, and some support from the development teams who were aware of the disaster they were courting. This created an environment that supported some degree of immediate change and a grace period for results to emerge. The new project manager implemented several initiatives that would lead the project to success. These were backed up by four milestone dates that each implemented components of the business solution.

Figure 6.3 shows the areas that were modified on this project. In the area of planning, the project plan was rebuilt at a high level so that it could be communicated, discussed, and modified with the other leaders on the project. Previous plans were very detailed and complicated or only focused on parts of the overall lifecycle. The new project plan had four milestones spaced three to four months apart. The executive, project teams, and business units bought into these key dates. The overall integrated plan revealed several points that had not been considered in the past. Planning activities for each of these were initiated as a result of this discovery.

The organization was supplemented by a new thin management and analytical layer that supported communication between the other groups. Four to five resources were dedicated to this role (out of 150+ resources).

Figure 6.3 New approach.

Being dedicated to their roles on a full-time basis, they were able to ensure that issues were tracked, information was communicated, meetings were executed, and all components of the extended project team were being represented. As shown in Figure 6.4, this management layer linked the various stakeholders together.

A status-reporting process was implemented as well. This included a regular status meeting every week with anyone who wanted to join the mandated core team. A telephone number was set up to support the geographically separated groups. An agenda was always sent out before the meeting. A facilitator ensured that everyone had an opportunity to speak at the meetings and also that the meetings proceeded efficiently. The attendees at each meeting reviewed the key points in a status report and followed up on the issues list. Another, executive-level, meeting was set up on an as-needed basis to deal with issues that could not be resolved in the status meeting. A status report was also distributed to the extended project team on a weekly basis. All of these changes were made with a minimal addition to the administrative workload of the attendees.

The project manager also ensured that expectations were revisited with the stakeholders. Rules were established that would substitute manual processes for automated processes if this was needed to meet the deadlines. Business requirements were also prioritized so that the initial releases would focus only on the core functionality.

A complete architecture picture was also developed with the extended project team through a series of workshops. This allowed bottlenecks and key stress points to be identified. Solutions were then designed and validated through proof-of-concept. Contingency plans for high-risk

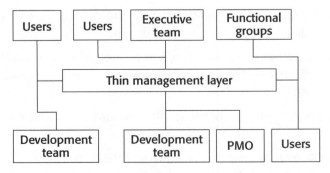

Figure 6.4 Organization chart—Case Study L.

areas were also developed. This proved to be important in meeting the delivery dates since a few stress points turned out to be unstable in the final solution.

Business requirements for all functionality that was being developed or integrated were gathered and documented. A simple rule was implemented: if it isn't written, it's not a requirement. An integration test environment was established and used throughout the project lifecycle. The original plan had called for a limited integration test cycle after system testing. The different development teams were required to unit-test their solutions and then to deliver them to the integration environment for further testing. This proved to be an excellent way to resolve the communication problems between the teams and uncovered a substantial number of integration problems that would have caused the deadlines to be missed.

The project manager reported the project status to the weekly PMO meetings along with the leaders of the other groups on the project. The PMO's firsthand knowledge of the project removed several critical obstacles before the project was implemented.

Summary of the Reasons for the Project's Success

This project was successful for the following reasons:

- ☐ Executive management wanted success and mandated a qualified project manager to pursue it.
- ☐ The project team bought into the change in direction.
- ☐ The thin management layer was able to overcome the previous project politics.
- ☐ Standards for status reporting and documentation captured a lot of the information that was previously unknown.
- ☐ The milestone dates were aggressive, but achievable. The time spacing between them allowed the project teams to continue to advance their personal skills.
- ☐ The PMO helped to remove obstacles that would have destroyed the project.
- ☐ The effective status meetings allowed the team to build an identity and have a regular forum for expression.

Summary

Understanding IT fads and trends is a critical role for the project manager. The IT industry, more than any other, sees the emergence of new techniques, technologies, and approaches on a frequent basis. Each of these is marketed and typed until the business community buys into the new trend as a panacea to solve all the problems that have plagued them for decades. A common practice employed by pioneers of a new technology is to build a small, limited success story, and then to make pronouncements that the IT world has changed for the better. In many cases, a look under the covers shows a lack of support for mission-critical applications, as well as other integration issues. The project manager must learn to differentiate between hype and reality. In the event that a trend lives up to the promises, the project manager must ensure a timely integration into a technical environment and ultimate adoption of the trend as a practice.

This chapter analyzed reasons for the success of IT projects by expanding the project manager's toolkit and through case studies. Successful projects involve avoiding factors that can cause project failure, but this chapter also demonstrated that project success involves additional variables. Case studies of a variety of successful projects were examined in an attempt to gain a more thorough understanding of project successes, and to provide a broader perspective for the reader. Some of the case studies involved multimillion-dollar budgets with multiyear project plans, divided into consecutive six-month phases. The project teams were large, numbering in the dozens to 100+ resources. In contrast, the remaining projects had less than six-month durations, with small, fully empowered teams.

It appears that the presence of a project champion with suitable authority is significant for a project's success. Project leaders, architects, or managers are appropriate choices for this role. Many of these projects followed one project methodology or another. Chapter 7 describes a methodology called Iterative Project Development Methodology (IPDM), which has been used on many successful IS projects.

This chapter also discussed viewing project results in terms of a gray area, where some factors were attained, but some other objectives were not met. The key was for the project manager to identify the key factors up front and to ensure that these were delivered according to metrics agreed to by the project sponsors. The effectiveness of a manager can be measured against the attainment of these factors. Soft success factors include such items as a happy staff, low staff turnover, and responsible training programs. Although it may not be obvious, lack of these factors can lead directly to failure conditions, so they too should be optimized for success.

Projects do not require absolute perfection in order to be successful. It is up to the management team and the customer to determine which factors must be 100 percent met and what value the others must attain in order to deem a project a success.

CHAPTER 7

Iterative Project Development Methodology (IPDM)

T his chapter focuses on project development methodologies and frameworks. It begins with a discussion of a generic development methodology
that is used in the marketplace. This methodology is combined with
Rapid Application Development and waterfall techniques to produce a
streamlined methodology that has been proven to work on projects of
varying sizes and complexity. This includes projects with a few resources
lasting a few months and projects with well over a hundred resources,
budgets in excess of $10 million, and a duration in excess of a year. This
methodology is called the Iterative Project Development Methodology
(IPDM). It is built on the principles of iteration, prototyping, and strong
user involvement. In this chapter the reader will learn about:

- Results-oriented project management
- Development methodology history
- Methodology strengths and weaknesses
- Standard Development Lifecycle (SDLC)
- Iterative Project Development Methodology (IPDM)
- Getting started with the methodology

Beyond a Process-Oriented View of Project Management

Project management involves the difficult task of balancing multiple factors in order to produce project deliverables. Many managers have historically met this challenge by adopting a process-oriented approach to their jobs. The process-oriented approach follows some particular development methodology in a precise way and requires regular status meetings (most of which report that work is progressing well) to track the project. A substantial number of projects still do not get delivered on time and within budget. A majority of those that seem to be on track often only satisfy a subset of the original business requirements. The authors are aware of one multimillion-dollar project that implemented a large application that produced no reports, even to satisfy auditing requirements. The opportunity for human error and fraud in this situation was significant.

Many organizations define rigorous detailed internal management principles for their managers. Much of the energy spent on these activities adds no value to the project deliverables, even though the activities may satisfy the needs of someone else in the organization. The end result is that a substantial amount of time is spent judiciously following the processes of project management, yet in the end, organizations are still plagued with chronic overruns and a general lack of project completion. In fact, many projects become revolving doors for managers, who take charge of a project, do all the right things according to generally accepted principles of project management and development methodologies, but end up achieving no tangible results even after many months or years on a project. Eventually the managers move on to other things, hoping to avoid damaging their careers, or they continue making the same mistakes and spend many years on the same project.

The authors have personally seen many examples where generally accepted project management principles were applied to information systems projects, yet after several years of effort nothing but reams of paper specifications, minutes of meetings, and isolated fragments of code were produced, after millions of dollars were spent. A close look at the participants generally shows hard-working, intelligent, dedicated professionals. Yet there are countless examples of these types of problems in organizations all over the world.

Fortunately the situation is far from hopeless. Many examples of successful IT projects are also found around the world. Some of these were discussed in chapter 6. The purpose of this chapter is to describe a powerful development methodology that has evolved over a variety of projects undertaken by the authors. The Iterative Project Development Methodology (IPDM) has been successfully used on both small and large development projects, including a variety of architectures such as mainframe, midrange, client/server, object-oriented, component, open systems, n-tier, Web-based, ERP, and others. IPDM also supports custom development, outsourcing, package search, and other IT development initiatives. One of its principal attributes is to change the traditional process-oriented view of project management to a results-oriented view. This requires a fundamental change in the current method in which projects are planned, as described in IPDM.

Project Development Methodologies

Project development methodologies have been around for centuries and were used to construct such objects as ships, houses, dams, and factories. In the last few decades, these methodologies were refined specifically to guide information systems projects. A project development methodology is like a recipe in a cookbook intended to allow the cooks to whip up a successful project. Many of these recipe-like methodologies read something like "spend one week reviewing the code, mix with an auditor, shake with an implementation schedule . . . " Inevitably, some recipes are better than others, and sometimes successful projects are implemented by strict adherence to a development methodology. In the last few years, many traditional methodologies have evolved into combined frameworks/ methodologies that are far more flexible and implementable than the methodology versions in isolation. We'll see the reason for this shortly.

Strengths of More Popular Methodologies

1. **A clear step-by-step roadmap from point A to point Z.**
   Methodologies provide an ordered list of all the activities that should be followed to complete a project. The difficulty with this is that a list of generic activities cannot be comprehensive enough to satisfy all possible types of projects.

2. **A tried and proven path to project implementation.** Methodologies generally have proven track records. That is the reason they are packaged and distributed in the first place.

3. **Important project deliverables are anticipated far in advance.** Projects that are conducted according to a methodology provide a manager with a list of expected deliverables at the start of the project, thus giving the manager something to work toward (e.g., data model, ER diagram) on a project plan.

4. **A checklist for project managers to follow.** A methodology allows project managers to build an inventory of the activities that lead up to the deliverables, and subsequently to check off completed items.

5. **A starting point.** Methodologies allow managers to start their projects without having a complete understanding of relevant issues.

6. **Transformation to frameworks.** Methodologies that have been transformed into frameworks provide a quick, proven, and reusable method for approaching projects.

Weaknesses of More Popular Methodologies

1. **Lack of flexibility in dealing with unexpected problems**. Managers who are following a methodology from A to Z may be incapable of handling an unexpected occurrence. For example, during acceptance testing, what happens if an operating system has a bug that disrupts communication to some PC clients? Similarly, other unexpected and complicated issues arise that cannot be resolved by looking for advice in a process box on a methodology document. The only answer is to have a hard-working, experienced project team tap into creative thinking.

2. **Focus on procedures, sometimes at the expense of results**. Procedures are intended to offer an effective approach for solving complex problems. This may be true; however, sometimes procedures can become a crutch for people trying to avoid making difficult decisions. Over a period of time, procedures can also become inefficient. Consequently, staff who follow procedures without questioning their applicability may be sacrificing results in their pursuit of dotting every "i" and crossing every "t."

3. **Unnecessary steps that are often ignored by project teams**. Methodologies are intended to be all-inclusive and universal. Such methodologies, by definition, will contain a comprehensive set of processes to support this. This is in direct conflict with being streamlined.

4. **Long durations for deliverables**. Deliverables in most traditional methodologies are the end product of a sequential, nonoptimized series of steps.

Things That Project Methodologies Will Not Do

Project methodologies are not magic wands for project development. They are simply roadmaps that could lead to successful projects. Some managers expect far more from them. In fact, some feel that the use of a methodology will pretty much guarantee the success of a project, with minimal effort from them. This would be similar to interviewing a few very successful people like Bill Gates to find out how they made their fortune and then expecting to repeat the process and achieve the same results. Of course, there is no guarantee that this would happen. The results will depend on many factors, such as opportunity, the state of the economy, personal contacts, starting capital, the product being sold, and of course, the abilities of the people involved. It is the same with project development methodologies. They will not do the following things:

1. **Instill a manager with vision**. A methodology may identify the need to do this, but it will only happen if the manager strives to make it so.

2. **Turn someone into a good manager.** A manager must develop multiple skills and experiences to make this happen.

3. **Build an actual deliverable**. Deliverables require effort from the project team to develop. Teams must be motivated and be able to produce deliverables. A manager must take responsibility for making this happen.

4. **Implement the project by automatically making things happen**. A methodology is not an animate entity that makes things happen by itself. Without input, a methodology produces nothing.

5. **Replace a talented project team**. The project team will make a project successful. A good project team will often develop or refine

a methodology as needed. A weak project team will not gain much value from any methodology, no matter its strength. Instead, it will serve as a crutch to the team, who will come to work every day and have something to work on until it becomes clear that the project is not on track. Some methodologies delay this for quite some time.

One final example that disproves the notion that a methodology replaces the need for a good project team is to consider a canvas, a paintbrush, and a how-to-paint book. Two artists using the "artistic methodology" in the book will probably produce two very different paintings. Ultimately, their talent will determine the quality of the final painting, even though they are using the same methodology. In fact, if they are not artists, they may end up producing garbage.

Project Manager Roles and Responsibilities in an SDLC

The Standard Development Lifecycle (SDLC) is an unofficial industry-wide approach for implementing IT development projects. It is based on several distinct phases that generally include "planning," "analysis and design," "development," "testing," and "implementation." In addition to the names and number of the phases changing, the precise contents, sequencing, techniques, and deliverables vary from implementation to implementation. This section describes a project manager's basic responsibilities in a generic SDLC that is independent of development tools, techniques, and technology infrastructures. Project managers are generally involved in all phases of the system development lifecycle. The next major section in this chapter describes a streamlined methodology that combines the successful elements of several major methodologies.

Project Confirmation, Initiation, and Planning

The project confirmation and initiation tasks include confirming the mission of the project, the steering committee, stakeholders, the scope, and milestone dates. This phase also sees the establishment of a project management office complete with standards, templates, status reports, an issue log, and a master copy of the project plan. This was the subject of chapter 4.

The project manager generally builds a living project plan, identifies team roles, and allocates resources at this stage. The project plan has a high level of detail for the near-term activities, but high-level descriptions and sketchy details for phases that are further out in time. Resources should be allocated to tasks and deliverables and must become available to the project as they are needed according to the project plan. The project manager should be careful to involve additional expertise in driving out the details in the plan, and should also solicit buy-in to the project plan from all stakeholders.

A recommended approach to the basic planning set of activities involves investing heavy effort at specific points in the project lifecycle, with regular iterations through the planning activities. Planning should have a heavy emphasis before the start of a project, at the beginning of every deliverable, and before the start of major phases.

Requirements and Analysis

Requirement gathering and early analysis activities are arguably the most important ones in the entire project lifecycle with respect to the end quality in the product. Invalid requirements negate the value of a system, no matter how brilliantly it is built. The project manager must ensure that requirements are gathered in their entirety for the application, technology, processes, and any other area that will affect the organization. The manger must ensure that users buy into these requirements. A variety of techniques, including prototyping and storyboarding, should be used to ensure that the users and the project team agree on the same interpretation of the requirements. This is an area of high risk since it is not uncommon for project teams and users to believe that they are agreeing on the same requirements, only to find, in fact, that they have entirely different interpretations. Using a visual technique, such as a storyboard or a prototype, allows both groups to focus on a picture that is more likely to highlight discrepancies.

Systems Architecture/Design

Systems architecture, consisting of data, application, and technology, is the foundation of the IT solution that is to be developed. Building an architecture is a highly iterative process that involves repeated refinements and extensive product evaluations and selection processes. Architecture moves from a high to a detailed level, based on the requirements that were captured in the earlier phase. Design is started after the architecture is accepted by project management.

The project manager is responsible for ensuring that the appropriate level of expertise is available while the architecture is being developed. This is especially a challenge when the architecture includes newer technologies, such as Internet/intranet, data warehousing, and component-based solutions. Furthermore, it is also important to receive active support and assistance from functional users, as well as ensuring buy-in from all stakeholders and those ultimately required to pay the bills. The project manager must understand the recommended architecture and design. The project manager may rely on expert opinions in terms of defining the system architecture, but is ultimately responsible and accountable for the recommendations.

Development

Development, regardless of the technology environment, be it third generation, fourth generation, code generators, CASE, or some other variation, involves managing technical resources through the process of building application code that functions in accordance with the business specifications. The project manager must ensure that developers adhere to standards and processes, as well as unit-test their code.

Testing

This encompasses a series of testing methods, including unit testing, functional testing, system testing, integration testing, regression testing, stress testing, acceptance testing, and benchmarking. The project manager must ensure that the relevant users see the results of the tests and get involved in setting up the tests. The project manager must also ensure that results are reported to senior management who make a final decision to accept or reject the system. Every test must be accompanied by a test plan, test cases, test scripts, and test results. There are subtle and not so subtle differences between industry definitions for the different types of testing. For example unit testing may mean one thing according to one group of practitioners and something entirely different to another group. Table 7.1 provides an interpretation that is consistent in many of the organizations we have operated in.

Table 7.1 Types of Testing

TEST	DESCRIPTION	OWNERSHIP
Unit	A set of informal tests conducted at the code level to prove the validity of basic functionality in an application.	Developers
Functional	A set of formal tests that are designed to thoroughly test business functionality according to business requirements.	Business users
System	A set of tests designed to test both the business and the technical solution without components built by other groups.	Technology group
Integration	This is sometimes referred to as end-to-end testing. The objective is to integrate all the components of a system and conduct a thorough business and technology test.	Technology group Business group
Regression	A set of iterative tests that are used to thoroughly retest the functionality of an application whenever changes are made to the code. These tests are good candidates for automation.	Business users
Stress	This set of tests is designed to test an application's maximum limits. This includes testing throughput, scalability, stability, concurrent users, and transactions flows. These tests require software tools.	Technology group
Acceptance	This set of tests is designed to conduct a thorough review of an application before it is accepted into production.	Business stakeholders
Benchmarking	This set of tests compares specific transactions to industry metrics.	Business users

Full lifecycle testing tools are critical in supporting Web-based applications. For example, the e-test suite from RSW Software (www.rswsoftware.com) can be used to simulate a high number of concurrent users, track statistics, identify bottlenecks, and monitor the site 24 hours a day, seven days a week to determine performance and evaluate system functionality.

Implementation

Implementation involves all the activities necessary to implement the system for use by end-users. This requires a tremendous amount of work in distributed computing environments. Some tasks include ensuring that the network is in place with the appropriate protocols and bandwidth support, implementing the production technology architecture, and ensuring the implementation of system management tools. Implementation also involves addressing disaster recovery concerns, contingency planning, parallel system operations for a trial period, user training, and rollout of a communication strategy.

Postimplementation Review

The project manager must conduct a review of the project and its major components, including the project plan, management style, performance of the team, and performance of the users. The objective is to identify lessons learned from the experience, and to share these with the organization to improve performance in future projects. If a formal methodology is in place, it is also useful to include the lessons learned within the methodology, either as additional tasks or as case studies. All the deliverables from the project should also be included in a central repository for future reference.

Relatively recent technology innovations, such as component-based computing, Web-based architecture, data warehousing, wireless solutions, package solutions, frameworks, mobile computing, and the Internet affect the specific deliverables produced during these phases. Similarly, project deliverables can be anything from a data model or process model, to the actual working applications. For example, an OO project produces an object model, while a data warehousing project produces a multidimensional data model.

Each of these phases must be supported by different roles and resources. The constant between them is that the project manager must coordinate the resources and have the expertise to ensure that the phases are conducted correctly. In order to do this effectively, the project manager needs to be the renaissance professional—the master of many skills and tools.

IPDM: A New Project Development Methodology

The iterative project development methodology is a derivation of the Rapid Application Development (RAD) methodology that gained widespread popularity in the 1980s and 1990s, the Standard Development Lifecycle, and the waterfall approach. IPDM has the following major characteristics.

Look and Feel Prototypes of Applications and Processes

This is a key component of this methodology. Prototypes allow clients to have a view of the final solution with minimal investment. In most non–IT projects, detailed models or prototypes are developed before full-scale construction is authorized to start. This is true of buildings, bridges, rockets, and even movies (e.g., demo tapes). None of these objects is generally purchased directly from drawings or scripts. Yet historically, many IT applications are built from nothing more than paper specifications. Users are expected to visualize a solution on the basis of flowcharts, decision tables, and words. Strangely enough there is surprise and disappointment when users look at the solution, which is sometimes delivered years later, and want something different.

There is also a widespread misconception that prototypes are an open invitation for users and project teams to design on the fly. In such cases, a prototype is built and demonstrated to users. The users accept the prototype and development begins. When users want to modify or add requirements, these are simply prototyped and incorporated into the development process. As this process repeats itself, the project team suddenly finds itself trying to hit a moving target. Requirements are coming in from all over the place and there is simply not enough time to finish development. This results in a bug-infested application, bruised egos, and missing requirements. Prototyping gets a bad reputation, when in fact, its purpose was misunderstood from the start.

Prototypes should be used as another tool to capture business requirements. IT prototypes should be used in the same way as models and prototypes are in non–IT industries. The prototype serves as a working model of the final application that the users can touch, feel, and understand. When they agree that the prototype is an accurate solution to the problem being addressed by a project, the prototype becomes the fixed requirements definition. Any changes to the prototype must be assessed to determine their impact, just as changes to requirements were historically handled in development projects that did not rely on prototypes.

Iterative Approach to Product Development

This is another important part of this methodology. Iteration is used to select a starting point, then repeatedly build on a solution until it is acceptable to the business. This is like going to a really dirty pane of glass, wiping it with a cloth, and noticing that it looks cleaner. Stopping this process will still result in the glass being cleaner than it was before the first swipe of the cloth. The glass can be shown to a client, and approval can be sought to continue. Additional swipes of the cloth across the pane of glass will continue to make it cleaner. Stopping at any time will result in a pane that is cleaner than it was at the beginning. Effort can be expended in this way until the client is satisfied with the cleanliness of the glass. Iteration on IT projects works the same way.

Flexibility in Dealing with Requirements

The objective of a project is to build the best and most useful product possible. Users will almost always come up with additional requirements, even after sign-off on the business requirements. The iterative nature of this methodology allows some flexibility in accommodating additional requirements within the project schedule. Requirements that cannot be incorporated without affecting the project plan can be rolled into a subsequent phase.

Direct Involvement of Users

Users have always been involved within the development cycle. But historically this has been limited to activities like answering interview questions and reviewing paper specifications. Users have not typically sat in a JAD session or at a PC actively painting GUI screens. By involving them in the design of the prototype, they are brought into the development process. This offers several benefits. First, they are able to actively lend their expertise to the process. Second, they become involved and thus become closer to the project and fight for its success. They gain a sense of ownership and familiarity. Last, the users are able to test-drive the application from the beginning, eliminating or dramatically minimizing surprises at the time of delivery.

Other Goals

IPDM has been shown to achieve the following additional significant goals: (1) deliver a completed application in a shorter period than was previously possible; (2) increase user acceptance of the final product; (3)

support a phased approach to implementation, where selected components of an application are delivered to users at regular time intervals instead of at the end of a long development process; and (4) achieve unconditional client satisfaction with the final product. In addition to meeting these goals, projects can be delivered with reduced costs and development time.

Despite these benefits, IPDM should not be viewed as a magic wand, but rather it should be given careful consideration as a development methodology or a framework for organizations involved in development projects.

A Description of IPDM

IPDM has evolved over a span of many successful projects, encompassing a broad range of business and technical environments. This methodology has successfully salvaged numerous projects that have gone grossly over budget and missed deadlines. It was successful in winning over badly scathed users and clients who had spent millions of dollars and many years without getting anything of value in return for their investment or patience.

The methodology contains 15 high-level processes that are manipulated in an iterative fashion. Some of these processes can be conducted in parallel, but this largely depends on the project specifics.

Level 1 (Highest Level)

Figure 7.1 provides a high-level view of the Iterative Project Development Methodology. Input/output files are not shown on this level, but they are included in the figures containing lower-level views of these processes later in this section.

An overview of the 15 processes in Figure 7.1 is provided here with a description of the process and deliverables from the perspective of the project manager.

Confirm Project Orientation Process

This orientation opportunity should be used by a project manager to become familiar with a project. Specifically, a manager should determine the importance of a project to the organization, identify the proj-

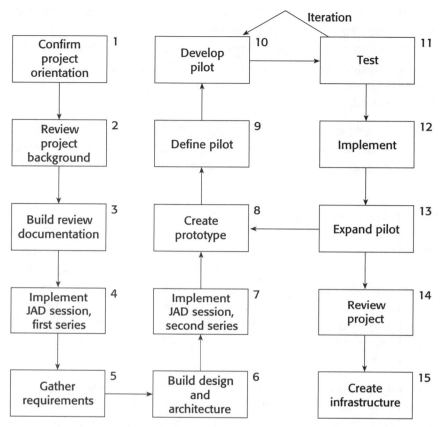

Figure 7.1 IPDM level 1 (highest).

ect sponsor, and ensure that an active steering committee exists. The manager should also get to know the people who will play key roles in the life of the project.

Review Project Background Process

All relevant background information concerning the project should be reviewed by the project manager. This includes the project mandate statement, written documentation, business documents, and the results of previous attempts at the project.

Build Review Documentation Process

The project manager should digest all the available project information and reformat it for discussion and JAD sessions. This allows the manager to begin sharing information with key players in the company and begin to build a consensus. The manager should not hesitate to involve other staff in this task if it is too large.

Another point to remember is that most people do not like to write documentation, which tends to be a time-consuming and arduous task. This step gives anyone an opportunity to begin this process and immediately make a positive impact that tends to mobilize others. An example of this was seen on a project that had been active for years, but with few written requirements being developed during that time. This was a point of great consternation for some members of the project team, who needed a definitive statement of business requirements to begin to satisfy their responsibilities. A new consultant on the project simply acted as facilitator and started recording requirements based on what was said by the players during JAD sessions. This act proved to be a great catalyst in moving the project forward.

Implement JAD Session, First Series Process

This is an iterative process that begins with the manager approaching key players (e.g., directors and managers of relevant business areas or departments) in one-on-one meetings to verify the documentation that was produced. The manager should assume that this documentation is incomplete or wrong, and should use these meetings to get a better understanding of the requirements or direction that the project is expected to take.

When the manager is comfortable with the documentation and information resulting from the small meetings, JAD sessions should be used to bring key users and IT staff together to revise and confirm what is known about the project.

This is an important planning process that will allow a project manager to build a reasonable project plan, ascertain resource requirements, determine infrastructure requirements, and obtain a first approximation of estimates.

Gather Requirements Process

This is a traditional process that builds business requirements and sometimes the technical requirements. A project manager can appoint business analysts, consultants, or other staff to assume responsibility for gathering and documenting this information.

Build Design and Architecture Process

This process involves technical staff, designers, and architects in building a solution to the project within the constraints of the organization. This will lead to a list of hardware and software tools for the project. The team may rely on feasibility studies and benchmarks that have already been done, or commission new ones to support the design and architecture process.

Some portions of the infrastructure solution will be implemented immediately (e.g., database creation scripts) to support development.

Implement JAD Session, Second Series Process

The solution being proposed for the project is shared with key individuals in the company to obtain the following benefits:

☐ Get their input and benefit from their expertise

☐ Gain their support

☐ Share information with them

☐ Get confirmation for the decisions already made on the project

☐ Confirm detail design

Create Prototype Process

A functional, reusable prototype is developed to support the requirements documentation produced in the previous processes. This should be done with extensive user involvement.

Define Pilot Process

The business requirements are divided into phases. Each phase is allocated a milestone called a pilot. This is an implementation of the core functionality within a phase without the bells and whistles. The pilot deliverable should be used as a proof of concept that runs a subset of the total data required for a phase. The completed pilot should be demonstrated to decision makers. Changes to the requirements should be anticipated, but they should be evaluated in terms of cost and impact on the schedule before being accepted into the current phase. If they cannot be handled, they should be incorporated into a future phase.

Develop Pilot Process

This traditional process requires analysis, design, specifications, coding, and unit testing for deliverables in the phase. This is an iterative process that involves building the pilot, going to the testing process, getting approval for the pilot from executive management, then completing development for the remaining functions in the phase.

Test Process

This is a rigorous testing process that includes system testing, regression testing, and acceptance testing. Each of these should be conducted with a testing kit that includes: a testing organization, testing approach, test scripts, test results, and test tools.

Implement Process

A plan is developed and followed to implement the application. A back-out plan is also developed in the event that the implementation is unsuccessful. A communication approach and user training strategy is also included in this activity.

Expand Pilot Process

Following a successful implementation, the functionality in the remaining phases is split off into additional pilots. This is an iterative approach that branches back to the prototyping stage.

Review Project Process

Following any implementation, a formal evaluation should be conducted to learn from the experience and share the results with the rest of the organization and other project teams.

Create Infrastructure Process

After a successful implementation, project staff is generally moved off the project. A manager should ensure that there has been appropriate skills transfer to allow this to happen smoothly. A help desk and support staff must also be retained to support users of the application.

Level 2

The level 2 flows provide a further level of detail for each process or phase in the streamlined methodology. Each phase is broken into component subprocesses or activities, inputs, outputs, and additional information that help describe the nature of the phase.

Confirm Project Orientation

Figure 7.2 shows that the project orientation process accepts several deliverables that are reviewed and used to confirm a project sponsor. The sponsor helps to identify members of a steering committee and key users who can define business requirements and ultimately accept the system. Other resources that may be included on the project team or assist the project are also identified at this stage. This information, along

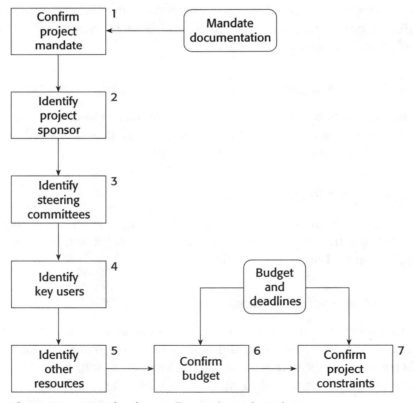

Figure 7.2   IPDM level 2: confirm project orientation.

with any project plans and budget information, are included in a project charter.

Input

Documentation mandate

Budget and deadlines

Project vision

Output

Project confirmation

Steering committee(s)

Identification of key users

Project charter

Subprocesses

Confirm project mandate

Identify project sponsor

Identify steering committees

Identify key users

Identify other resources

Confirm budget

Confirm project constraints

Review Project Background

Figure 7.3 shows a process to review the background information available for a project. This could be descriptions of the current system, manual processes, or results of other attempts at the same project that did not succeed. Background information can be found in central repositories (e.g., Lotus Notes or intranets), in binders, and at people's desks. It may also be necessary to interview key users to extract or clarify background information.

Input

Project documentation

Output

Understanding and confirmation of the project

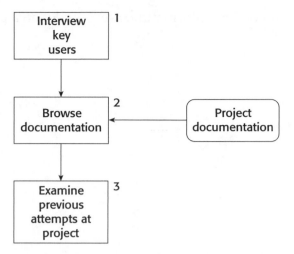

Figure 7.3 IPDM level 2: review project background.

Subprocesses

Interview key users

Browse documentation

Examine previous attempts at project

Build Review Documentation

Figure 7.4 shows how background information and interview results can be analyzed and converted into other forms for further clarification and validation. This can include creating high-level data models, process models, and drafting business requirements.

Input

Project documentation

Project charter

Output

Data models

Requirements

Process models

ER diagrams

First cut project plan

Quality plan

Risk plan

Subprocess

Assemble documentation

Refine and validate documentation

Additional Information

There is no secret to doing this analysis properly. It takes hard work, talent, and dedication. This is the hardest thing to do and is often the weakest link in a project. Business requirements are rarely straightforward, and users often need assistance in establishing them. To understand this, imagine a person buying a car. The person may have decided to buy a sports car, but needs assistance in choosing one model over the others. Even after choosing a model, the buyer needs assistance in understanding the implications of getting a lease or a loan, insurance options, mileage considerations, and warranty possibilities.

An ineffective method of capturing business requirements is for an analyst to ask a user a set of questions and to meticulously write down what was said exactly and go away believing that a good job was done. Instead, an analyst should show initiative, internalize the requirements to determine consistency, and offer suggestions to the business users. This process is iterative in that the requirements are fine-tuned over a series of passes, improving each time.

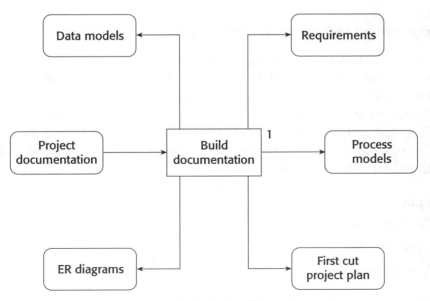

Figure 7.4   IPDM level 2: build review documentation.

The business analyst (BA) must be careful to avoid confrontation during the process of defining business requirements. After a few projects, effective business analysts learn enough about a set of business cases to allow them to intuitively understand and develop business requirements for a wide variety of business cases. The analyst, who often acts as a consultant in this phase, has a backlog of knowledge that allows him or her to distinguish between what has been known to work from what has not been known to work. During this process, the business analyst should also endeavor to be consultative rather than combative. A BA or consultant should also avoid being perceived as too passive or having little to offer in this phase. A BA or consultant must lend experience and wisdom to a project without becoming overbearing. This can be done by organizing a series of JAD sessions with the users.

A manager should be careful to ensure that a business analyst is performing this job function correctly. Managers who do not have the technical or business skills to ensure that this is happening should seek out a suitable project leader or architect for assistance.

The common method of conducting this phase consists of empowering a one- to three-person project team. Outside expertise is sought as required.

Skills Required

Architects, business analysts, systems analysts, data modelers

Implement JAD Session, First Series

Figure 7.5 shows how the background project documentation and the newly created models can be reviewed with business users and other members of the project team through a set of JADs. The project manager should facilitate or hire a facilitator to run the JADs effectively. This will allow the project plan, estimates, and the project charter to be updated. The models and requirements themselves will also be revised and could drive another set of JADs.

Input

ER diagrams

Data models

Process models

Requirements

First cut project plan

JAD members

Output

Confirmation of documentation

Updated versions of input (models, project plan)

Project estimates

Risk analysis

Quality plan

Subprocesses

Select JAD members

Confirm documentation

Update documentation

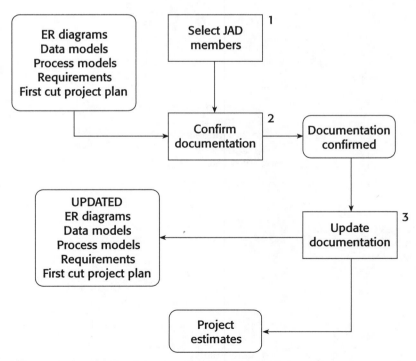

Figure 7.5   IPDM level 2: implement JAD session, first series.

Gather Requirements

Figure 7.6 shows how the high-level models and requirement statements can be used to drive to another level of detail. Business users must be identified and used in this process with the support of the organization's management. Requirements can be described in terms of business, technical, organization, and other categories.

Input

ER diagrams

Data models

Process models

Requirements

Project plan

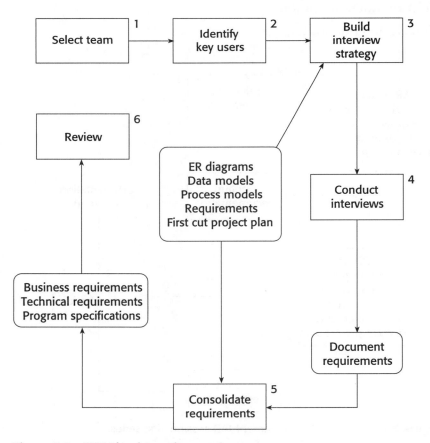

Figure 7.6 IPDM level 2: gather requirements.

Output

Business requirements

Technical requirements

Draft program specifications

Subprocesses

Select team

Identify key users

Build interview strategy

Conduct interviews

Consolidate requirements

Review

Build Design and Architecture

Figure 7.7 shows how the requirement statements can be used to build a high-level architecture and design for the solution. This is then iteratively refined until the requirements are satisfied.

Input

Project charter

Business requirements

Technical requirements

Corporate infrastructure

Output

Updated business requirements

Updated technical requirements

Architecture

Design

Infrastructure requirements

Subprocesses

Appoint design team

Design JAD

Review JAD

Contact H/W, S/W vendors

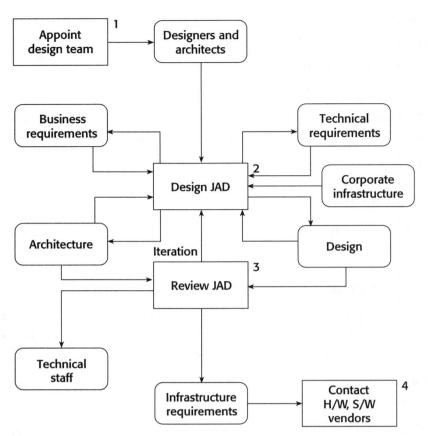

Figure 7.7 IPDM level 2: build design and architecture.

Additional Information

Conduct careful reference checks and analyze benchmarking results when selecting the technology. Establish performance criteria and system availability requirements (e.g., Is a fault-tolerant system required? What is online response time? What are throughput requirements?).

Just as the act of gathering business requirements is not a "by-the-recipe" process, this step also involves hard, but properly focused, work that cannot be done by following a recipe. If the knowledge and experience to do this effectively is not available in-house, it is wise to hire consultants to bring it in. In the 2000s, there are many technology options available, such as client/server, legacy systems, pen-based systems, voice systems, and distributed systems, to name a few. Each of these can be the subject of at least one textbook. An error in judgment in this stage can have costly repercussions in the other phases.

Skills Required

Architect, systems analyst

Implement JAD Session, Second Series

Figure 7.8 shows how the architecture and design documents can be iteratively refined and approved through another series of JAD sessions. At this point in the project, a lot more information has been gathered and is ready for final verification.

Input

Project plan

Design documentation

Architecture documentation

Output

Approved documentation

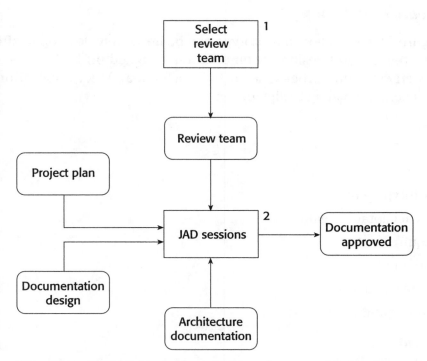

Figure 7.8 IPDM level 2: implement JAD session, second series.

Subprocesses

Select review team

Implement JAD sessions

Additional Information

Confirm that the business users understand the business requirements and their impact (through JADs, functional prototypes, ER diagrams, dataflow diagrams, and process charts).

Remember that change appears to be a big and unavoidable part of life. Changes to business requirements should therefore come as no surprise, and a method mutually agreed upon between users/clients and the development team should be established at the onset of the project. Perhaps the project team can accept changes, but only apply them in a subsequent release. Implementation can be done in phases of six- to eight-month durations.

Skills Required

Architects, systems analysts, business users

Create Prototype

Figure 7.9 shows how a prototype can be iteratively developed after the architecture and design documentation is signed off by the users. The objective of this process is to build a look-and-feel application that the users are willing to sign off on.

Input

IS staff

Users

Prototyping tool

Key acceptance team

Requirements

Data models

Process models

Prototyping standards

Output

Prototype

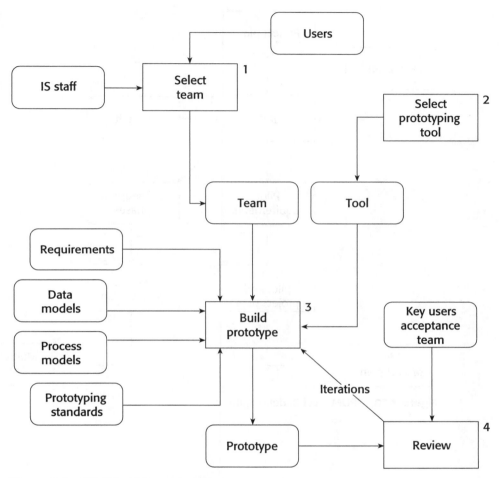

Figure 7.9   IPDM level 2: create prototype.

Subprocesses

Select team

Select prototyping tool

Build prototype

Review

Define Pilot

Figure 7.10 shows the pilot subprocesses. The size of a pilot determines whether a big bang approach or a series of limited implementations are favored by a client. In scoping out a pilot, it is necessary to identify the

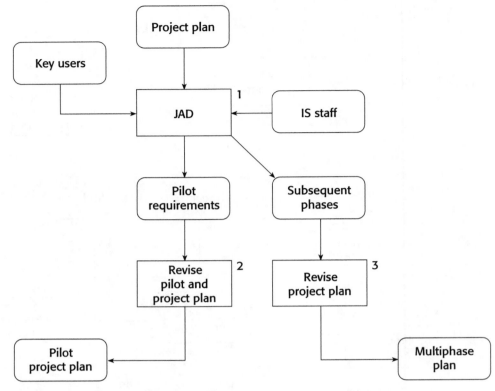

Figure 7.10 IPDM level 2: define pilot.

implementation architecture, data, users, and acceptance criteria for each part of the solution that is being implemented.

Input

IS staff

Key users

Project plan

Output

Pilot requirements

Revised project plan for pilot

Multiphase plan

Subprocesses

JAD

Revise pilot project plan

Revise project plan

Additional Information

Every project can be divided into several subreleases. The nature of application development in the 2000s has evolved from earlier decades. Traditionally, projects tended to be an all-or-nothing proposition. Large projects required large budgets, lots of staff, and long development cycles. The current approach is to support full development through a series of phases in order to provide value to the customers as soon as possible. Each phase has deliverables that can be implemented so that users can start testing, parallel running, and using them. The first phase could be designed to serve as a pilot.

A pilot should include the critical functionality of the whole project, but limit the number of test cases and noncritical features. A pilot project does not need to be implemented, but should be presented and confirmed with key users. Changes should be encouraged and incorporated into the application through normal channels at this time, in order to build a superior product.

The project plan should lead to full release implementation after the pilot is successful.

Skills Required

Full project team

Development

Figures 7.11 and 7.12 show how the development specifications based on the pilot are used to develop the parts of the application that will initially be implemented.

Input

Specifications

Output

Revised specifications

Physical program design

Unit test plans

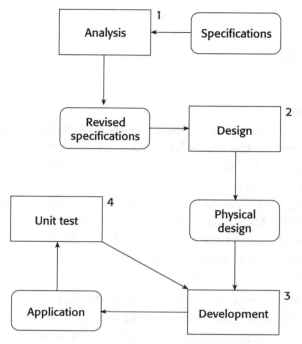

Figure 7.11 IPDM level 2: development, part A.

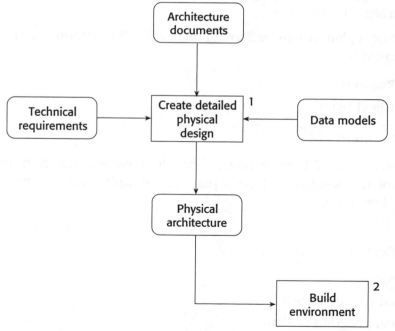

Figure 7.12 IPDM level 2: development, part B.

Subprocesses

Analysis

Design

Development

Unit test

Input

Architecture documents

Technical requirements

Data models

Output

Physical architecture

Subprocesses

Create detailed physical design

Build environment

Testing

Figure 7.13 shows the testing process for the components that are under development. Each testing cycle should be supported by an approach, a team structure, and scripts. Test results should be carefully documented and reviewed at project status meetings. The project plan should reflect the time it may take to make system changes due to testing results.

Input

Test plans

Key users

Test team

Volume data

Application

Output

Test results

Updated application

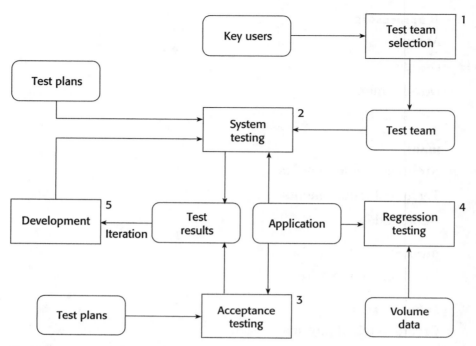

Figure 7.13 IPDM level 2: testing.

Subprocesses

Test team selection

System testing

Acceptance testing

Regression testing

Development

Additional Information

Never accept a piece of code from a developer if it has not been unit tested. In fact, it seems silly at team meetings to hear someone say that they are 75 percent finished, all programs are compiled, and unit testing will be starting soon. In fact, such members are 0 percent finished, but have just keyed everything into a file. Managers must be careful to resist accepting these statements at face value. Insist that all programs be unit tested as they are written, and not at some point in the future.

The testing process should be divided into phases and should incorporate the following:

- ☐ Unit testing
- ☐ System testing
- ☐ Acceptance testing
- ☐ Regression testing
- ☐ Integration testing

Testing is often done in teams led by a resource external to the project team to obtain objective results.

Skills Required

Testers, business users, technical backup

Implementation

Figure 7.14 shows the subprocesses required to support a system implementation. This includes a communication strategy, testing materials, and a contingency approach. Lessons learned from the implementation should be examined to ease subsequent implementations of the application.

Input

Implementation plan

Backout plan

Output

Communication strategy and materials

Implemented application

Training materials

Lessons learned

Contingency strategy

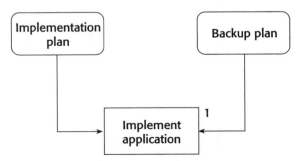

Figure 7.14 IPDM level 2: implementation.

Subprocess

Implement application

Additional Information

An implementation plan should gradually bring an application online, while ensuring that an organization is protected against any type of system crash. This is often done by running a previous system (if there is one) or a manual process in parallel with a new system until it is deemed acceptable.

Implementation is also frequently done on different hardware than development, especially in client/server projects. This means that all operating software and connections must be reestablished on the new hardware. Other issues, such as licensing agreements and vendor support, must also be considered. The development environment may still be required, so it must be kept intact and in sync with the production environment. The project manager must also determine which team members are required to stay on the project, which are required part-time, and which not at all.

Skills Required

Development team + implementers

Expand Pilot

Figure 7.15 shows the subprocesses required to identify additional functionality to include in the next implementation of the solution.

Input

Application

Key users

IS staff

Output

New pilot plan

Updated project plan

Subprocesses

JAD

Revised plan

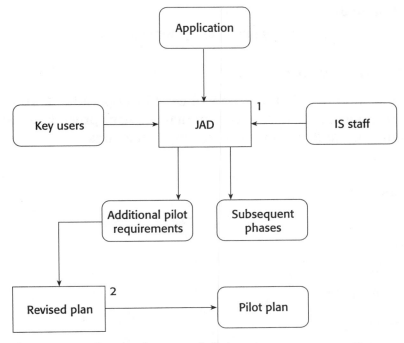

Figure 7.15   IPDM level 2: expand pilot.

Project Review

This collection of subprocesses will capture lessons from the collection of pilot subprojects that were implemented and, subsequently, share these with other project efforts in the organization.

Input

Test plans

Error list

Output

Lessons and recommendations

Subprocess

Project review

Additional Information

This is a review of the project, perhaps in the form of JAD sessions, with a view to improving future projects. This should be passed to the next release.

Skills Required

Project manager, business analysts, systems analysts

Create Infrastructure

This collection of subprocesses will establish operational procedures, support groups, help desks, system management procedures, systems environments, and ongoing user training procedures.

Input

Trainers

Team

Output

Standards

Operational plans

Subprocess

Infrastructure

Easy Steps for Getting Started

Using this methodology, the following steps were used for a one-year project. A six-month pilot was successfully developed and implemented, followed by the other phases of the project.

1. A project sponsor was selected. The sponsor selected a project manager and a steering committee.

2. The project manager selected a lead architect to oversee the design aspects of the application.

3. Prototyping tools were selected. The following tools were evaluated: JAM from Jyacc, Powerbuilder from Powersoft/Sybase, Vision from Unify, SQLWindows from Gupta, and Microsoft Access.

4. The architect worked with the users to build and confirm business requirements.

5. The project manager worked with a technical team to select a technical architecture that was consistent with the organizational standards.

6. The principal users of the project were identified.

7. The architect facilitated JAD sessions to confirm the business requirements. The architect ensured that the users understood the business requirements. The users ensured that the architect understood the business requirements as well. This enabled both groups to have a common understanding of the project.

The architect worked with the project team to accomplish the following:

    a. Talked with the users, read background documentation about the project

    b. Developed dataflow diagrams, ER diagrams, flowcharts, and a project plan to describe the project's business requirements

    c. Modified documents to reflect changes identified during the JAD sessions

    d. Built a project plan

    e. Identified a six-month pilot

    f. Built a multiphase project plan

8. The architect worked with a team to build a reusable prototype that reflected the business requirements.

9. The prototype was confirmed with the users.

10. The prototype was enhanced and reconfirmed with the users on an iterative basis.

11. Program specifications were written to accompany the prototype.

12. The project manager selected a project team.

13. Training and support was provided for the project team.

14. The project plan was divided into milestones that delivered the application in short phases of a few months or less.

15. The deliverable from each phase was given to the users so that acceptable testing could begin.

Regular status meetings and memos were used to inform the project manager and the project team about issues and status per the experiences captured in chapter 7.

Potential Pitfalls

IPDM is unlike many other development methodologies in that it focuses on deliverables instead of on processes. This could leave an exposure for managers who are dependent on following a recipe-like approach. IPDM is unsuccessful when used incorrectly, as shown in the following cases:

1. **Prototyping should not be equated with having no defined requirements.** A prototype in the computer industry is similar to one created in other industries. An architect builds a scale model of a building to show clients what the product will look like, without incurring the total costs of actually constructing the building, only to discover that rooms or hallways are too small. Similarly, engineers build various specifications on paper, on CAD, and as scale models to show what a car will look like before actually starting up the assembly lines.

    In the IS industry, prototypes are often not used in the same manner. They sometimes become a license to be lax with business requirements. A prototype should be built iteratively until it is signed off. From that point on, the prototype becomes the functional specification for the project, and any other changes to it should be carefully assessed for impact on the project plan.

2. **Choosing the wrong development tool for building the prototype.** A prototype should be developed using the same development tool as the rest of the system. This will make it reusable. The development tool should have the following features:

    □ Easy-to-use painting tool supporting GUI or character-based screens. The character-based screen methodology is useful in applications that must be ported across platforms for a variety of clients (some of whom do not have architectures capable of supporting GUIs) and also in applications that require quick response time.

    □ Broad database support (e.g., Informix, Oracle, Sybase, Ingres)

    □ Event-driven functionality

    □ 4GL support

Other Considerations

Project managers should also be aware of several other considerations that can help them achieve their project objectives. These are discussed in this section.

Select Project Team

This requires a careful mixing of skills and attitudes, based on the business requirements and the technology. A project manager must be careful to hire a mix of full-time staff and consultants who work well together and offer the technical skills that are necessary to implement a project. Project managers should not be bashful at this point. Prepare a detailed questionnaire or quiz to gauge a candidate's set of skills. Also keep in mind that bright professionals with good attitudes are capable of learning new skills relatively quickly. For example, a consultant who had one year of "C" development experience was hired as a senior developer on a client/server project. Within three weeks, the developer was able to learn entirely new skills, without specific training, in areas such as Sybase SQL Server, TCP/IP, JAM (a screen management product), and a new operating system, sufficiently to fulfill the requirements of the assignment. Attitude and aptitude were the important characteristics this developer possessed, and hiring someone with more specific experience may not have saved time and money. Many such examples justify the position that soft skills are sometimes more important than specific skills. The best fit may be a candidate who can offer both soft and specific skills to a project.

Skills development should be an ongoing process during the development cycle. This can be done through a variety of means, such as magazines, textbooks, and in-house training courses.

Skills Required
Project management

Regularly and Critically Monitor Progress

In a meeting, a project manager inviting disaster goes around the table and asks everyone to give his or her status as a way to measure the overall status of the project. In many environments, the most wonderful things are said, such as: "There is no inflation," "World peace is around the corner," "Only ethical politicians are elected," and "Everyone is competent in his or her job." Yet, at implementation time, every conceivable problem confronts the project team.

The reality is that human beings have an affinity for wanting to do the easy things first and ignoring the difficult ones for as long as possible. The weekly status meetings that report continued progress often cite only these successes, and the classic "almost-done" syndrome easily applies. The manager should not be surprised to find that the project will always remain 80 percent complete and 20 percent incomplete.

A manager can solve this dilemma by complementing weekly status meetings with regular walkabouts and requests for demonstrations of work in progress. Managers who are too senior or uncomfortable to do this can have a team leader or other team member do it instead. One effective manager the author worked with used to walk around every several days, look at what was being done, and talk to all the team members on a one-on-one basis. This allowed him to see the current state of the application and the ongoing ability of the developers, and it also allowed the developers to gain from his experience. In one instance, a developer was working on a user interface screen using JAM. Functions coded in C language were connected to events on the screen. The application was connected to Sybase SQL Server. The developer unit tested the application and declared that he was finished. The manager walked to the screen and performed what all the team members affectionately began to call the "Mitch test." This involved holding down a key at random and filling all the fields on a screen completely. Without exception, this test has always uncovered a problem somewhere in an application.

Managers who adopt this walkabout strategy should be careful to be noncritical. If it is done incorrectly or harshly, your team will spend more time dreading your presence and less time actually getting work done.

Skills Required

Project management, system architecture, project leadership

Build Team Synergy and Loyalty

A group of individuals working together as a team will produce a better product than individuals looking after their own interests. A manager should consider different forms of team building, perhaps bringing in a facilitator to promote this. It is important for the members of your team to respect each other's abilities.

In the computer industry it is possible to build loyalty, but do not expect to keep all your key players on the team for the length of a project. Ensure that at least two team members (who are not buddies, since they often leave during the same time period) share the same knowledge. Also insist on good ongoing documentation that must be shared with all the members of the team. Implement a regular review of the documentation so that team members have an incentive to keep it current.

Skills Required

Development team

Summary

The last few years have seen many traditional methodologies transformed into frameworks that are easy to use, flexible, and reusable. These have addressed some of the historical limitations affecting the larger methodologies. However, organizations should be careful to realize that frameworks, while easier to implement, are also not as thorough as a fully prescriptive methodology.

This chapter identified the role a project manager should fill in each of the phases of the Standard Development Lifecycle (SDLC). This chapter also presented an implementation of the SDLC based on the techniques of prototyping and Rapid Application Development (RAD), which is technology-independent. This is an effective methodology that is called the Iterative Project Development Methodology (IPDM), which has a solid track record of success. IPDM will support projects in a variety of business areas and technical environments. It supports mainframe, client/server, open, n-tier, Web-based, and distributed systems, to name a few. This methodology was presented in two levels of detail. Level 1 was an overview consisting of 15 processes. Level 2 provided more detail per process, including input and output deliverables.

CHAPTER 8

Project Resourcing: Roles, Responsibilities, and Monitoring

This chapter deals with defining and managing resource requirements on projects. It focuses on the human side of project management and deals with the roles and responsibilities of the project manager, project team, sponsors, and stakeholders who are affected by the results of the completed project. In this chapter the reader will learn about:

- Project resourcing
- Roles and responsibilities
- Resource estimation
- Project reporting
- Staffing projects
- Project monitoring

Resourcing Stages of a Project

Projects are resourced at two levels and in several stages. There are two levels: the core project team and the extended project team. They are differentiated in terms of their time involvement on the project, their accountability, and their level of responsibility. Resources can be allocated to these levels for the entire duration of the project or for a limited time until a milestone is reached.

There are at least three stages of project staffing on most projects. The first of these involves the formation of a core team to get the project started and to offer support in the planning phase. This was discussed in chapter 4. The second stage involves what most people would describe as project-level resourcing. This stage increases the resource complement on the core project team to support the other project phases.

The third resourcing stage includes implementation and postimplementation support. This includes resources to roll the application out, implement a contingency plan, host a help desk, train the users, and operate the systems. Technical resources to correct bugs and code enhancements are also included in this group.

Projects are resourced from a variety of sources, usually at the discretion of a project manager or a designate(s). Staffing can come from internal sources, other departments, or external sources. External sources can include former colleagues of the manager or other team members, consulting agencies, contracting agencies, and independent contractors.

The difference between the core and the extended project team is sometimes hazy. One set of guidelines stipulates that core team members should be dedicated to the project, spending most of their time on project activities. They should also be directly responsible for delivering at least a portion of it. Core team members should also report directly to the project manager and expect to receive a performance appraisal at the end of the project. The collective core team should satisfy the following elements:

☐ A project manager with the right leadership, management, and technical skills

☐ A project manager who can identify issues, communicate them effectively, and resolve them in a timely manner

☐ A project team that can work together under the direction of the project manager

☐ A project team committed to deliverables and deadlines

☐ A project team where members learn from each other and contribute to an improved quality end result

☐ A project team focused on delivering results

☐ A project team that understands the business processes and respects users' concerns

The project manager is typically either from the systems department or works closely with them to complete the project. A primary role of the systems department is to ensure that projects are delivered in accordance with user requirements.

Organization

Project organization deals with a project manager and the team members responsible for the delivery of the project. The project manager has the overall responsibility for attaining the project goals on schedule, within cost, and in accordance with the requirements and expectations set out by the project sponsor. Typically, the project will involve staff from the systems department and representative staff from the user departments. For example, if the project is to develop a human resources information system, the project team may comprise:

☐ A project manager, usually from the systems department

☐ Several analysts from the systems department, including a systems analyst, a data analyst, a programmer analyst, and programmers. The roles and responsibilities of these positions are described in more detail later in this chapter.

☐ External consultants for specific skill-sets, such as software package selection and evaluation, integration testing, and conversion

☐ User analysts from the human resources department with the expertise in the business of planning and managing human resources

Consequently, most projects do not follow the typical hierarchical or functional organization structure, but rather follow a matrix organizational structure. In a matrix organizational structure, a project team cuts across several functional units to get the appropriate mix of team members whose contribution is essential to the success of the project. The team members report directly to the project manager for project-related work. In addition, each of the project team members from the user departments continues to report to his or her functional manager for department-specific tasks. At the completion of the project, the respective team members return to their original departments.

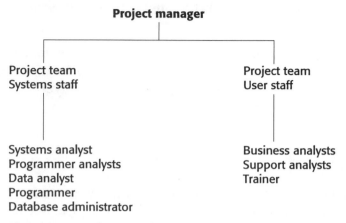

Figure 8.1   Project organization.

Figure 8.1 shows the reporting relationship between the project manager and the team members.

Resourcing

An integral part of managing projects is to build a clear understanding of resources required to complete the project, including developing a budget to plan and manage the resources. Budgetary items include salary and related benefits, equipment and supplies, travel, and consulting dollars. Examples of nonhuman resources include the following:

☐ Salary and related benefits associated with project team members

☐ Hardware and software tools to enable the project team members to complete their tasks in an effective and efficient manner

☐ Travel and related expenses for the project

☐ Physical facilities, such as space for offices and meeting rooms

☐ Time commitment of the project sponsor

☐ Acquisition of appropriate project management tools and methodology (if not already available) to guide the development and implementation of the project

Project resources are directly related to completing projects in a timely manner, in conjunction with other factors as shown in Figure 8.2.

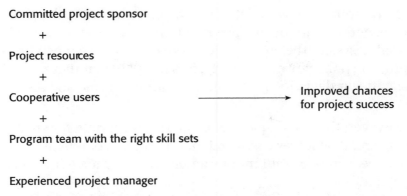

Committed project sponsor

+

Project resources

+

Cooperative users ———————————→ Improved chances for project success

+

Program team with the right skill sets

+

Experienced project manager

Figure 8.2 Project resources.

The provision of project resources is fundamental to the successful delivery of the project. However, to determine resource requirements for a project requires experience in managing both similar projects and a diverse range of projects. Lack of resources will typically have an impact on the quality and timeliness of the project. But how does the project manager determine the size of the project team and the right mix of skillsets required to resource the project? For instance, how many analysts, programmers, data architects, and so on are required, and will they be required on a part-time or full-time basis to get the job done in a timely and cost-effective manner?

Several estimating approaches are available to the project manager, depending on the complexity of the project, the quality of resources available, and the commitment of the project sponsor. Typically, estimating techniques include the following:

1. Project estimation based on prior experience of working with projects of similar size and complexity. Under this approach, the project manager is estimating the costing requirements based on his or her past experience in working with similar projects. The key advantage of this approach is that the cost estimation process can be approximated rather quickly, based on the project manager's knowledge base. The project manager would have typically normalized the estimates to ensure that the project complexity and the project environment are comparable to the present environment.

   The disadvantage of this approach is that all variables may not have been considered, and this may result in underestimating the effort required to complete the project. In addition, the project manager may not be in a position to fully assess the strengths and weaknesses of the current project team and the expectations of the project sponsor. Consequently, it is possible that there could be significant deviations between the estimated cost and the actual costs.

However, this technique may be quite appropriate for smaller projects entailing lower cost and limited project complexity, and may be also relevant for determining order-of-magnitude costing estimates.

2. Project estimation based on a detailed breakdown of tasks and estimation of resources required to complete those tasks. This approach requires a good understanding of the detailed tasks required to complete a project, as well as availability of the appropriate skill-sets within the project team to complete the deliverables. Under this approach, a detailed spreadsheet could be developed for each team member, detailing the tasks and the time and costs required to complete those tasks. Allowance for coordination and monitoring of these activities, time for administrative tasks, such as attending department meetings, vacation, and sick time, should be also included in the overall estimates. After developing these detailed estimates, the project manager can still apply his or her judgment and experience to validate and fine-tune the figures.

   This approach is typically used by consulting companies and systems integrators who are involved in fixed-price application development projects. It can also be used for managing in-house projects.

3. Project estimation based on in-house standards. As an organization gains more experience in completing projects, a database of projects could be developed that identifies the key project attributes and defines complexity in a quantifiable manner. Such a database of projects could help an organization in developing standards for project estimation based on project and organizational characteristics. Some of the elements for developing an in-house project database are:

   □ Number of project tasks

   □ Number of business functions and processes addressed by the application

- Project complexity (e.g., determined on a scale of 1 to 10, where 1 = not complex and 10 = very complex)
- Number of screens developed for conducting various functions and tasks
- Number and size of programs (e.g., lines of code)
- Number of data elements and number of records, files, and tables
- Number of hard-copy and soft-copy reports
- Methodology and tools used (e.g., use of computer-aided software engineering tools, tools for developing prototypes, and Rapid Application Development techniques)
- Type of technology environment (e.g., legacy application or client/server application)
- Number of project team members
- Number of changes to the original requirement specifications

A database of projects could be helpful in establishing benchmarks when a new project is undertaken. In addition, the project manager can still exercise his or her judgment to ensure that the project estimates are realistic and incorporate new project characteristics.

4. Another method to build estimates for a project is to use estimating tools. The principle behind such a tool is to supply a set of attribute values (e.g., for project complexity, project duration, skills of the staff, degree of project politics) and receive an estimate of the types of resources and their roles needed to complete an activity. Estimating tools are discussed in more detail in chapter 10.

Roles and Responsibilities

A primary role of the systems department is to provide information technology services to support business goals and objectives. This is usually done in the context of a project. These services include, but are not limited to:

- Preparing, coordinating, and maintaining information technology strategic, tactical, and operational plans
- Providing and maintaining hardware, software, and communications infrastructure to capture, process, and retrieve information

- ☐ Developing, maintaining, and supporting computer applications to enable better delivery of business functions and processes

- ☐ Developing and maintaining standards for developing applications in stand-alone and multiuser environments

- ☐ Acquiring and installing hardware and software products in accordance with the standards

- ☐ Developing and administering data management practices to facilitate capture, store, and retrieval in a timely, secure, and reliable manner

- ☐ Providing computer technology training to organizational users

- ☐ Managing computer professionals in the delivery and support of information technology services

- ☐ Managing vendors of computer products and services to ensure that timely and cost-effective services are received

In the project management context, the systems department is responsible for managing systems resources, facilitating projects by working in partnership with the user departments, and providing coordination and support for the timely delivery of projects.

Depending on the size, scope, and complexity of projects, a number of stakeholders are involved in the progress of the project and its successful outcome. Descriptions follow of some of the formal structures that can provide guidance to the project team and monitor the progress of the project to ensure that it meets the stated goals and objectives.

Executive Committee

This committee is composed of the senior management of the organization, and has an overall responsibility for accepting and approving the project initiatives outlined in the information technology strategic plan, including the funding and prioritization of projects before they are initiated. They are usually the ones who launched the project in the first place.

Project Steering Committee

This committee provides general business direction to the application development project, and reviews and accepts deliverables. The steering committee is typically chaired by a user manager or director, with the system director functioning in an advisory role on the committee. The project manager is part of this committee and receives input regarding project direction, priorities, and project funding. The steering committee usually provides a mechanism for reconciling conflicts between different user groups.

Project Manager

The project manager is directly responsible for the successful delivery of the project. The project manager reports to the steering committee on the status of the project and seeks advice from the committee on a variety of project-related issues, including direction, scope, and funding.

After the project manager has been assigned to the project, one of his or her primary tasks is to select the team members who will be responsible for completing the project deliverables. The project manager may be offered several resources from other departments; however, he or she should be careful in accepting these resources. The primary purpose of resource allocation is to ensure that there is a fit between the tasks to be completed and the corresponding skill-sets needed to achieve the tasks. It should not be the project manager's responsibility to accept surplus staff from other departments. Utilizing staff without the appropriate skill-sets is bound to affect the quality and timeliness of the project. If the project manager cannot find sufficient internal resources, then external resources with the appropriate skill-sets should be acquired.

A project manager provides the glue linking a number of players, including project sponsor, stakeholders, project team, and user groups. Depending on the size and complexity of the project, the extent of the project manager's involvement may vary. For instance, for larger projects, project coordinators may be required to manage specific subsystems and to ensure that the subsystems are integrated.

Typically, the responsibilities of the project manager include the following:

- Clarifying the scope of the project, including technologies to be used and interfaces to existing systems
- Defining system functions to support the business functions, generating technology options, developing implementation strategies, and preparing an implementation plan
- Identifying the business functions and processes requiring either change or improvement through automation, and identifying new or changed information needs

☐ Obtaining approvals from the steering committee in accordance with the project plan

☐ Working with the project team to identify/refine and prioritize project tasks and the responsibilities for the timely completion of those tasks

☐ Monitoring the project and communicating the status to the steering committee on a regular basis. Regular project reporting provides a vehicle to communicate the project status to the steering committee. Regular reporting also tends to diffuse any communication problems that may have surfaced and require the attention of the steering committee. Such problems could include change in system specifications, changes in the hardware or software environment, a change in business direction because of mergers, loss of certain key project team personnel, and lack of funding.

With the above responsibilities, the project manager must continually operate by building relationships with the project team and winning their respect. There will be situations in which the project manager is required to negotiate terms with the team members and motivate them to accept the new arrangement and responsibilities. The project manager is a key influencer and, consequently, must have superb communication and interpersonal skills to manage a team with diverse skills. Wherever possible, the project manager should use influence and persuasion instead of authority to get results from the project team.

Project Team

The project team members report to the project manager. The project team has responsibility for completing the project tasks and ensuring that the deliverables are completed in a timely and effective manner.

In addition to specific technical skills, the project team requires a good understanding of various business skills to enhance the chances of project success. Some of these business skills include, but are not limited to:

☐ **Understanding of the business.** This means that if the project is concerned with a financial services industry, such as a bank or an insurance company, it is essential that the project manager and some of the analysts have competence in that business sector. Analysts need a good grasp of the business and technical skills in order to deliver the project.

☐ **Communication skills.** A project involves teamwork. Usually, a variety of ideas and alternatives are discussed before formulating a plan of action. Communication skills include the ability to capture and analyze data, document the results, and provide feedback to the clients to ensure that there is a correct understanding of the tasks.

☐ **Technical skills.** There is no substitute for technical skills. For instance, if programming skills are required for developing applications in an Oracle database environment, it is necessary that the programmer have experience in that environment. Sometimes, programming skills under a specific operating system environment, such as UNIX, may be required to streamline and expedite the application development process.

☐ **Analytical and problem-solving skills.** A new project involves change. The project team members must be proficient in anticipating and responding to change and developing change-management practices and procedures to ease client concerns.

☐ **Team-building and team player skills.** A project involves a multidisciplinary team to complete the tasks and deliverables. Consequently, a high level of coordination and communication is required to minimize misunderstanding. Typically, a project will produce results in a timely manner if the team's efforts are synergistic. Conversely, with a technically proficient team that has little team-building and team player skills, the results will likely be less than successful.

The following list provides a brief description of a representative project team's functions and responsibilities for developing an *n*-tier, Web-based application using relational database management technology. The typical roles and responsibilities of the project team members are described. For each of the project team positions, a detailed job description may be required so that the relevant skill-sets are obtained to work on the project.

Developer

The developer's roles and responsibilities include the following:

☐ Assist in the definition, analysis, and refinement of application requirements

☐ Provide input to estimates for work plans

☐ Develop, test, and document programs/modules per specifications

- Review application performance to ensure that it meets the expectations

The developer's skills include the following:

- Detailed knowledge of programming languages and database products
- Good knowledge of user interface tools and utilities
- Good knowledge of CASE tools
- Ability to work in individual and team environments and produce deliverables

Architect

The architect's roles and responsibilities may require several individuals to satisfy. These include the following:

- Technical architecture—logical and physical
- Data architecture—logical and physical
- Application architecture—logical and physical

The architect's skills include the following:

- Best practices
- Industry solutions
- Modeling tools

Data Modeler

The data modeler's roles and responsibilities include the following:

- Use business requirements to build logical data models
- Build a physical data design based on the data architecture

The data modeler's skills include the following:

- Data modeling approaches and syntax
- Modeling tools

Systems Analyst

The systems analyst's roles and responsibilities include the following:

- Define, analyze, and refine requirements
- Provide input to estimates for work plans

- ☐ Prepare program and module specifications
- ☐ Test program modules to achieve the specified objectives
- ☐ Set up user test plans

The systems analyst's skills include the following:

- ☐ Analytical and problem-solving skills
- ☐ Good experience in the use and applications of database software
- ☐ Knowledge of graphical user interface (GUI) tools for screen design and navigation and prototyping
- ☐ Good communication skills

Database Analyst/Administrator

The database analyst's roles and responsibilities include the following:

- ☐ Install and maintain the database management system
- ☐ Conduct physical design of the database
- ☐ Maintain system files
- ☐ Communicate physical database changes to project team
- ☐ Conduct performance tuning on the database management system
- ☐ Review and document the physical schema
- ☐ Adhere to systems development standards and procedures
- ☐ Adhere to security standards and procedures

The database analyst's skills include the following:

- ☐ In-depth knowledge of the database
- ☐ Solid knowledge of access language
- ☐ Good knowledge of the client/server operating systems and networks
- ☐ Good communication skills

Technical Analyst

The technical analyst's roles and responsibilities include the following:

- ☐ Investigate and address technical problems
- ☐ Identify hardware and software elements and define the technology environment

- ☐ Determine system configurations based on application's planned requirements
- ☐ Provide solutions to data transport and internetworking issues
- ☐ Resolve hardware, software, and network issues

The technical analyst's skills include the following:

- ☐ Excellent knowledge of current and planned technology
- ☐ Ability to resolve problems in timely manner
- ☐ Good communications and interpersonal skills

Object/Component Modeler

The object/component modeler's roles and responsibilities include the following:

- ☐ Build an object model (including messages and methods)
- ☐ Identify use cases
- ☐ Implement an object methodology

The object/component modeler's skills include the following:

- ☐ Object-oriented experience

Network Administrator

The network administrator's roles and responsibilities include the following:

- ☐ Maintain physical network
- ☐ Support architects
- ☐ Maintain physical security

The network administrator's skills include the following:

- ☐ Troubleshooting
- ☐ Low-level knowledge of a network operating system (NOS)
- ☐ Knowledge of WANs/LANs
- ☐ Knowledge of system management tools (e.g., sniffers)

Business Analyst

The business analyst's roles and responsibilities include the following:

- ☐ Identify key business functions and processes
- ☐ Provide relationships between these functions
- ☐ Provide input to project team regarding processes, procedures, and expected results
- ☐ Provide feedback to project team based on its analysis
- ☐ Assist the data and systems analysts with data attributes

The business analyst's skills include the following:

- ☐ Excellent knowledge of business processes and planned direction
- ☐ Good problem-solving skills
- ☐ Good communication skills
- ☐ Working knowledge of technology tools
- ☐ Ability to work well in individual and team environments

Data Analyst

The data analyst's roles and responsibilities include the following:

- ☐ Provide input to data standards and procedures
- ☐ Interact with business and technical analysts
- ☐ Define data and their attributes based on the requirements
- ☐ Prepare, update, and maintain the data integrity matrix (i.e., create, read, update, and delete)
- ☐ Translate functional requirement specifications and produce conceptual and logical data models
- ☐ Resolve conflicts pertaining to logical data elements

The data analyst's skills include the following:

- ☐ Good knowledge of CASE tools
- ☐ In-depth expertise in developing data models and logical designs
- ☐ Good problem-solving and communication skills
- ☐ Ability to represent data properties independent of system constraints

Organization: Position Number:

Project Name: Position Name:

Project Number: Project Effective Date:

Client Contact: Planned Completion Date:

Project Manager:

Project Description:

Deliverables:

_____   _____
Prepared by: Approved by:

Figure 8.3   Job description form.

Job Description Form

Figure 8.3 shows a form that can be used for preparing a detailed job description for each project team member, to define and document each project team member's role and responsibility. This job description can be used as a basis to discuss the specific skills of the team member and seek appropriate budgetary approvals.

Types of Application Development

The previous section detailed a full suite of roles along with their appropriate deliverables and skill requirements. The composition and timing of the use of those resources will depend in part on the nature of the development effort, the technology in use, and the business being automated. Most application development efforts will fall into one of three broad categories:

1. Automating new business practices
2. Replacing a legacy system
3. Benefiting from a new technology

Though a core set of resources is needed across each of the preceding examples, some exceptions do occur. One such example is an n-tier application that seeks to replace small portions of a legacy system.

Automating New Business Practices

This type of development effort typically draws upon a standard set of development tools, standards, and methodology (although the use of a methodology such as the IPDM discussed in chapter 7 provides a faster and more focused path to implementation).

A standard team structure for development projects is provided in Table 8.1.

The project manager is ultimately responsible for the success of every project. In this particular development effort, the areas of exposure lie in the business environment. The successful design and implementation of such a project hardly stops at the point at which code has been written and the software finds itself into the hands of the users. The project manager must ensure that the appropriate business practice documents have been developed and accepted by the user community. This is especially critical in instances where a new business is being automated.

As a final note, the automation of a new business practice is sometimes viewed as an opportunity to introduce new technology into an organization.

Table 8.1   Team Structure: Automation of New Business Practices

TITLE	INVOLVEMENT	DETAILS
Project manager	All	Manages project from inception to postimplementation
Senior architect	All	Ensures that there is a balance between application and technology architectures
Business analyst	All	Takes conceptual design down to detail requirements
Technical analyst	Analysis	Verifies technical architecture's ability to support application
Systems analyst	Design coding	Converts detail requirements to design specifications
Programmer analyst	Design coding	Designs algorithms, libraries, object classes, and constructs
Programmer	Coding	Constructs per specifications
Database administrator	Analysis	Designs database environment, database tables, and rules
Data analyst	Analysis	Manages data and standards from corporate perspective

This is a risky combination, since many new variables are introduced into an organization. A new technology brings with it a host of uncertainties that must be managed in a separate project. If a need has been identified (through some justification process) to implement a new technology (whether it be a toolset or an infrastructure) while designing a new business system, a great deal of care must be taken to stagger the work effort to allow time for the new technology to be incorporated into the infrastructure of an organization prior to the implementation of a new application.

Replacing a Legacy System

The design of an application aimed at replacing a legacy system requires details on the functionality of the existing system, as well as some knowledge of the evolution of the system. At times, the business processes automated by legacy systems are modified to fit the limitations of the technology available at the time. The level of sophistication of the development tools today is far greater that those of 10, or even 5, years ago.

As in the previous example, a great deal of emphasis will be placed on the business-planning stage, where the business processes are modeled. The replacement of legacy systems has typically presented opportunities for reengineering. This will again place additional stress on the business-planning resources from both the development team and the business community. The team structure for such a design will look similar to that of Table 8.1 except for minor additions (see Table 8.2).

Two key differences worth noting at this point are in the areas of business planning and technology planning. The information architect will work closely with the business analyst and the user team to do workflow analysis. The primary purpose of this exercise is to verify the existing business processes and look for ways to introduce improvements. The technical analyst will concentrate on the technology infrastructure and its ability to support the new business processes. Statistically, the redesign of legacy systems has also meant the migration of an application to another platform. A typical path is from a mainframe or minicomputer to a microcomputer/LAN architecture. This activity requires careful analysis and capacity planning. The technical architect has a tough task at hand in trying to translate the MIPS and DASD over to 80_86 and megabytes.

Table 8.2   Team Structure: Replacing a Legacy System

TITLE	INVOLVEMENT	DETAILS
Project manager	All	Manages project from inception to postimplementation
Information architect	Planning	Will review business workflow and recommend reengineering opportunities
Senior architect	All	Ensures that there is a balance between application and technology architectures
Business analyst	All	Takes conceptual design down to detail requirements
Technical analyst	Analysis	Verifies technical architecture's ability to support application
Systems analyst	Design coding	Converts detail requirements to design specifications
Programmer analyst	Design coding	Designs algorithms, libraries, object classes, and constructs
Programmer	Coding	Constructs per specifications
Database administrator	Analysis design	Designs database environment, database tables, and rules
Data analyst	Analysis design	Manages data and standards from corporate perspectives

Benefiting from a New Technology

Though there are numerous examples of this type of development, the client/server technology will be profiled in this section because of its relevance to real-world applications. Moving to client/server architecture involves a number of key issues, as shown in the following list:

☐ Evaluation and selection of an appropriate development toolset

☐ Design of an integrated development environment for the development team

☐ Design of a technology infrastructure able to support client/server applications

☐ Appropriate training for both staff and clients to be able to undertake the design and support of a new technology

Although the preceding activities can easily be separate projects, they can be designed in phases with the appropriate settle-in time allowed for each major phase. An example of this is the design of a wide area network (using routers) to enable the distributing of business processes across some geographic area. This is clearly a strength of client/server (C/S) and the WAN will basically provide the supporting platform for this to happen.

In undertaking such a project, it is typically wise to do the following:

☐ Bring in consulting services to fast-track the development work. Also, establish a knowledge transfer protocol so that internal staff can benefit from the consulting services.

☐ Use a three-tiered approach to mustering the team. First, equip the team with the appropriate resources to design and implement the application. This team will typically consist of a number of consulting resources in order to bring in the new technology expertise. Second, have a separate team charged with being the support group for the application once it goes into production. This team will essentially be training and learning as the project evolves. Last, from a corporate perspective, it is wise to prepare a few staff for the next undertaking of this type of development. There are a number of good reasons for this, including the fact that with new technology there will be staff turnovers. This is a fact of life and should be accommodated. Also, while the first team is still tied down with the postimplementation issues of the first application, it likely will be necessary to fire up a second application in your organization. With the people already trained, it will be a matter of simply moving the staff over to the next area of development.

Table 8.3 outlines a typical team structure for this type of development. The role of the technical analyst will be crucial. This individual will have to come up with a measurable technical solution for a proposed business problem. Further, this technical solution will have to fit into the overall infrastructure of the organization and be able to support future developments.

The role of the business analyst will become more complex in that the business process can now be distributed across the business environment. This will in turn lead to the distribution of data across the business infrastructure. This is a key advantage to be attained by client/server technology.

Table 8.3 Team Structure: Benefiting from a New Technology

TITLE	INVOLVEMENT	DETAILS
Project manager	All	Manages project from inception to postimplementation
Business analyst	All	Takes conceptual design down to detail requirements. With C/S technology, BA will also look into distributing business processes across business environment.
Senior architect	All	Ensures that there is a balance between application and technology architectures
Technical analyst	Analysis design	Profiles new technology. Provides capacity planning and ensures that application is supportable on new technology
Systems analyst	Design coding	Converts detail requirements to design specifications
Programmer analyst	Design coding	Designs algorithms, libraries, object classes, and constructs
Programmer	Coding	Constructs per specifications
Database administrator	Analysis design	Designs database environment, database tables, and rules
Data analyst	Analysis design	Manages data and standards from corporate perspective

Monitoring and Reporting

After the project has been launched, it is important to keep track of its progress and to communicate its status on a regular basis to the project sponsor and the stakeholders. The project manager is concerned with the quality and performance of the project—this means that the progress of the team members is monitored and that appropriate feedback is provided to them so that the team is properly aligned and working in unison to achieve the project goals.

The purpose of project monitoring is twofold: first, to describe the project progress to the project sponsor and the stakeholders, and second, to use regular reporting concerning project progress as a means to obtain consensus among stakeholders and also to better manage their expectations and seek their support. Depending on the audience, the details regarding project monitoring and reporting may vary. The steering committee may be only interested in a monthly status report as outlined in Appendix E, but a detailed report indicating the progress by specific business function and subsystems may be of more interest to the user groups directly affected by the project.

Typically, for larger projects, the project is monitored in accordance with the methodology used by an organization. For instance, the methodology may require that before proceeding to the next task, the analyst must ensure that the work is reviewed by the project manager or the data architect. If team members have encountered problems with given tasks, regular project meetings may provide an opportunity to address these problems and understand their implications on other tasks. In addition, the use of tools such as an electronic bulletin board for the project and email to communicate with members of the project team may also be effective for communicating problems and seeking ideas for possible solutions.

Project reviews are usually undertaken in one of the following ways:

☐ **Periodic project review.** This type of review is driven by time, and typically conducted on a weekly or monthly basis. For instance, the monthly status report is an example of a time-driven review to communicate status and report on progress and obstacles, if any. The project manager can use reviews on a periodic basis to deal with specific problems, including issues related to the project team, changes to specifications, and problems with obtaining user consensus or resources.

Project reviews provide opportunities for the project manager to find timely and acceptable solutions. Reviews also help the project manager to stay on schedule and prevent future problems. We have found that project review meetings help the project team to clarify its expectations and requirements. Periodically, meetings should be conducted by the project manager with user and management groups to keep them informed about project progress and issues.

☐ **Deliverable-based review.** Typically, this type of review is based on the completion of deliverables, including: review of documented user requirements, review of the application prototype, review of the documented functional specification, and review of the documented detailed design.

At the completion of each deliverable, the project manager reviews the progress with the project team and the appropriate user groups. It may be necessary to review key deliverables with senior management to ensure that key issues are communicated to and accepted by them.

☐ **Technical reviews.** These are peer reviews undertaken by project team members, such as programmers and analysts, with the objective of reducing errors and improving the overall quality of design and code. These reviews could be undertaken periodically—either weekly or monthly or based on completion of specific tasks, such as testing the logic of a program module. The project manager usually participates in some of these reviews and provides advice regarding approach and use of quality assurance tools and techniques such as structured walk-throughs.

Standardized project management forms are typically used to monitor projects on a consistent and effective basis and communicate both with the project team and various user and management groups. Samples of various forms are provided in Appendix E to monitor and track project activities. Each of these forms can be customized to specific environments, as appropriate to the type of project and the nature of the organization. As a result, these forms should be used as a guideline.

Summary

This chapter described the resources required for completing projects and techniques for managing and monitoring projects. The roles and responsibilities of key players in project development were also described to give the reader a better understanding of the skills required to complete a project. In an organization, senior managers rely on project managers to execute projects in accordance with the business objectives of the organization. The project manager relies on the project team to deliver the deliverables and tasks in a timely and cost-effective manner. Project management discipline is based on a team approach and, consequently, requires delegation, effective communication for follow-up and feedback, and delegation of tasks to the appropriate team members.

If a project is staffed appropriately and provided with adequate resources, it will have a better chance for success. Staffing can be either internal or external, depending on the availability of expertise. Internal staff is typically obtained from the systems department. External resources can be obtained from a variety of sources, including consulting companies, outsourcing companies providing systems integration services, or individual fee-for-service consultants. In assembling the project team, the skills and the expertise should be of paramount concern. Use of surplus staff from other departments is not necessarily a good practice to top-up resourcing levels.

Appendix E contains a variety of forms that can be used for describing and monitoring projects.

CHAPTER 9

Outsourcing of Information Technology Projects

This chapter focuses on outsourcing as an option to either offload business needs to a proven vendor, or to temporarily augment in-house resource levels. This chapter also examines the Application Service Provider (ASP) as a vehicle to leverage third-party infrastructures, reduce operating costs, or bolster resources at peak times. In this chapter the reader will learn about:

- A definition of project outsourcing and Application Service Providers (ASPs)
- Advantages and disadvantages of outsourcing
- Modes of delivery
- A methodology for evaluating outsourcing providers
- Outsourcing case studies

Understanding Outsourcing

Outsourcing can be defined as a method of acquiring services from an external organization or company instead of using internal resources for a set of tasks. In our day-to-day lives, we use outsourcing or contracting to acquire the services of tradespeople such as plumbers, carpenters, and auto mechanics to meet our needs. Outsourcing is also used to meet an organization's needs. An alternative to outsourcing is delivering the required services with in-house personnel. Although it might be appealing for some organizations to rely mainly on in-house staff, it may not be economical and practical to keep them busy and gainfully occupied after a project is implemented.

With the benefits of economies of scale, outsourcing enables vendors to provide services at a competitive price. Outsourcing also implies that another organization can provide similar or better services at a lower cost compared to using in-house personnel. Recently, another term, Application Service Provider (ASP), has also been used analogously with outsourcing vendor. However, the fundamental premise is still the same—a vendor providing a range of services to their clients more cost-effectively than the client could normally provide using their in-house resources.

In the global, new technology economy, better products and services are introduced faster than ever before and market success is often enhanced by bringing the product and/or service to the market first. New product introduction is important for organizations to remain competitive even though product lifecycles have shortened. To bring the product out first requires forming alliances with several players. With competitive pressures, it is just not possible to do it alone and be first; this approach allows organizations to keep focused on their core competencies.

Outsourcing allows organizations to work together with their supply chain partners (suppliers, subcontractors of component assembly, and information technology vendors offering a variety of services such as application hosting and support, network management support, and hardware/software rentals and support) in bringing new products to the market. With this approach, the partners become part of the virtual corporation providing capacity for volume production, timely delivery of products and services, and post-sales support.

Outsourcing is part of the overall supply chain management function in the organization. In a supply chain, there should be a free flow of information between customers, and company staff dealing with customers and suppliers on issues ranging from receiving and processing orders to receiving payment and shipping orders. For instance, companies such as Amazon.com require a successful supply chain so the products are available when ordered by customers, inventories are managed to respond to sales, order entry and shipping functions are in sync, and payment is received so that the transaction is processed in a timely manner. Web-enabled tools can be used to help the customer understand the status of the product to be shipped or the service to be rendered, and encourage collaboration.

Supply chain management is about providing seamless, value-added services at every stage of the process. To have a successful supply chain, organizations typically acquire external services for one or more of the following reasons:

☐ The outsourcing vendor has the required special knowledge to provide services more cost-effectively than in-house personnel.

☐ In-house personnel lack flexibility and expertise to keep abreast of changes in the marketplace and to implement solutions requiring new and perhaps unproven technologies.

☐ The outsourcing vendor can use economies of scale to serve its clientele and build up skill-sets to meet needs in a timely manner.

☐ The outsourcing vendor can provide services on an as-required basis consistent with the needs of the organization.

☐ Using outsourcing services provides organizations with an opportunity to focus on their core business.

Typically, the external vendors can be regarded as specialists and wholesalers of information technology services to the marketplace. Over the past 10 years, there has been a gradual shift to outsourcing services. Some of the services normally provided by in-house company staff have been moved to outsourcing vendors, including cafeteria services, printing and publication services, legal services, check-printing and distribution services, check-processing services, cleaning and maintenance services, property management services, and, of course, information technology services.

The primary issue in outsourcing is whether the required service is part of the core business. If the answer is no, then cost-effective alternatives to acquiring these services should be considered. It may make business sense to retain a small staff to provide coordination and basic services, but any significant requirements should be supplemented with resources from the outsourcing vendor.

In the information technology sector, with the pressures to remain competitive in the global economy, many organizations have streamlined their operations and focused their attention on their core business by outsourcing services that do not add value directly to the organization. Information technology departments are becoming more vulnerable to a combination of budget cuts and the need for greater services, and consequently are looking at outsourcing as a viable way of delivering services to the organization. As the information technology function continues to mature, it makes good business sense to consider outsourcing as a viable option to in-house systems services.

Outsourcing is about partnerships between providers and recipients of services and the way these services can be delivered effectively to meet the business goals of the organization. If this partnership approach is going to be successful, the outsourcing vendor has to know the organizations it services and strive to continuously provide added value. Figure 9.1 outlines the elements of the outsourcing environment and the linkages.

Since the early 1980s, organizations have explored and considered outsourcing opportunities with the objective of achieving the following benefits:

☐ Reducing overall information technology costs without sacrificing service levels

☐ Achieving flexibility and responsiveness in acquiring services according to the needs of the organization

☐ Dealing with a vendor who is an "expert" in the field and manages diverse and changing technologies instead of hiring in-house staff

☐ Driving business needs by requirements instead of being constrained by existing hardware and software environments

☐ Focusing on managing the core business—using information technology to complement the core business without using internal staff

☐ Capitalizing on significant cost savings through the economies of scale achieved by outsourcing vendors

Outsourcing is based on a fundamental premise that an outsourcing vendor can provide equivalent or better services to an organization at a lower cost and with increased flexibility. Outsourcing can be acquired in various forms, ranging from the complete outsourcing of information technology functions to selective outsourcing on a project-by-project basis, depending on business requirements.

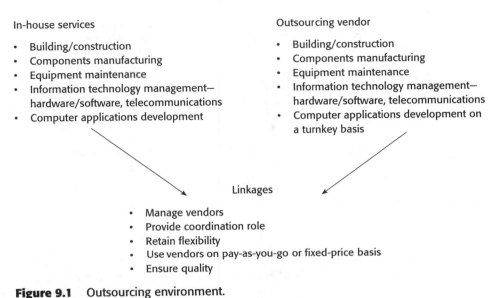

In-house services

- Building/construction
- Components manufacturing
- Equipment maintenance
- Information technology management—
  hardware/software, telecommunications
- Computer applications development

Outsourcing vendor

- Building/construction
- Components manufacturing
- Equipment maintenance
- Information technology management—
  hardware/software, telecommunications
- Computer applications development on
  a turnkey basis

Linkages

- Manage vendors
- Provide coordination role
- Retain flexibility
- Use vendors on pay-as-you-go or fixed-price basis
- Ensure quality

Figure 9.1   Outsourcing environment.

Outsourcing Information Technology Functions

Outsourcing enables organizations to work together in providing information technology services. Outsourcing is a partnership between the provider of services and the recipient of services—both parties have to understand each other and work together to make it work effectively. To better understand the relationship between the outsourcing players, an outsourcing model is described in Figure 9.2. The figure depicts the partnership arrangement between the organization and its outsourcing vendors to deliver products and services to the customers. The organization is focused on its core competencies by providing products and servicing them, and managing the customer relationship. The outsourcing vendor provides the services to the company to enable delivery of products and services. The vendor services include Web hosting, application development, and management of the information technology infrastructure.

The need for a particular skill-set, particularly in Web-based and e-commerce application development, is the primary reason for seeking a partnership arrangement with a vendor, which allows in-house staff to focus their time and efforts on strategic projects. It is not uncommon to find that in addition to Web and e-commerce management, other functions that are outsourced include desktop management and intranet/extranet

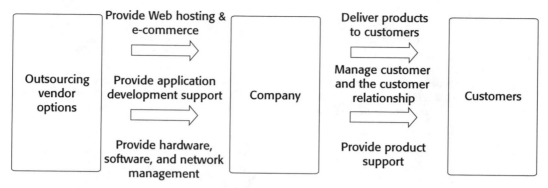

Figure 9.2 Outsourcing model.

management. With the declining cost of hardware and software, it is becoming more difficult to make a case for outsourcing on the basis of cost alone; instead, the need for utilizing specialized e-skills is more appealing than cost. The following list shows technology functions that can be provided in-house versus functions that could be outsourced; use this list as a guide, because the specific outsourcing activities will be dependent on the objectives and needs of the organization.

If portions of a business problem are being outsourced, some of the functions that are provided in-house are included in the following list:

☐ Project coordination between the user and the outsourcing vendor

☐ Quality assurance throughout the system's development lifecycle—e.g., from project initiation to project implementation

☐ Determination of functional requirements

☐ Development of a logical design for an application

☐ Selection of an application software package—e.g., selection of a database management system software for the enterprise

☐ Testing beta versions of the application

☐ Development of service level agreements

☐ Performance monitoring based on service level agreements

☐ Outsourcing vendor management

Some of the functions provided by the outsourcing vendor to the organization are shown in the following list:

- System construction
- Web hosting and implementation
- Application testing, including unit and integration testing
- Application training
- System and user documentation
- System maintenance and enhancement
- Any overload-related functions of the information technology department
- Complete system integration and turnkey application development
- Electronic component manufacturing for electronic manufacturing service companies
- Electronic component assembly

Outsourcing has also permeated the electronic component manufacturing area, enabling large computer vendors to outsource most of their manufacturing processes to electronic manufacturing service companies. With shorter product lifecycles in the hardware industry (e.g., chips, processors) increased sophistication in specialized component manufacturing systems, and ability for mass production, outsourcing has become an obvious cost-effective alternative.

Application Service Provider (ASP)

Application Service Providers help small and midsized companies to gain access to technology that they could not otherwise afford. ASP customers can receive a variety of specialized information technology services such as intrusion detection technologies, tunneling, and firewalls. ASPs can also rent out software based on the number of users, and charge organizations on a monthly or quarterly basis. With an ASP, customers get the best of both worlds—for example, they have networking experts running the hardware and the network, software experts running the applications, data center infrastructure for hosting applications, installation of e-commerce hooks including credit card and security functions, and branding of Web-based applications.

Customers can also have access to the latest storage area networks to manage large databases. Customer service can be delivered through customer relationship managers and a self-service portal such as an e-help desk. Organizations can also access their enterprise applications using an ASP channel. In addition, the ASP channel can be cost-effective for hosting a number of applications, depending on vendor support. Large software vendors (e.g., Oracle, SAP) have established the ASP channel as a more affordable way to offer enterprise applications, application hosting, and support to many small and midsized companies.

With the increasing demand for creating industry-wide Internet portals (e.g., an all-in-one solution), there will be greater opportunities to integrate the back-end systems. However, integration will not be a trivial undertaking. Some of the challenges include connecting disparate systems, opening up pricing and inventory systems, linking suppliers and distribution center, coordinating shipping, acquiring the right resources of systems integrators, and continuously enhancing these systems. Such challenges will be addressed by the ASP marketplace to enable a more flexible and cost-effective solution.

The rapid growth in business-to-business e-commerce demand will require ASPs to develop portals for specific markets. For instance, a global industry portal for retailers provides the various national and global partners with opportunities to join and work cooperatively, with the expectation of reducing inventory costs. One of the advantages of such a portal is the ability to use a Web browser as a primary interface to conduct business on this retail exchange. The Web browser is all the supplier needs to buy and sell, and do demand planning, capacity planning, and delivery scheduling without any additional applications. The Web browser facilitates the retailing e-marketplace exchange and thereby significantly reduces the overall cost of sales, up to a factor of 10.

ASPs can provide software developers with a facility to post their applications on the ASP site, where interested companies can browse and rent the services they desire. Smaller software vendors who have good ideas but lack the marketing muscle of the bigger players can make their products available for rent over the portal. For example, instead of selling accounting software, some accounting software vendors are offering to rent their software for as little as $50 per month—customers access the software from a Web browser over the Internet.

Advantages and Disadvantages of Outsourcing

Outsourcing should be viewed as one of the modes of managing services required in an organization, and should be driven by specific business needs. It is not a panacea and may not be suited for all organizations. Some of the advantages and disadvantages of outsourcing are described here.

Advantages

If properly planned and managed, outsourcing offers several important advantages to an organization:

1. Costs can be predicted and fixed over a period of time. Outsourcing services can be defined and measured. It is easier to predict fixed costs with the outsourcing vendor over time. For instance, the outsourcing vendor can provide a fixed-price estimate for developing and implementing a computer application servicing 2,000 users by managing a help desk, or for providing a performance uptime guarantee for a computer network and providing comprehensive application security.

2. The client organization has an opportunity to focus on their core business instead of splitting their energy between that function and infrastructure development. If the organization's business is to manufacture products, such as office furniture, it may not be critical to have another vendor manage its information technology requirements. In such a situation, the role of the organization would change from providing information technology services with in-house personnel to managing the outsourcing vendor to ensure that performance and service levels are delivered in a timely and cost-effective manner.

3. Workload can be better managed—service levels can be monitored on a regular basis. If the organization's workload is seasonal or requires greater flexibility due to changes in the marketplace, the outsourcing vendor can satisfy the need by offering services on a demand or as-required basis.

4. No increase in staff will be needed if the workload increases. Having an outsourcing vendor provides flexibility to an organization,

allowing it to pass on the extra work if there is an increase in business activity. A partnership approach with the outsourcing vendor provides an opportunity to transfer more workload over time, if there is an acceptable level of service at a competitive price. For noncore business functions, it may be prudent to expand the business without expanding the staffing levels.

5. Service agreements can be reviewed frequently—for example, every year or every two years. The contract expiration date provides a logical point to review with the outsourcing vendor the types and value of services acquired. The duration of the contract is dependent on a number of factors, including the type of services acquired, the value of all services, the cost and risk associated with changing the outsourcing vendor, the service responsiveness from the vendor, the viability of the outsourcing vendor, the reliability of the vendor, and the vendor's ability to meet deliverables when promised.

   For instance, a contract duration of two years with a one-year extension may be appropriate to monitor service levels with the vendor. A desktop computer maintenance agreement to service microcomputers and peripherals throughout the country could be for two years with an option to renew for one year. On the other hand, a service agreement to manage a computer center and telecommunications services could be for a longer time period, say, up to five years, because the vendor may have to make capital investments in hardware and software to deliver the service and performance levels.

6. Accountability can be tied to performance and service levels; unacceptable performance could be subject to financial penalty. An outsourcing vendor is in the business of providing services at a competitive price. Since these services are distinct and measurable, it is important that service levels be monitored and reported. Typical measures of service levels include the following:

   ☐ Timeliness of service. If a desktop computer maintenance agreement requires service within four hours of placing a telephone call to the vendor, then this activity can be measured and reported. If the service level is not met, financial penalties may be imposed, provided that they are specified in the service agreement.

☐ Availability of service. If the computer center is required to be available 24 hours a day, seven days a week, the service availability can be measured and monitored. Again, there could be financial penalties associated with lack of availability.

☐ Response time of the computer system. This is a visible factor for determining the effectiveness of a computer system. A subsecond response time for 95 percent of transactions is normally expected by a user. Again, this measurable indicator could be an integral part of the service agreement.

☐ Quality of service. Although quality is difficult to measure, it can be experienced by the users of the service. Quality can include responsiveness to a request, ability to meet deadlines when promised, preparing the users for a change of software release before it is implemented, testing a product before it is released, providing support services for problem resolution, and so on. Quality of service could be measured by customer surveys, for example, once a year, to determine some of the problem areas and ensure that they are addressed adequately.

Disadvantages

There are several disadvantages to outsourcing that can cause an organization a lot of difficulty and risk, if the process is not managed properly:

☐ Outsourcing may be costly in the long term—after the outsourcing vendor has acquired the understanding of the client organization, both unit costs and total costs may increase as the outsourcing vendor seeks additional revenue-generating opportunities.

☐ Requirements that were not anticipated would be contingent on the availability of funds—the vendor can demand additional funding to incorporate these unanticipated requirements.

☐ Limited skills transfer may occur from the outsourcing vendor to the client—the vendor may not be cooperative in skills transfer to the client organization.

☐ Difficulty may arise in measuring and managing quality.

☐ Staff morale at the client organization may be affected—with a greater amount work being transferred to the outsourcing vendor, the more interesting work could be potentially outsourced.

- ☐ The outsourcing vendor retains control over the ultimate level and quality of services provided.

- ☐ A higher level of risk is incurred if there are changes at the outsourcing vendor organization.

- ☐ Typically, a higher price results when the client organization decides to change the outsourcing vendor—e.g., conversion and migration costs, training costs, greater coordination, and risk of downtime.

Outsourcing—Modes of Delivery

There are several delivery models for managing outsourcing services. The two distinguishing characteristics between these delivery models are the level of control over the service and the amount of risk the organization is prepared to take with the outsourcing vendor. Any organization planning to use outsourcing services must make sure that it has a service level agreement (SLA) in place with financial penalties for noncompliance. SLAs are key because that is where the user organization can set the expectations for the services it requires. Figure 9.3 depicts the relationship between the various outsourcing factors.

It should be noted that when the work is contracted out to an outsourcing vendor, it often makes sense to transfer the in-house company staff associated with the work to the outsourcing company. Typically, such a move would ensure greater stability during the transition and provide a

---

Key Constraints

Greater exposure to risk
(e.g., security risk, lack of data integrity)

Limited degree of control

Difficulty in measuring performance and service levels

Limited control over costs and quality

Limited understanding of the client's business and priorities

---

Figure 9.3 Key constraints.

more manageable working environment. In addition, there is no training required because the transferred staff would be familiar with the organization and its business practices. An organization can rely on three primary modes of delivery when acquiring outsourcing services and products, as described in this section.

In-House Project Delivery

This delivery model includes the provision of services by in-house staff, based on the priorities and requirements of the internal client within the organization. The degree of responsiveness and the associated allocation of resources could be driven by priorities set by the senior management of the organization or, alternatively, based on internal pricing to recover costs and overhead.

Of the three modes of delivery, the in-house project delivery model is typically the most expensive but most effective. Depending on the requirements of the organization, it might make business sense to deliver high-priority services by in-house staff and acquire less critical services from the outsourcing vendor.

Use of Supplementary Consultants and Systems Integrators

This delivery model includes the selective use of consultants and systems integrators on an as-required basis. Typical examples of using consultants and systems integrators would include developing computer applications; maintaining computer applications; implementing computer systems; and acquiring a complete turnkey system, including hardware and software.

This model is effective for specific project-related activities where the scope and deliverables are clearly understood. Many organizations use consultants to acquire specific skill-sets that are not readily available in the client organization. Sometimes consultants are also used to supplement in-house resources to get a job done in a timely manner. This mode of acquiring outsourcing services would also include using services to jump-start support capabilities, followed by skills transfer to in-house staff.

Systems integrators are used when there is a need to acquire specific solutions for the client organization. For instance, systems integrators may be considered for vertical market applications such as systems for the dental office, insurance broker, property management office, or advertising office.

Complete Outsourcing of Projects

This delivery model includes the provision of all designated services by the outsourcing vendor, at a predictable cost. In-house systems provide a coordinating function. The nature and scope of services are determined by the senior management of the company in accordance with the requirements of the organization. Service parameters would include cost, quality, and timeliness of services. Figure 9.4 depicts the outsourcing delivery model and its relationship to the project manager.

The ASP approach is consistent with the complete outsourcing of applications and related services. For instance, ASPs can become business-to-business hubs and provide a variety of applications and utilities through a partnership arrangement. ASP service delivery could be described as meeting the service needs of the customers on the Internet—whatever service, whatever resource or application customers want to access over the Internet would be available at an affordable price. The ASP industry is moving toward providing that application support and network access to a community of buyers and sellers.

Organizations do not have to be concerned about running and operating application hosting services on their own, but can look to ASPs as part-

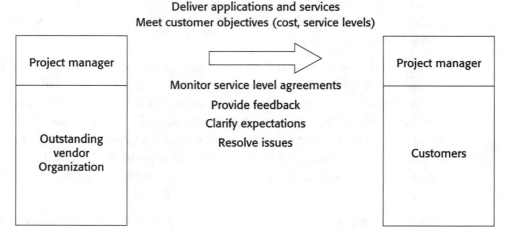

Figure 9.4   Outsourcing delivery model.

ners capable of providing that service. The user organizations can pay on a per user basis or on a per transaction basis. The ASP model is becoming similar to other existing service delivery models we are used to—for example, similar to getting water and paying for usage, or getting your electricity and paying for it on a usage basis, or using taxi services and paying for it based on time and distance.

As the demand for skilled resources increases in the information technology sector, there is a growing trend to take the work to offshore companies. Also, time-to-market pressure has companies racing to locate skilled developers at a lower cost.

Offshore outsourcing can be found in numerous locales, including Taiwan, Singapore, India, China, Malaysia, and Ireland. The demand for knowledge workers has grown due to explosive growth in e-commerce applications. Offshore outsourcing offers several advantages:

☐ Lower cost in developing and maintaining applications

☐ Greater flexibility in managing the workload based on market demand

☐ Ready availability of skilled resources to respond to increasing demand for resources

☐ Faster introduction of new applications to the market

Typically, an offshore project involves the onsite liaison staff for overseeing the project and ensuring that the client and the outsourcing vendor understand each others' requirements. Application coding and testing functions are well suited for offshore outsourcing. Project status reports can be communicated via the project Web site. It is important to have available high bandwidth to the North American offices to facilitate a quick turnaround.

Organizations are working hard to be Web-ready and transact e-commerce. As a result, there is an increasing demand for skilled workers who can build applications with Web storefronts quickly, and link them with existing legacy applications.

Request for Proposal (RFP)

Outsourcing services are usually acquired from vendors on a competitive basis. Depending on the size and complexity of the services required from the outsourcing vendor, a Request for Proposal (RFP) document is prepared to outline the business and systems requirements of the client organization. An RFP is a formal document sent to a list of qualified vendors, inviting them to propose a cost-effective system solution to meet the client's requirements. Identical copies of the RFP are sent to vendors so that all the vendors are responding to similar requirements. The RFP process typically involves the following steps:

1. The client organization prepares a Request for Proposal including a description of the company's background, a description of how the RFP process will be conducted, and a description of its current information technology environment. In addition, the RFP will include a description of hardware, software, network, and services that the client organization intends to acquire as part of the RFP process. The RFP provides a detailed listing of mandatory and desirable items for the proposed goods and services. A description of how the vendor proposals will be evaluated is also provided for the vendors.

2. A list of qualified vendors is prepared.

3. The RFP is distributed to the qualified vendors. Vendors are usually allowed 10 to 20 business days to respond.

4. Vendors submit their proposals to the client organization.

5. The client organization evaluates these proposals based on an evaluation methodology.

6. The successful vendor proposal is determined and the vendor advised.

7. A contract is negotiated between the vendor and the client to finalize the arrangements between the two parties.

8. The vendor provides information technology goods and services in accordance with the contract.

Evaluation Criteria

Some of the key factors to be considered when acquiring the services from an outsourcing vendor follow.

1. **Overall cost to the client organization.** The overall cost to the client organization can be determined on a yearly basis for a minimum of three years. Understanding the costs over a three-year

period provides a better understanding of the cost variables and their relationship to time. Wherever appropriate, cost factors should be tied to specific services required from the outsourcing vendor. Unit costs should also be clearly understood by the client organization, to assess the cost variation with volume.

2. **Level of risk.** Outsourcing projects requires greater coordination, especially if various parts of the project are assigned to different vendors. In addition, projects developed by one vendor may require maintenance changes that are implemented by another vendor. It is important to plan the outsourcing projects so that the deliverables are distinct and manageable as such. It may also make sense to deal with a limited number of outsourcing vendors to enhance consistency of standards and integration between systems.

   Outsourcing projects also involve financial risks to the client organization in terms of cost overruns due to incomplete or unclear specifications. If the system specifications are clearly and adequately defined, the outsourcing vendor would assume the financial risk of delivering the system at a fixed cost and time. The information technology organization would be responsible for ensuring that the outsourcing vendor can actually deliver the system as originally proposed.

3. **Performance measurement.** Vendor management is an important function to ensure that systems that are delivered meet well-defined performance criteria. Performance criteria include response time of the application; the ability to process a minimum number of transactions per specifications; user-friendly applications including GUI design principles; and an intuitive application interface that facilitates efficient navigation throughout the application.

4. **Flexibility and responsiveness.** Outsourcing vendors are an extension of the services provided by the in-house information technology organization. Consequently, it is easier to manage the information technology workload with increased flexibility and responsiveness by partnering with an outsourcing vendor. By supplementing resources with the outsourcing vendors, in-house client requirements can be met in a more timely manner.

5. **Accountability.** The ultimate responsibility for the definition, design, and delivery of systems rests with the information technology organization. Accountability includes the costs and benefits of

implementing information technology and ensuring client acceptance for the completed applications.

6. **Skills and knowledge transfer.** As part of vendor management, skills and knowledge transfer should be an integral part of vendor responsibility. Skills transfer includes supporting documentation, user and system training, and ongoing communication of system problems and how they were resolved.

A Methodology for Evaluating Outsourcing Vendor Proposals

When evaluating different vendor proposals, it is useful to have an approach that is defensible and fair to vendors. Such a methodology also helps the evaluation team to obtain consensus from their management and the project stakeholders before undertaking a detailed evaluation.

The key elements of an evaluation methodology are described here:

1. **Evaluation team.** A team is usually established to evaluate the proposals submitted by the vendors in response to the RFP for acquiring hardware, software, and services. Depending on the size and complexity of the project, additional team members may be required. The team is typically composed of a project manager, a business analyst, and a systems manager. The primary responsibility of the evaluation team is to evaluate each proposal and make final recommendations to the steering committee.

2. **Vendor qualification.** The evaluation team evaluates each of the proposals submitted, and can use the criteria outlined in this section to prepare a short list of proposals that qualify for further evaluation.

3. **Vendor viability.** The vendor proposal provides details on stability and viability. Proposals can be disqualified because

   □ The company has been in relevant business for less than one year.

   □ The company is financially unstable, according to analysis of data in the vendor-supplied annual report. The company is deemed to be financially unstable if it reported a loss for each of the last three fiscal years. If annual reports are not available, analysis may be performed on the basis of vendor-supplied financial statements.

☐ There is a lack of demonstrated experience in similar-sized accounts.

4. **Mandatory requirements.** The vendor's proposal must meet the requirements outlined in the RFP. The evaluation team must be satisfied that the proposed solution meets all the mandatory requirements. If any of these requirements are not met, the vendor's proposal is rejected.

5. **Viability of implementation and operation.** The project team will evaluate the viability of the implementation and operation of the vendor-proposed solution. Information relating to the analysis can be obtained from a number of sources, including, but not limited to, client references, published research reports, and performance data. The evaluation team will assess the vendor's ability to meet the requirements as outlined in the Request for Proposal. Proposals will be disqualified if, in the opinion of the evaluation team, the recommended solution is not viable from an implementation or operational point of view, or for organizational, environmental, or technological reasons, or if the proposed solution cannot be implemented in a reasonable timeframe.

6. **Credibility and quality of proposals.** The proposed solution will be accompanied by models or statements of experience in similar-sized accounts, which will demonstrate that the proposed solution has been configured in a manner that will meet the workload and performance requirements of the client organization. Should the supporting documentation not support the workload and performance requirements, the vendor proposal is disqualified.

7. **Contractual compliance.** Each vendor is requested to indicate compliance with the terms and conditions outlined in the RFP. All contract modifications requested by the vendor may be assessed to ensure that the long-term interests of the client organization are served.

8. **Detailed evaluation of vendor proposals.**

☐ **References.** Typically, vendors are requested to submit three to five references, depending on the project. Reference checks are usually conducted for qualified vendors based on a detailed evaluation of their proposals. Reference checks performed by the evaluation team will not be necessarily restricted to the supplied references. Proposals will be penalized for the following reasons:

- [ ] References provided are not being served by the vendor in any manner similar to the approach proposed by the client organization.

- [ ] Service and support has not been provided recently by the vendor at the referenced client.

- [ ] A claim made in the vendor proposal is found to be inaccurate.

- [ ] The vendor has been unable to fulfill commitments made to the client, whether initially or during the term of the contract.

References will be evaluated based on response to a series of questions relating to vendor's performance and service levels. References will be scored on a scale of 1 to 10. The average score will be determined; if the score is less than 90, a penalty of up to 15 percent of the total evaluated cost of the vendor's proposal will be assigned. Some of the sample reference check questions are included in Figure 9.5.

- [ ] **Evaluation period.** The evaluation team will evaluate proposals for the duration of the contract, for example, over 24 or 36 months.

- [ ] **Financial factors.** The evaluation team may consider using financial factors such as net present value (NPV) or the internal rate of return (IRR) to account for the value of money over time.

- [ ] **Evaluated cost.** The evaluated cost of each proposal will include the following components:

  - [ ] Charges proposed by the vendor, as adjusted by the evaluation team. This includes all hardware, software, support, and maintenance charges.

  - [ ] Charges related to installation, upgrade, or hardware relocation charges.

  - [ ] All charges incurred directly by the client during the implementation of the vendor proposal—for example, conversion costs and telecommunications costs for the network.

  - [ ] Application of any other credits or charges, as provided in the proposal. For instance, the vendor proposal may include

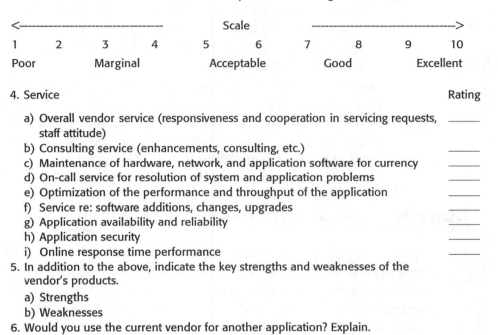

Reference Check Questions

1. How long have you been using the vendor's services?
2. Briefly explain the nature of services provided by the vendor.
3. Please indicate the level of satisfaction experienced in using these services.

```
<---------------------------          Scale          --------------------------->
1      2      3      4      5      6      7      8      9      10
Poor          Marginal          Acceptable          Good          Excellent
```

4. Service   Rating

   a) Overall vendor service (responsiveness and cooperation in servicing requests,   _____
      staff attitude)
   b) Consulting service (enhancements, consulting, etc.)   _____
   c) Maintenance of hardware, network, and application software for currency   _____
   d) On-call service for resolution of system and application problems   _____
   e) Optimization of the performance and throughput of the application   _____
   f) Service re: software additions, changes, upgrades   _____
   g) Application availability and reliability   _____
   h) Application security   _____
   i) Online response time performance   _____
5. In addition to the above, indicate the key strengths and weaknesses of the
   vendor's products.
   a) Strengths
   b) Weaknesses
6. Would you use the current vendor for another application? Explain.

Figure 9.5   Reference check questions.

the provision of 100 training hours to the client at no extra cost.

☐ Cost for all desirable items requested by the client and proposed by the vendor. Vendor proposals will not be disqualified for failing to respond to desirable items. The number of desirable items met, and those included in the standard price, will be determined for each proposal during evaluation. For vendor proposals that do not include desirable items, the evaluation team will assign an evaluated cost to the vendor's proposal.

☐ Business risks associated with implementation. A potential cost associated with implementation includes disruption of the client's business operations if the implementation is incomplete or results in unanticipated delays because of time needed to resolve problems. Depth in a vendor organization represents an asset to the client in meeting unanticipated requirements during the term of the contract. Alternately, the lack of depth in an organization may restrict the client's ability to request additional service from the successful vendor. The evaluation team will assess business risk and assign a quantifiable figure that will be included in the evaluated cost of the vendor proposal.

☐ **Determination of the successful proposal.** After identification and inclusion of all costs as identified in this section, the best proposal—that is, the proposal with the lowest evaluated cost that has met all other criteria indicated above—will be designated as the successful proposal. The successful proposal can then be presented to the steering committee for approval.

Outsourcing—Case Studies

Two outsourcing case studies are described in this section. The cases have been generalized to protect the privacy of organizations. The cases illustrate some of the key considerations for organizations to adopt outsourcing including greater flexibility in managing the workload, opportunity for client organizations to focus on their core competencies, improved quality of services, and more effective management of costs.

A Consumer Products Company

A large, diversified consumer products company was considering whether to continue managing its system department as it had done in the past, that is, to provide virtually all services using in-house personnel from its systems department. The organization was going through a restructuring exercise and looking for ways to streamline its business processes and practices by focusing on its core business.

As part of the focusing exercise and after adequate deliberations, the senior management team decided that it would be worthwhile to review alternate ways of delivering information technology services to support its business. Outsourcing of some or most of the information technology services would be another viable way of providing services.

Some of the key issues in considering whether to outsource work to a vendor included the following:

☐ A growing number of users who required support in the use of productivity tools such as email, word processing, and spreadsheets

☐ An increasing number of requests for application development, ranging from building local databases to managing business functions and processes

☐ A greater demand on end users of computer technologies to be more productive through improved coordination and integration of activities between departments

☐ Rapid advances in the information technology marketplace placing more demands on company's systems staff to stay abreast of these developments and deploy these solutions in a cost-effective and standardized manner throughout the organization

☐ Increasing demands placed on systems staff to find solutions that are stable and work well in a production environment

☐ Demands on the systems department to cut costs and provide improved services to a growing number of users

Faced with these issues, the company decided that it would be prudent to achieve its objectives through outsourcing of several key services, including the help desk, maintenance of its computer servers and peripherals, and application development. The company finalized agreements with an outsourcer, after a competitive selection and evaluation process, to provide these services for a period of three years. Most of the company staff involved in application development would be absorbed by the outsourcing vendor as part of the outsourcing agreement.

The net impact of this move to an outsourcing vendor was an immediate savings of 25 percent per year for three years. The application development portfolio was agreed on as part of the agreement, including maintenance of all existing applications. Outsourcing vendor management and the coordination of all their work would still be the responsibility of the systems department.

The company staff is now busy analyzing the key business processes that have an impact on the core business, preparing recommendations and solution strategies in areas they never had time to approach, and providing more timely services to their users. The staff have more time to examine high payoff areas and assess where their efforts will have the greatest value to the company.

The company is prepared to try this arrangement for three years. It recognizes that there are risks associated with outsourcing, but the management has come to the conclusion that given their objectives, such risks do not pose a major threat to the company. The contractual arrangement includes a monthly review at two levels—a performance review between the operational managers of the company and the outsourcing vendor, and a review with senior management. The company also has the option to terminate the contract if the performance measures are not achieved. The performance measures include actual time to respond to and resolve a problem, application development times for each application, software assurance, levels of system and application testing, and user acceptance criteria.

A Public Sector Agency

A large public sector agency was processing its batch and online applications on a usage-sensitive basis by acquiring computer processing services from an outsourcing vendor. The agency was faced with increasing pressures to streamline its business processes and deploy information technologies wherever appropriate, to provide a more responsive service to the public, and to reduce the total computer processing and network management costs.

With changing market and business conditions, the agency had an opportunity to explore all service alternatives to ensure that it receives an excellent return on technology investment as well as improved service levels. The agency considered using facility management services employed by several organizations, including acquiring computer services at a fixed and predictable operating cost.

The agency was determined to move to acquiring services on a fixed-price basis dependent on anticipated resource utilization on the host computer and related network usage based on the following objectives:

- To reduce and contain costs
- To provide timely, affordable, and easy-to-use host services to users
- To retain flexibility to accommodate changes in the computer processing workload
- To deliver improved services to agency staff by offering additional tools and applications aimed at enhancing staff productivity

Based on a competitive acquisition process, the agency acquired all host processing services from the outsourcing vendor, including computer processing, disk and tape storage, backup and recovery services, contingency planning and disaster recovery, province-wide help desk support through a toll-free number, and all network management functions. As a result of this process, the agency reduced its processing and network management costs by 20 percent in the first two years, and capped its costs for the third year despite an increase in processing and network workload.

Outsourcing in the 2000s

Outsourcing will continue to be a viable option in managing the information-processing workload in organizations as pressures to rationalize service offerings continue. Outsourcing will provide organizations with the flexibility of managing information-processing requirements with a modicum of staff, adapting from mainframe-centric to distributed-centric operating styles, and maintaining or improving service throughout this transition. We believe that in most organizations, outsourcing services will become an integral part of the information technology operating budget. Organizations are already utilizing selective outsourcing such as training, computer application development, maintenance of computer applications, and maintenance of the computer center to meet their resourcing requirements at a manageable and predictable cost.

Based on an organization's specific requirements, those involved in the outsourcing of computer services will continue to focus on the following objectives:

- [ ] To predict, control, and contain costs
- [ ] To provide timely, affordable, and easy-to-use computer services to users
- [ ] To retain flexibility to accommodate changes in the computer processing workload at the least cost, should business requirements or technology change
- [ ] To enable the organization to focus on its core services and use information technology to support those core services
- [ ] To deliver improved services to the organization by offering additional tools and applications aimed at enhancing staff productivity

A proactive outsourcing strategy will become an integral part of the delivery of total information technology services in organizations and will include developing processes for identifying outsourcing services; managing outsourcing vendors; ensuring that outsourcing contracts include performance factors and skills transfer to in-house staff, where appropriate; and maintaining continuity and a nonthreatening work environment. Outsourcing projects will become successful if they are managed in a partnership mode between vendor staff and in-house staff.

Outsourcing is, and will continue, making dramatic changes in information technology departments. It is reasonable to expect that there will be a shift in the budgets of IT departments—a shift from IT departments to the outsourcing vendor organization. Some of the services that will likely continue to be outsourced include application development and hosting, help desk and related support, network management, and e-commerce applications, as organizations strip down to their core competencies. Even business processes such as procurement and order processing could be potentially outsourced. For instance, the auto industry e-marketplace set up by the big three automakers is an example of moving some of the information technology workload to large business-to-business Web sites.

Outsourcing has made significant changes in the manufacturing sector. For example, a large telecommunications company recently announced that it would outsource several manufacturing plants to an electronics component manufacturer. In addition, it announced that a variety of corporate services, including payroll, employee training, human resources centers, and the accounts payable function, would be outsourced. Such outsourcing arrangements would enable the telecommunications company to focus on what it does best—delivering state-of-the-art telecommunications products to its customers.

Summary

This chapter answered the following questions:

- ☐ What is the significance of outsourcing to project managers?
- ☐ What does outsourcing mean and what is its scope?
- ☐ What are key business issues when considering outsourcing?
- ☐ Is an Application Service Provider similar to an outsourcer?

☐ What are the skills required to manage a project that is outsourced?

☐ Is outsourcing a panacea? When should it be considered and how will it improve the organization's competitiveness?

☐ What are the risks associated with outsourcing and how can these risks best be managed?

☐ Is there merit in offshore outsourcing?

☐ How does an organization know that it is receiving value from the outsourcing vendor?

This chapter also described the importance of outsourcing to an organization. With increasing pressures on organizations to focus on their core competencies in order to maintain competitiveness, and with greater demands to producing better products and provide value-added services, it is not possible to do it alone. Outsourcing enables organizations to work together with their partners in bringing new products to the market faster, providing services and support on a timely basis, and responding to market pressures quickly and efficiently.

This chapter described the business reasons for organizations to utilize outsourcing and Application Service Providers as an effective strategy in providing products and services. The advantages and disadvantages of outsourcing were described, along with the project management perspectives so that the benefits from the partnership can be realized. Offshore outsourcing, if properly managed, is another extension of the partnership process and can provide organizations with significant cost savings.

With Application Service Providers, organizations no longer need to worry about running and hosting applications on their own, but can potentially provide that functionality through partners on a per user basis, a per transaction basis, or a time basis, or some combination of these. The ASP model is similar to other existing models—paying for water on a usage basis, paying for a taxicab on a time-and-distance basis, and paying for professional services based on time. However, any organization planning to use an ASP must make sure that it has a service level agreement in place with service levels and financial penalties clearly spelled out.

The motivation to outsource is driven by a number of factors: the desire to focus on core competencies, faster turnaround of end product from concept to delivery, a more cost-effective alternative to providing products or services than using in-house personnel, and greater flexibility in making changes. Outsourcing is here to stay and will continue to evolve over time. Outsourcing is a partnership between the provider of services and the recipient of services—both parties have to understand each other and work together to make it work effectively. When services are outsourced, there is a distinct change in role for the organization from a doer to a coordinator of vendor services. Vendor management becomes another job function with its associated risks and accountability. There will be continued pressure on information technology departments to provide value to the organization, and outsourcing will be one of the ways to achieve that objective. Outsourcing is not a panacea—it requires a solid understanding of the business by the vendor and the commitment to deliver results at a competitive price.

CHAPTER 10

Introduction to Project Management Tools and Microsoft Project

I n this chapter, the reader will learn about establishing the technical infrastructure required to implement the approaches and techniques already discussed in this book. The primary focus in this chapter is on defining approaches for building effective project plans. This involves an examination of project estimating and management tools in the context of reasons to use them and what to expect from them. The advantages of using project templates and standards are also examined. This chapter also provides criteria that can be used to select management tool vendors to establish an enterprise-wide architecture. Finally, the chapter gives the reasons to select Microsoft Project 2000 as an organizational standard and then provides a roadmap to the remaining chapters that focus on this tool. In this chapter the reader will learn about:

- Project estimating tools
- Project management tools
- Selection criteria
- Standard features
- Basic planning templates
- Alternatives to Microsoft Project
- A Microsoft Project roadmap

Estimating and Management Tools

Estimating and management tools can be used together to build metrics for a project in the planning stages and to track them throughout the project lifecycle. Metrics can be gathered or built under a set of parameters, such as project cost, duration, number of resources, project complexity, skills of a project team, project politics, and organizational support for the initiative. The metrics can be used to select specific values for a project, usually by using a value in a weighted range or a descriptor that will drive out the following estimates:

☐ **Tasks.** This can include a hierarchy of "work units" such as phases, activities, and tasks. Each unit of work consists of a collection of lower-order work units. For example, a phase may have three activities. Each activity further divides into a set of tasks each. The names for this sort of hierarchy can change with the methodology or framework; however, the principles remain the same.

☐ **Resources.** This can include specific resource names or roles (e.g., project manager, consultant, network administrator, business analyst) that are specified for a unit of work.

☐ **Durations.** This can include a range or specific values for each unit of work expressed in terms of weeks, days, or hours. The general approach is to begin by specifying durations at the lowest unit of work in a hierarchy (e.g., task, instead of phase).

Estimating Tools

Many project managers do produce estimates based on intuition and experience. A variety of tests conducted by colleagues on a limited set of test cases have shown that some project managers can produce fairly accurate projections using this method. Estimating approaches can also be more tool-oriented. As shown in Figure 10.1, an estimating tool accepts specific values for a set of predetermined parameters that are believed to affect the metrics for a project. These metrics are applied to a methodology or framework to generate a first cut at a project plan with estimates for resources and task durations. These can then be fed into a project management tool and used as the project plan. Any of the generated results can be adjusted on the basis of the project manager's experience.

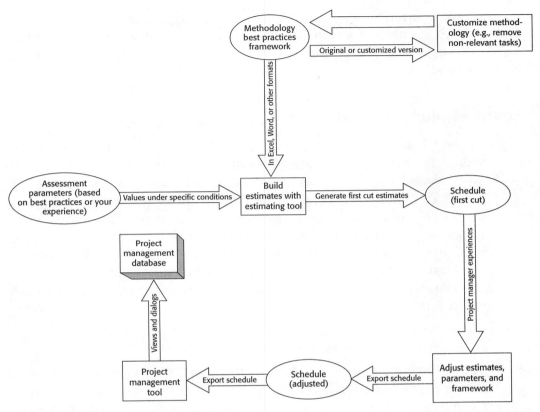

Figure 10.1 Estimating tool process.

Estimating tools can be useful for producing first cuts at a project schedule that can then be customized for the project. The accuracy of the estimates depends on the discreteness and depth of the parameters that can be selected to generate the first draft of the project plan. Too much detail becomes very difficult to manage, while too little detail offers limited assistance. We have discovered that about three values (e.g., high, medium, low) for about a half dozen parameters are a reasonable place to start.

A project can be defined within an organization to gather metrics from existing best practices or from a number of projects, or can be purchased from third-party sources. The project plan for this would include a confirmation of the parameters, the values they can assume, and major activities in a project development lifecycle. This information can be entered into a packaged estimating tool or used to create a few different spreadsheets that reflect the common values that an organization wants to support. Every project within the organization can then use the spreadsheets or tools to start with a standard version of a project plan and customize it from there.

Project Management and Tracking Tools

At the most basic level of project management tools track "portions of work," resources, and deliverables during a project. A work effort can go by many names, such as phase, activity, subactivity, tasks, and subtasks. The important thing is that each work effort has an associated start date–time, end date–time, and associated resources. The work effort can also be divided into levels or a work hierarchy, where larger work durations are divided into two or more subdurations. This process can be repeated indefinitely; however, in practice it makes sense to proceed to maybe four or so levels deep. An example of defining a work effort follows:

```
Work effort 1, start date/time, end date/time, resource list
Work effort 2, start date/time, end date/time, resource list
```

The following generic example demonstrates three levels of a work effort that consists of two phases. The first activity identifies the subactivities for getting started. The second activity identifies the subactivities for producing and distributing invitations to a workshop. The third activity contains no additional details, but specifies the facilitator and the time of the meeting. The fourth activity specifies who is responsible for compiling the feedback received from the workshop. This collection of activities could be included under a phase, say "Manage workshops." Resources and durations are specified at the lowest level of the hierarchy. Some, but not all, project management tools allow these to roll up. Also notice that in some cases, some portions of a project plan can be effectively replaced with a checklist that only contains milestone dates.

```
Phase: Manage Workshops
Getting started
     Define Infrastructure requirements Feb 1, 1 day, B. James
     Implement hardware enhancements    Feb 2, 2 days, B. James
     Add userids and privileges         Feb 8, 2 days, T. Carry
     REMARK dependency on subactivity "Collect rsvps"
     Test Infrastructure changes        Feb 10, 1 days, B. James
Distribute Invitations
     Draft Invitation                   Feb 1, .5 days, J. Terry
     Build invitation list              Feb 1, .5 days, J. Terry
```

```
        Gather email addresses        Feb 1, .5 days, T. Busie
        Send first Invitation         Feb 2, .5 days, T. Busie
        Collect RSVPs                 Feb 3, 5 days, T. Busie
        Send reminder                 Feb 10, .5 days, T. Busie
   Conduct meeting                    Feb 15, 2 days, J. Terry
   Compile attendee feedback          Feb 17, 3 days, T. Busie
```

Your choices for what constitutes a phase, activity, and subactivity, and their relative ordering, will have a large impact on the plan's readability, usefulness, and tracking support. Other properties can also be allocated to the work effort, such as whether it is a mandatory activity and the dependencies it has with other activities.

Showing less information can make it easier to follow a project plan. You can roll up the plan to a phase or activity level. Some, but not all, project management tools will allow you to track the resources at the rolled-up level. Other tools will allow the roll-up to be done, but will not show the resources at the higher level. For example, the "Manage Workshops" project plan can be rolled up to the activity level with resources showing, as follows:

```
Phase: Manage Workshops (Rolled up to activity level)
Getting started            Feb 1, 11 days, B. James, T. Carry
     REMARK: dependency on subactivity "Collect rsvps"
Distribute Invitations     Feb 1, 10.5 days, J. Terry, T. Busie
Conduct meeting            Feb 15, 2 days, J. Terry
Compile attendee feedback  Feb 17, 3 days, T. Busie
```

Although the rolled-up view shows fewer details, it is easier to read and understand from a key milestone perspective. It can also highlight areas for greater clarity. For example, it may be useful to move some of the "invitation" building subactivities from "Distribute Invitations" into a second activity called "Prepare Invitations" that precedes the original activity.

Another useful variant is to combine aspects of a project plan and a checklist to include key dates and milestones, but not to be too concerned about the time element of simple activities, just when they need to be completed. This is shown in the following example:

```
Phase: Manage Workshops (combines project plan with checklist view)
Getting started               Feb 1 to Feb 11, B. James, T. Carry
     Define Infrastructure requirements
     Implement hardware enhancements
     Add userids and privileges
     Test Infrastructure changes
Distribute Invitations        Feb 1 to Feb 11, J. Terry, T. Busie
     Draft Invitation
     Build invitation list
```

```
            Gather email addresses
            Send first Invitation
            Collect RSVPs
            Send reminder
      Conduct meeting              Feb 15 to Feb 16, J. Terry
      Compile attendee feedback    Feb 17 to Feb 19, T. Busie
```

The other functionality offered by project management tools manipulates the basic project plan throughout the project lifecycle. The plan must be saved as a baseline at some point to establish a comparison point for future tracking against the actual experience.

Limitations

A major weakness with project management tools becomes visible when a manager begins to act as an administrator by allowing the tool to do the planning and decision making for him or her. Many of the problems that occur on a project require the experience, judgment, and intuition of the project manager to resolve. Managers should avoid allowing the tool to replace their own roles, and instead restrict it to being a tool. For example, resource overutilization should be avoided in general, but trying to eliminate every such indication on a plan can be a waste of time. This is because overutilization may be shown when a resource is booked on several activities on a part-time basis. Trying to slice their time exactly to fit so that the daily sum is within a full-time range cannot usually be done accurately—it is a guess at most. It is better to indicate part-time involvement and accept the warning the tool produces.

Tools can end up producing views that are phenomenally complex—even though they are intended to simply project planning and tracking. By the time you take a moderately complex project, update a calendar, add the resources, update the budget, and insert the detailed tasks and deliverables, the resulting project plan can become complex enough to require a few hours to maintain on a weekly basis. A few additions to the functionality, and the updates can require an exponential amount of time to incorporate them into the rest of the plan. It can become difficult to visualize mentally, time-consuming to track, and difficult to walk through with a team. This is usually the time to produce a one-page high-level plan and use it to track the project instead.

We have observed many cases in which a great deal of time and energy was spent creating a detailed project plan, only to have it ignored and replaced by a much simpler one. The larger plan has the value of making the people building the plan think about the subtler aspects of the project. The problem is that it is difficult to track and conceptualize at that level.

Standard Functions and Features

Figure 10.2 shows the type of data and relationships that are required to build a project plan. The major components include a master resource list, project details, basic templates, and calendar information. Various views can be constructed from this basic data. Standard features required to manipulate this data are as follows:

- □ **Calendar functions.** Ability to establish the standard length of the workweek, the number of hours in the working day, and standard holidays.

- □ **Resource list.** Ability to maintain a list of resources by name and role. The ability to include rate information will support project accounting and project cost controls.

- □ **Templates.** Ability to reuse a set of project templates as a basis for creating project plans. It is useful if the templates are available from a shield or a wizard.

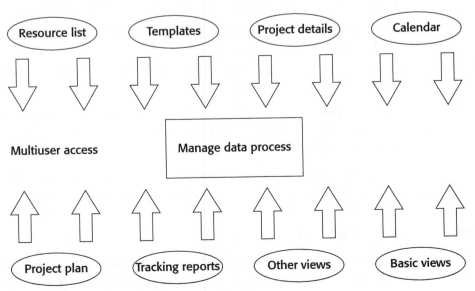

Figure 10.2 Processing project management data.

- **Gantt chart.** Ability to represent project data as a graphical view that shows the project plan consisting of units of work (in the hierarchy), resources, dependencies, start dates, end dates, and durations. Ability to support a baseline to compare against actual project details. Ability to support master project plans and subproject plans.

- **Views, lists, and reports.** Ability to extract project data in a variety of views including: activity list by week, activity list by resource, overallocated resource list, master milestone list, milestone list by resource, planned versus actual reports, and a critical path list. The views should be accessible by different date ranges and legends.

Approaches for Building a Project Plan

There are many approaches for building a project plan. Each approach offers its own risks and rewards that must be ultimately balanced to build an effective project plan. An effective project plan must be:

- **Understandable.** It must be possible to understand and explain the project plan in its entirety. A plan that is so complex that it cannot be comprehended, end-to-end, is not effective.

- **Trackable.** It must be possible to track project events in a timely and consistent manner. A plan that requires an inordinate amount of time to update and explain will probably be abandoned.

- **Acceptable.** The project plan can only be effective if resources have bought into it and are committed to meeting its dates.

- **Reasonable.** The project plan must have achievable goals and be reasonable to accommodate.

- **Flexible.** The project plan must be flexible to allow activities and deliverables to be adjusted without necessarily changing any of the implementation dates.

Some popular approaches for building project plans are described here. They are differentiated in how implementation dates are determined.

Time-Limited Planning

This approach is based on a specific delivery date(s) established by the business due to any number of legitimate reasons. The project phases are then configured to meet the specified delivery date. This will rarely be a clean fit and will require several passes to complete. Some parameters that are available to support the fit into the timeframe include increasing resources and reducing functionality to the meet the deadline. Milestone deliverables should be used to track the project.

This approach can face resistance from team leaders, especially on larger projects. There is no sure method of overcoming these objections, but some approaches that have been successful include: (1) an open dialogue with the teams to understand their issues and demonstrate the importance of meeting the deadlines; (2) offering more resources to meet the deadlines; and (3) creating an open dialogue between the business and the project teams.

Bottom-up Planning

A more popular approach with project teams is to poll team leads and have them build project plans for their pieces based on their resources and abilities. These individual plans are then consolidated into a master project plan. The project delivery is driven by the results of this consolidation.

This approach helps to build consensus from the start of the planning efforts. Getting reasonable delivery dates will require several passes through the planning activities. This usually requires cutting back on the individual project plans by the team leads. The same parameters used to adjust the timeframe in the time-driven approach can be used here.

It is useful to combine this approach with the earlier one to do a sanity check, while building consensus among the project teams. The project manager can then have a standard for comparison with the team-based consolidated plans.

Index of Useful Planning Templates

Building a project plan does not always need to be done from scratch, although this is sometimes the most efficient way to proceed. It is useful to have access to a set of project planning templates that can be used for a quick start, either from your own personal files or from a central repository that is available to managers across the organization. The templates should include some of the major phases and activities that should be included in a custom project plan. The templates should also include a list of resources and milestones. Some useful project planning templates include the following:

- **Full development lifecycle.** High-level phases and activities for the full development lifecycle. The IPDM methodology can be used to construct this template.

- **Testing.** These activities are underrepresented on most projects. You should have templates for unit testing, system testing, integration testing, regression testing, capacity planning, performance testing, and acceptance testing. On Internet and Web-based applications, a lack of testing can be catastrophic. Other competing applications are only a mouse click (or a voice command) away. Capacity planning and performance testing on the Internet requires a view to unprecedented concurrent user volumes.

- **Training.** This involves a plan to train the development team and users on the application during and after its deployment.

- **Application deployment.** This involves a plan that deploys an application across one or more sites. The plan should also provide for a single large (e.g., big bang) implementation or a phased or limited rollout based on a pilot approach.

- **Product selection project plan.** A basic template to support product selections for the organization.

A Wide Selection of Tools to Choose From

There are several leading project management tools in the marketplace, in addition to Microsoft Project, that could be used to manage projects. They are differentiated by a variety of criteria that are described in the following section. Some of the other management tools that you might want to consider are:

- Project QuickStart, which can be accessed at www.projectkickstart .com at the time of writing, is suitable for projects that are not large.

- Primavera Systems offers a suite of project management solutions suitable for the enterprise. These solutions can be viewed at www.primavera.com at the time of writing.

- Open Plan, from Welcom, which can be accessed at www.welcom .com at the time of writing, offers a project management solution for the enterprise.

☐ Planview, which can be accessed at www.planview.com at the time of writing, offers both project management and some workflow support.

Other project management tools that operate on non-Windows platforms include the following: Autoplan, Compass, Gecomo Plus, MasterPlan, SIZE Plus, Cobra (from Welcom), and Ultra Planner (from Productivity Solutions).

Tool Selection Criteria

Selecting a project management tool for an organization involves considering a lot of competing interests. It is appropriate to establish a set of standards for project management tools for an organization. This allows deliverable and experience reuse at a management level, eliminates the need for conversions, and encourages managers to seek out other experiences. Establishing these standards requires executive support and a selection procedure. It is not unusual to engage an external consultant to lead such a search in order to demonstrate a nonbiased perspective. Selection procedures are a combination of science and art. The final answer requires compromises and consensus among a coalition of stakeholders. The roles and responsibilities for all these resources is as follows:

☐ **Executive management.** Empowers the selection committee and ratifies the final decision. This team is always responsible for resolving obstacles and conflicts.

☐ **Selection committee.** Provides business requirements, makes decisions, and manages the process. This team makes the final selection.

☐ **Selection team.** Brings the process knowledge to the project, finds vendors, establish meetings, and executes the work tasks.

An approach for a project tool selection that has worked well for us requires a few weeks at most, while other approaches may take a month or more. In the streamlined approach, executive management is required to identify members of a selection committee that has representation from key stakeholders. The working team (which may be led by a consultant) works with the selection committee to identify a set of criteria to differentiate between the tools that are available. For example, this could result in the following list of criteria:

- ☐ **Product functionality.** A rating of the functionality in the product compared to a "wish list" that is drafted by the selection committee.

- ☐ **Cost.** There are several levels of cost, including the purchase price, technical support fees, renewable license fees, future upgrade costs (estimated), technology upgrade costs, training costs, rollout costs, and any other costs that will be incurred in installing and rolling the tools out across the organization.

- ☐ **Availability of skills.** An assessment of how easy it will be to locate resources with knowledge of the software. A more important assessment might to be to evaluate the number of managers in the organization that already have the knowledge to operate the software.

- ☐ **Ease of use.** An assessment of the intuitiveness of the tool, the elegance of the user interaction, and level of effort required for an experienced user to use the tool.

- ☐ **Ease of learning.** An assessment of how easy the tool will be to learn for new users. This can include an assessment of the training courses and materials that the vendor offers or that are available through third parties.

- ☐ **Market penetration.** An assessment of the popularity of the tool in the marketplace, the stability of the vendor, and the momentum of the software in the industry.

- ☐ **Cultural fit with the organization.** An assessment of how well the tool's philosophy fits within the organization. This can include an examination of the detail the tool expects and its navigation and a comparison of this to the way the organization generally manages projects.

- ☐ **Technical compatibility.** An assessment of the ability to implement the tool within the technical infrastructure of the organization and the cost of doing so.

- ☐ **Limitations.** An assessment of the limitations the tool faces within the organization. This includes the number of concurrent users, data, complexity, and other measures that are determined by the selection committee.

- ☐ **Vendor support.** An assessment of the vendor's ability and willingness to support the organization after the sale. This can include an examination of the vendor's local presence and help-line support and hours of operation.

An easy-to-use rating system can be devised for this list of criteria. This may include something like: high, medium, low, where high is the most desired rating. A numeric rating can also be used. It is obviously faster to work with a simple rating system with a few rating points, say 1 to 3 (with 1 being the best), than to have a more complex one with many rating points. This is the decision of the selection committee.

The criteria list can be used to identify and categorize a long list of potential tools. Initial vendor contacts should also be made at this time. Depending on the size of your organization, it may be necessary to issue a Request for Information (RFI) to the potential vendors. The selection committee should also identify between three to five criteria as key to the final decision. Providing weightings to the set of criteria can be done; however, this can complicate the process and in many cases does not provide a more scientific answer in the end. In the streamlined approach, the key criteria can be used to quickly narrow the scope of the long list to a shortlist of maybe three or four suitable options. The process after the shortlist is defined involves product demonstrations, reference checks, and perhaps a short pilot.

Why Microsoft Project?

Microsoft Project has proven itself to be a good and effective project management tool. It occupies a large space in the marketplace and is obviously backed by a large vendor. It is a favorite of many of the managers that we interviewed for the book. Applying the selection criteria from above yields the observations shown in Table 10.1 based on our personal experiences. The rating for the criteria can be a number between 1 and 3. A "1" suggests a market leader. A "2" suggests a strong rating. A "3" is below average.

Bolt-ons for Project

The market offers a substantial number of bolt-ons for Microsoft Project to enhance its functionality. This includes the tools in the following categories, most of which are available on the Internet:

☐ **Visual products.** Some examples include Project Reporter, PERT Chart Expert, and WBS Chart.

Table 10.1 Microsoft Project Selection Criteria

KEY	CRITERIA	RATING	DESCRIPTION
✔	Product functionality	1	Comprehensive, proven, and capable of full lifecycle support.
	Cost	1	Purchase cost. Additional product update cost. Number of users included in discussion.
	Availability of skills	1	Large installed base and a very mature product has resulted in a large pool of experienced Project resources in the marketplace.
✔	Ease of use	1	Intuitive interface, COM+ compatible, and cut/paste support for Windows-based tools.
	Ease of learning	1	Online tutorial, lots of third-party support, and excellent courseware is available.
	Cultural fit with the organization	2	New version of Project supports workgroups. Supports top-down and bottom-up management approaches.
	Technical compatibility	2	Supports the Windows platform. Lots of value-added bolt-ons are available in the market.
✔	Limitations	1	Few limitations encountered in projects from 3 to 200 resources.
	Vendor support	1	Help line, third-party training courses, free Web sites on the Internet, and active newsgroups.

☐ **Analysis tools.** Some examples include Project ResourcePlanner and @Risk for Microsoft Project.

☐ **Controls.** Some examples include Project Partner and Time Disciple.

☐ **Estimating.** Some examples include Workload Arranger and MicroFusion.

☐ **General.** PM Office, ProjX, TimeWatch, Office Timesheet 2000, ProjX Timesheets, Project Commander 98, Teamwork 98, and Workload Arranger.

A Roadmap to Project

As with any mature tool, there is a substantial amount of information available on Microsoft Project on the Internet, within its own help files, and in technical books and journals. This in itself is a strong statement on the successful market penetration this product enjoys. However, too much information does not necessarily help the project manager who is under time pressure to manage a project and must learn to use the essential features of a product well enough to be effective—and learn the more advanced features for a just-in-time learning philosophy. The remaining chapters in this book focus on providing a technical base for the discussions in earlier chapters of this book. As shown in Figure 10.3, chapter 11 focuses on the basics. This includes establishing the project management environment, entering a project plan, saving a baseline, and maintaining

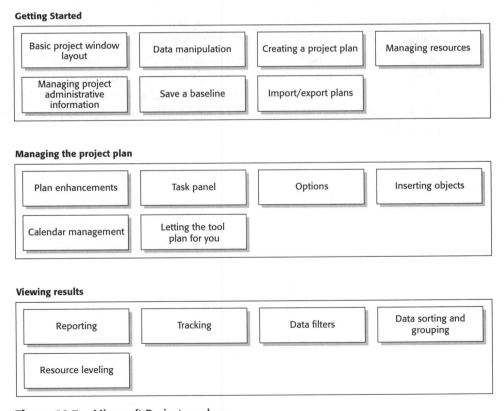

Getting Started

| Basic project window layout | Data manipulation | Creating a project plan | Managing resources |
| Managing project administrative information | Save a baseline | Import/export plans | |

Managing the project plan

| Plan enhancements | Task panel | Options | Inserting objects |
| Calendar management | Letting the tool plan for you | | |

Viewing results

| Reporting | Tracking | Data filters | Data sorting and grouping |
| Resource leveling | | | |

Figure 10.3   Microsoft Project roadmap.

the plan's integrity. Chapter 12 focuses on producing various views and reports for a project plan. Chapter 13 examines some of the other features, including the use of master project plans, rollouts, and other customer features.

Summary

This chapter examined the essentials of building an effective project plan. This was done in the context of establishing a technical infrastructure that supported the techniques and approaches that were discussed in the earlier chapters of this book. Reasons to leverage project estimating tools during the planning stages were examined. The chapter also examined the purpose of project management tools, what to expect for them, and how to select a tool suitable for the organization. Other issues, such as templates and guidelines for building a plan, were also discussed.

The technical infrastructure to implement management approaches includes Microsoft Project 2000. This is the year 2000 release of this powerful toolset that has satisfied many managers in the past decade. This chapter provided reasons to use this tool and provided a roadmap for learning some of the essentials to implement the management techniques already discussed. A list of bolt-ons and other project management tools were reviewed as well.

CHAPTER 11

Creating the Project Plan with Microsoft Project

I n this chapter, the reader will learn how to implement the concepts learned earlier in this book, using the new version of Microsoft Project. You will be shown how to install and navigate through the essential features of this powerful tool to build and resource a project plan based on a business case. Some of the new features that will help you develop more effective project plans immediately are also discussed in this chapter. Readers who are familiar with Microsoft Project should still review this chapter because it focuses on using the tool for implementing good project management techniques as opposed to providing a tutorial view that examines only product features. This chapter focuses on the following topics:

- What's new in Microsoft Project
- Getting started
- Creating a project plan
- Entering phases, activities, tasks
- Modifying a project plan
- Managing resources
- Saving a baseline

- Importing and exporting plans
- Using GanttChartWizard

What's New In Microsoft Project

The latest release of Microsoft Project is an incremental release that is designed to take advantage of Windows 2000, the Internet, and the Web. It offers the following enhancements and improvements to its core functionality.

Functional Enhancements

There are many strong functional enhancements and extensions in the core product, many of which are aimed at improving scheduling capabilities, data validation, ease of use, and improved flexibility. Some specific examples of these are shown in the following list:

- General improvements to the product's scheduling features
- Ability to phase resource availability over time
- Ability to split a task in the same line (e.g., very useful for specifying regular status meetings)
- Support for time-phased resource availability
- Improved data validation and data definition (e.g., identifying a value as an estimate with "?")
- Per task authorization before inclusion in the master project plan
- More generous availability of pick (selection) lists. Custom formulas can also be specified for data fields.
- Improvements to existing features (e.g., resource leveling, tracking, scheduling, printing)
- Support for flexible resource reallocation
- Ability to fill multiple cells with a pattern to improve input capabilities
- Ability to group task and resource information
- Ability to define outline codes
- Ability to roll up subtasks to a task line
- Ability to specify a month value as a duration
- Management of material resources (e.g., computers, furniture)

Reports, Views, and Diagrams

Some of the enhancements to reports, views, and diagrams are described in this section:

☐ Improved Gantt chart functionality. Gantt charts can also be produced for individual team members.

☐ Improvements to diagram views

☐ Wider assortment of views and rollups

☐ Reusable project templates

☐ Views across multiple projects

☐ Printing improvements (e.g., improved scaling)

☐ Network Diagram replaces the PERT chart.

☐ Numerous visual improvements and filtering capabilities

☐ Calendar improvements that create views for specific tasks only

☐ Reporting capabilities for non-project-team staff

Visual Improvements

There are significant visual improvements incorporated into the current release of the product, as follows:

☐ Numerous presentation improvements

☐ An administration module is included to improve visual affects, security features, time administration, and views.

☐ New capability to attach graphical indicators to custom fields to improve identification of key indicators

☐ Visual warnings are available about impending deadlines.

☐ Variable row heights are supported.

Supports Multi-Users

The current release supports multi-users and workgroups with the following features:

☐ Multi-user/workgroup support through the central workgroup system

☐ Ability for team member notification

☐ Interaction with email servers

☐ Manipulation of central messages

Web and Internet Capabilities

The current release is Web-enabled, offering the following capabilities:

☐ Web-based "project central" allows resources to maintain their own tasks on a master plan.

☐ Project Central allows status updates to be rolled up into group reports.

Additional Capabilities

The current release of Project offers the following capabilities in addition to those already mentioned:

☐ OLE DB access and COM add-ons

☐ Integration with Outlook

☐ Single Document Interface support

☐ Active Accessibility programming interfaces for third-party support

☐ Performance improvements, roaming support, support for the MS Windows Object Model

Getting Started

Building your first project plan with Microsoft Project can be done relatively quickly and painlessly—including product installation. This section shows you how this is done.

Installing Project

Installation of most desktop Windows-based products follows a standard process, namely:

☐ Insert the CD-ROM into the drive (one that can automatically display the install shield) or select the INSTALL/SETUP option from a directory listing or menu.

☐ Wait until the install shield appears and select the installation option.

The remainder of the process is menu-driven and proceeds smoothly as long as the Windows 2000 components are accessible, there are no software conflicts, and the hardware environment is robust enough to support Project. Microsoft Project, however, is no longer a stand-alone

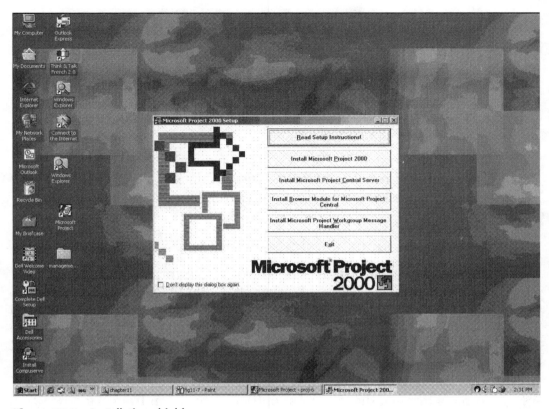

Figure 11.1 Installation shield.

product, and it supports a multi-user environment that adds some complexity to the standard process under a full, distributed installation.

The initial screen offers several options to reflect the functionality in the new release, as shown in Figure 11.1. This list contains options to install the Project Central Server, a browser for the server, and a global message handler. The instructions option will contain the most current installation details available at the time your CD was burned.

System Requirements

The new release of Microsoft Project has the following system requirements:

☐ **CPU.** Minimum requirement is a Pentium 75. However, trying to install Windows 98+ on this configuration and running any substantial application is terribly inefficient. Our recommendation is a minimum of a Pentium 166 MHz or higher. Project Central requires 200 MHz or higher.

☐ **Operating system.** The Windows 2000 environment is highly recommended. A Windows NT Workstation 4.0 or higher with Service Pack 4 or higher is also supported.

☐ **Hard disk space.** This varies between 40 and 210 MB, depending on the components being installed.

☐ **RAM.** At least 40 MB of RAM is recommended. The Project Central component requires 128 MB+. We recommend 132 MB of RAM for either operation to receive good performance from the application.

Working with Previous Versions of Project

Microsoft Project 2000 saves files in Project 98 format, as well as in other Office formats (e.g., Excel Workbook, Excel Pivot Table, Access Database). It can also save data in a tab-delimited text or comma-delimited format in a flat file. These options are available under File, Save As in the "Save as type" field on the panel that appears. Project 2000 can read .MPX files from Windows 95 versions of the product, but not .MPP format files. This will require conversion of Windows 95 .MPP format files to .MPX formats through the "Save As" option. Conversion from Windows 98 is more straightforward. Project 2000 can read these .MPP format files directly and will convert them for you.

Be sure to validate all your information after every project file is opened in Project 2000 because some data may be lost in the process, specifically custom fields, views, macros, and tables.

Getting Help

Several levels of support are available under the Help menu option in the tool's main window, consistent with options offered in most Microsoft packages. This includes basic Project help <F1>, which starts by allowing you to search for specific topics. Clicking on the Office Assistant also provides this level of help. You can choose the appearance of the Office Assistant (e.g., whether it appears as a paperclip, puzzle, or globe) from its properties panel (e.g., right-click on the Office Assistant icon).

You also have the option of displaying the entire help contents and index panel, as shown in Figure 11.2. A "Getting Started" option allows quick

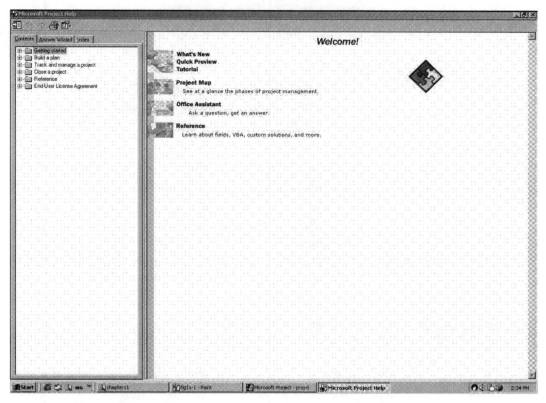

Figure 11.2   Help dialog box.

entry to a tutorial and a project map. Another option, "What's This," offers a method to retrieve information on any object in the Project window. This is done by selecting the option from the pull-down menu (the pointer changes to an arrow and a question mark) and clicking on an object to display information about it.

Basic Layout

Project's basic user interface layout is intuitive and effective, and supports project managers in planning their projects. The basic Project window is divided into three main areas. The largest area consists of two panes. Another area consists of the standard Windows pull-down menus and action icons that are present in most Microsoft applications. The third area consists of a set of icons that provide quick access to specific views.

In the largest area of the window, the left pane manages a task-oriented view of a project plan as a hierarchy. The right pane manages a Gantt diagram view of this data. The size of either pane can be modified by dragging the center window lines to the left or right. The task pane can display additional columns of information, such as task duration, start date, finish date, resources, and predecessors (dependencies). As shown in Figure 11.3, the main Project window also consists of several other areas.

The icons on the left side of the window offer other standard views that project managers will want to regularly manipulate. The most commonly used ones are the Gantt Chart, Tracking Gantt, and Resource Sheet. Each of the views reflects modified information automatically. For example, if you enter a task in the Gantt chart, it automatically becomes visible in the Tracking Gantt. The contents of the views can be passed through a

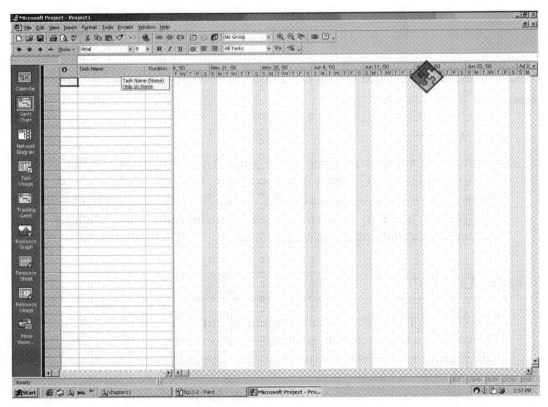

Figure 11.3   Basic project window layout.

variety of filters—for example, all tasks, completed tasks, milestones, critical tasks, in-progress tasks, and summary tasks—depending on the context you want to express. The purpose of each of these views is described here:

- **Calendar.** This view provides a common view of a calendar month in a block format with the project tasks superimposed on top of it. The calendar also provides access to other views, such as the Task Information dialog box. Double-clicking on a day provides access to a Timescale dialog box that allows you to modify the appearance of the calendar through titles, shading, patterns, and formatting.

- **Gantt chart.** This is arguably the most common format for expressing a project plan. This view contains two main components. Project information is usually entered in the columns on the left side of the view. The other component is a chart that represents the project activities graphically. This displays activities as horizontal bars with superimposed resources, start and end dates, dependencies, and other characteristics. The table view of the project plan includes the following standard columns: Task Name, Duration, Start, Finish, Predecessors, and Resource Names. The visual component of the Gantt chart is automatically updated with information that is manipulated in the columns.

- **Network diagram.** This provides a task-dependency view of the project plan in diagram form. The visual presentation helps you understand the dependencies and the critical path of the project. Task information is displayed in boxes, with the shape of the box indicating the type of information. The shapes of the boxes can be customized through the Format, Box command from the main menu or by highlighting a box and right-clicking on it. For example a standard task might be represented as a square, while a milestone could be represented as a diamond. The mouse approach also conveniently shows you the definition of the box that is selected. Dependencies are represented by lines connecting the boxes. You can use the Zoom feature to increase or decrease the amount of information visible in a view.

- **Task usage.** This offers a task-oriented view that shows the resources that are allocated to a task. This allows you to manage the roles and skill-sets available at a task level. This provides a good approach to support week-to-week planning on the project.

☐ **Tracking Gantt.** This is based on the common Gantt view that many practitioners use to visually represent a project plan and track planned versus actual figures against a saved baseline.

☐ **Resource graph.** This view consists of a graph that shows resource usage across the project against time. This will allow you to visually identify periods of time when resources are overutilized and under-utilized. This view can be used with the Gantt Leveling view to reduce resource overallocation.

☐ **Resource sheet.** This view shows information about resources, such as their names, billing information, and role. This and the Resource Form are frequently used dialog boxes in most planning sessions. A change made to a name in this view is automatically reflected in all its occurrences in the project plan (e.g., changing Katie to Kathleen).

☐ **Resource usage.** This view offers a chart-oriented perspective of resource allocation across the project.

☐ **More views.** There are additional views, including Pessimistic Gantt (based on Pert Analysis), Optimistic Gantt (based on Pert Analysis), Resource Name Form, Task Details Form, Task Form, Task Name Form, Descriptive Network Diagram, Bar Rollup, Milestone Date Rollup, Detail Gantt, Leveling Gantt, and Relationship Diagram.

The top portion of the Project window includes the standard pull-down menus and toolbars that are common in Windows-based applications. The basic functionality offered under the primary menu options is as follows:

☐ **File.** This menu option provides functions to manage information at the file level. The "Save As" and the "Save As Web Page" options are used to save the project information in various formats.

☐ **Edit.** This menu option provides access to the standard clipboard copy/paste/cut suboptions. This option also allows you to link/unlink tasks on the Gantt chart to reflect task dependencies.

☐ **View.** This menu option provides access to a collection of diagrams, views, and reports. It also provides access to header and footer customization. A "Zoom" command is available to manipulate the amount of information shown in the window. Since project planning involves moving between details and the big picture, this is a highly useful option.

□ **Insert.** This menu option allows tasks, project plans, and other objects to be inserted into a project plan.

□ **Format.** This menu option provides functions to manipulate the visual appearance of the results shown on the screen. It also contains a "Timescale" function that is frequently used to manage the amount of information that is visible in a Gantt chart according to the duration of the tasks.

□ **Tools.** This menu option provides access to workgroup functions, resourcing options, and other customization features.

□ **Project.** This menu option provides functionality affecting the project environment, including the ability to set filters for data, groups, task information, and project summary information.

□ **Window.** This menu option provides access to the standard functions available to manipulate the Project window(s).

□ **Help.** This menu option provides access to various help functions, including an index, context level help, and an option to repair detected errors in the application.

Data Manipulation

If you're new to Microsoft Project, you'll quickly get used to the dialog boxes and some of the time-saving features it offers. This section gives you a head start in understanding or recognizing some of the methods available to you for manipulating the user interface more quickly and efficiently.

Entering Information

Fortunately, Project is not a process-driven application, and consequently it is not dependent on the order of the information that is entered. It is relatively tolerant of oversights and mistakes, offering opportunities to fix these problems with minimal effort after they are generated. For example, you can set up the resource lists and tasks, and then connect them, or start with the tasks and proceed there.

Mouse Clicks

Double-clicking on the left mouse button generally brings up a context-sensitive dialog box to capture detailed information. For example, doing this operation on a task line on the Gantt chart displays a Task

Information panel. Clicking on the right mouse button displays panels to manage object properties.

OLE Support

You can copy data from Excel and Word directly into Project. For example, you can enter a list of tasks in Word, each separated by a new line, and then block copy them into the Gantt chart. Each task gets its own line in the Gantt chart.

Inserting/Deleting Tasks

You can quickly insert or delete a task line in the Gantt chart by pressing the INSERT or DELETE keys respectively. The insert operation pushes tasks down and produces a new blank line. The delete option deletes the selected task. Insert is also available from the pull-down Insert menu.

Manipulating Task Levels

Earlier chapters of this book discussed the activity or task hierarchy. Microsoft Project manages project details at the task level. You can create nested levels by clicking on the left and right arrows in the formatting toolbar. Selecting a task and clicking on the left arrow button promotes a task to a higher (parent) level. Selecting a task and clicking on the right button demotes it to a lower (child) level. These operations affect all corresponding lower-level tasks. For example, consider the following set of activities to create a test plan:

```
Review business requirements
Build test scripts
Build test cases
Conduct unit test
Gather results
```

Since these activities have a common theme, it is useful to create another task to precede the other ones, as follows:

```
Unit Test
Review business requirements
Build test scripts
Build test cases
Conduct unit test
Gather results
```

"Unit Test" can now be promoted by selecting it and clicking on the left arrow button. The other tasks could also be highlighted and demoted by clicking on the right arrow button. As shown in Figure 11.4, two hierarchy levels are created.

Now suppose you want to group the Unit Test task hierarchy under a higher-level name for more general testing. Positioning the cursor on the Unit Test line of the Gantt chart and pressing the INSERT key a few times inserts a few blank task lines. You can enter "Testing" above the "Unit Test" task to produce the following task list:

```
Testing
Unit Test
     Review business requirements
     Build test scripts
     Build test cases
     Conduct unit test
     Gather results
```

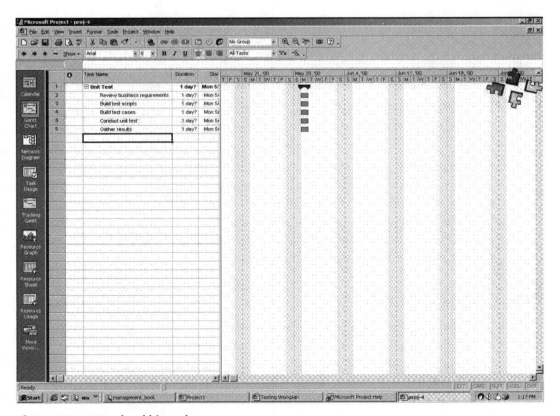

Figure 11.4   Two-level hierarchy.

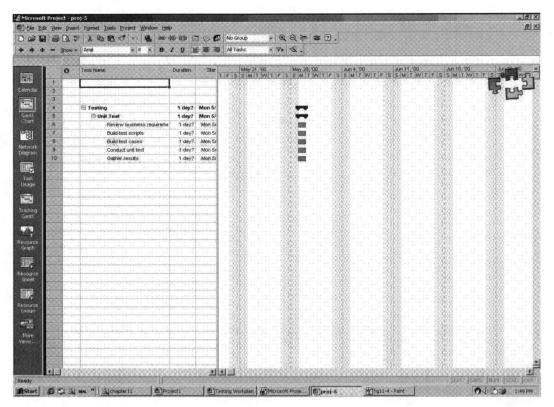

Figure 11.5 Three-level task hierarchy.

Selecting "Unit Test" and clicking on the right arrow moves it and all its dependent tasks under Testing as a single group. Figure 11.5 shows the results of this action. Figure 11.6 shows the Testing function expanded to include a set of tasks to establish a test environment and another set of tasks to conduct a system test. The dates have also been adjusted to reflect some of the task dependencies.

Rolling Up Task Levels

As shown in Figure 11.6, parent tasks are preceded by a "-" sign when lower-level tasks are visible in the window. Clicking on the "-" hides these tasks, and changes the symbol to a "+." The result of doing this for the "Test Environment" and "Unit Test" activities is shown in Figure 11.7. Clicking on the "+" toggles back to the detailed task display view. The +/- symbols from the toolbar can also be used to do this task manip-

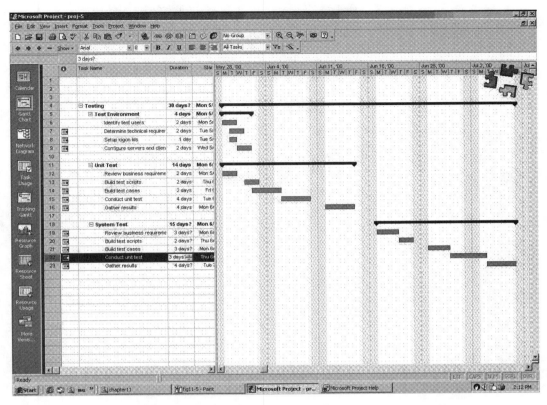

Figure 11.6   Expanding the Testing function.

ulation. The Show option on the toolbar provides a double + (i.e., ++) option that expands all detail tasks at once and makes them visible in the window. The same option allows you to display task levels up to a nested level of nine. Realistically, nesting beyond five or six levels deep becomes cumbersome to manipulate and should be avoided on your project plans.

Manipulating Time Bars

Modifying time that is already allocated to a task is a frequent operation in project planning and tracking. You can visually inspect a task's timeline on the Gantt chart diagram. More detailed information, such as the task name, start date, duration, and finish date, can be observed by leaving the mouse cursor hanging over the time bar. This information can be modified in several ways, as follows:

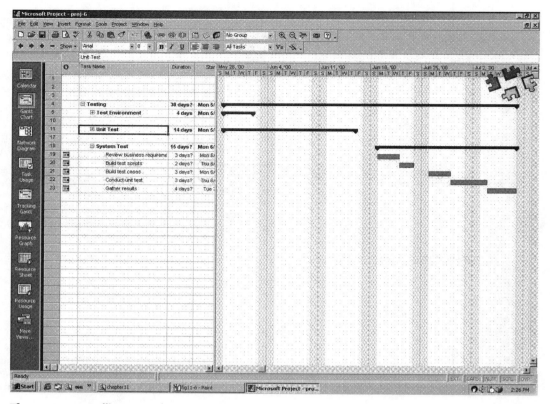

Figure 11.7 Rolling up tasks.

☐ To drag and drop, position the mouse pointer on the right side of the time bar you want to modify and click on the left mouse button to select the task. If the cursor turns into an arrow that points right, you can hold the mouse button down and drag the time bar to the right to reflect the new timeframe. This change is automatically reflected in the duration column. Dragging the time bar to the left will shrink the task duration.

☐ Position the mouse pointer on a task and click on the right button. This provides access to a task information panel that can be used to explicitly enter task time information.

☐ Double-click on the task in the Task Name column to gain access to the task information panel.

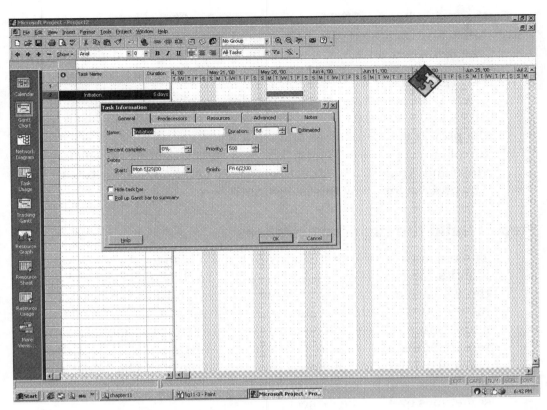

Figure 11.8 Task Information panel.

You can also shift a task's effective dates by using the methods above with a slight modification to the process. Using the drag and drop method, move the mouse cursor on top of the task time bar until it changes into a four-way arrow icon. As shown in Figure 11.8, you can also simply enter the Start and Finish dates in the Task Information dialog box.

Creating a Project Plan

To demonstrate the project-building capabilities of Project, consider this short business problem. Suppose a business wanted to build a Web-based component to enroll users into a bonus plan that gives them loyalty points on every visit they make to the corporate Web site. Further suppose that the project has received the full support of executive management, which has in turn identified you as the overall project manager for the initiative. The delivery deadline is two months away, driven by a digital marketing campaign to draw traffic to the Web site beginning on that date.

There is, of course, no correct, absolute, or single answer for building a project plan for this initiative. However, a plan that allows us to deliver the project successfully as defined in chapter 5 is the primary driver of the planning process. The project plan can be built iteratively in several steps and would likely take a complete eight-hour day or two to build. The process for doing this is described here.

Step 1: Build the High-Level Phases

The objective of the first step is to build a high-level project plan that identifies major phases and deliverables, as shown in Figure 11.9. Since the delivery date is already known, this establishes the project imple-mentation date, which is shown as a milestone on the plan. The other major phases in the expected lifecycle of this project include initiation, requirements, development, integration, testing, and rollout. It is not unusual to miss a few phases at this stage of the lifecycle. Inconsistencies in the plan will be caught through the iterative planning process, and sometimes even as the project progresses.

The task names can be entered directly under the Task Name column in the Gantt chart with a blank line separating each phase name. You should start with a new project file and save it under the name example1 with the Project file format. The usual good practices of regularly saving the project file and making regular backups apply here.

It is useful to modify the timeline of the Gantt diagram to make it easier to visualize the whole project through the Format-Timescale option. Get a sense of whether the planning is being done at the right level of detail by selecting a Major scale in Months and a Minor scale in weeks. A time-line can also be built using the deadline dates that the executive has spec-ified—namely, that the implementation is two months away. Assuming a start date of May 28, the implementation date is then July 28. This is expressed as a milestone date by specifying a duration of zero days in the Task Information panel.

Working backwards from this time, we want to express the duration for the other high-level phases. Testing should be less than half of the over-

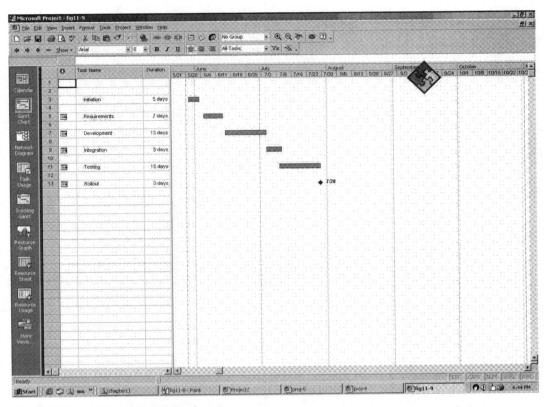

Figure 11.9   High-level project plan.

all project lifecycle, but still substantive in duration. The other estimates are based on experience of managing projects that sound like they are of the same order of complexity as this one. This analysis results in the following estimates for the task durations:

- [ ] Initiation: 5 days
- [ ] Requirements: 7 days
- [ ] Development: 13 days
- [ ] Integration: 5 days
- [ ] Testing: 15 days

The result of this first step shows the overall timeline and complexity of the project, and allows the manager to start building the project team and establishing important user contacts.

Step 2: Add Detailed Tasks

If the high-level plan appears to be satisfactory, the next step is to drill down on the detailed tasks. This will promote the existing tasks to a phase level, making room for the details to be identified. For initiation, we want to confirm the stakeholders, assemble the project team, build a testing approach, and conduct a risk assessment.

For the requirements phase, we want to gather technical requirements for the different infrastructure environments, as well as the business requirements for the solution. Since one of the major pieces of the solution is to connect to a third-party vendor that manages the loyalty point program, the interface requirements must be gathered as well.

In the infrastructure phase, users who are expected to work on the application in some capacity are identified and provided with appropriate logon privileges. The development and testing, and potentially the production environment, infrastructure are also identified. There may be a need to send out purchase orders for new software or hardware equipment. The development and testing environments are also established.

A new phase is needed to be added to the project plan, namely, "Analyze and model requirements." This will produce business specifications, an updated object model, and a component specification. The interface requirements will also be modeled in this phase. Another phase needs to be added to the project plan to update the corporate architecture and to get formal approval for the changes.

The development phase requires the development specifications to be built, the components to be coded, and unit testing to be conducted. The code will need to be updated iteratively as bugs or inconsistencies are identified as testing progresses.

The integration phase is used to integrate the different components and to introduce the link to the third-party vendor. This phase will require interaction with third-party resources and may involve a series of meetings and discussions.

The testing phase is used to identify testing users, establish user IDs, and conduct several levels of testing. Integration and system testing provide an end-to-end test of the application. Stress testing is used to evaluate the application's stability, performance, and scalability. Acceptance testing is the final level of testing before a decision is made to accept the system, make more changes, or take some other action. Any problems discovered in the testing activities will probably need to be corrected and will require a pass through the testing phases again. The project plan includes some time to accommodate several iterations of this process. If too many problems are detected and the iterations are not getting the system to a cleaner state, the project manager will need to take some corrective action immediately.

Another phase was added to the project plan to assemble the test results, documentation, and any other information that is needed to help get the stakeholders and steering committees to make a go/no go decision. This should preferably be captured in writing.

The rollout activities have been rolled into an implementation phase. This also includes building an implementation approach, a training strategy, and a contingency plan.

One additional level of detail has expanded the project plan from less than a dozen tasks to 92 or so tasks. We still have not included every step that is likely to be followed in this project. For example, the business requirements activities may require several meetings that will themselves require several organizational steps each. Adding this additional level of detail will make this plan too cumbersome to build, maintain, and use. A project manager will then spend too much time tracking, and not enough resolving problems or issues that inevitably come up on every project. A value judgment needs to be made when determining the level of detail to include in a project plan.

The number of tasks in this project plan are sufficient for a project of this size and complexity. The plan still requires additional details in terms of resources and task dependencies. These are described in the next section of this chapter. The task list should be reviewed and vetted a few times with key resources and stakeholders to reduce the likelihood that major items are missed at this stage. The following text list shows the task hierarchy for these phases. This list was extracted from the project plan created in Project using the Export features described later in this section.

```
Initiation
      Confirm stakeholders
      Assemble project team
      Identify key users
      Identify external vendors
      Establish status requirements
      Revise project charter
```

```
        Revise project plan
        Conduct risk assessment
        Build testing approach
        Identify high-level requirements
        Build high-level test cases
        Identify acceptance criteria
        Get user sign-off

    Requirements
        Gather development environment requirements
        Gather vendor interface requirements
        Gather business requirements
        Get sign-offs

    Infrastructure
        Identify logon users
        Create Logon IDs
        Update infrastructure documentation
        Establish development environment
        Establish testing environment

    Analyze and model requirements
        Develop requirement specifications
        Update object model
        Define component interfaces and methods
        Define user interface interaction

    Architecture
        Update architecture documentation
        Approve changes

    Development
        Build development specfications
        Code component modules
        Update user interface
        Build control reports
        Develop unit test scripts
        Conduct unit testing

    Integration
        Build integration plan
        Quality assure vendor interface
        Integrate Components

    Testing
        Integration & System Testing
            Identify testing users
            Build testing approach
            Build test scripts
            Build test cases
            Conduct tests
            Gather results
```

```
          Stress Testing
             Identify testing users
             Build testing approach
             Build test scripts
             Build test cases
             Conduct tests
             Gather results

          Acceptance Testing
             Identify testing users
             Build testing approach
             Build test scripts
             Build test cases
             Conduct tests
             Gather results

          Final Sign-off
             Assemble test rsults
             Assemble project documentation
             Distribute package to stakeholders
             Conduct final presentation
             Make go/no go decision

    Implementation
             Build implementation approach
             Define training strategy
             Define backout/contingency strategy
             Train users
             Implement solution
             Product rollout
```

Step 3: Adjust Timeline

With the task list pretty much complete for the present, the start dates, durations, and end dates can be adjusted for each task. As long as two of these three pieces of information are known, the remaining one can be derived. With the addition of the new phases, the original task (now called phase) timelines will need to be adjusted. However, every attempt will be made to preserve the original delivery date. Figures 11.10, 11.11, and 11.12 show the timeline for the project plan. The two-month steering committee delivery date is still preserved. The timeline is clearly very tight with little slack or room for time overruns. The integration phases are very tight. Final acceptance of the project is also tight and will require the stakeholders to make themselves available as specified in the plan if the implementation date is to be met. Development activities are

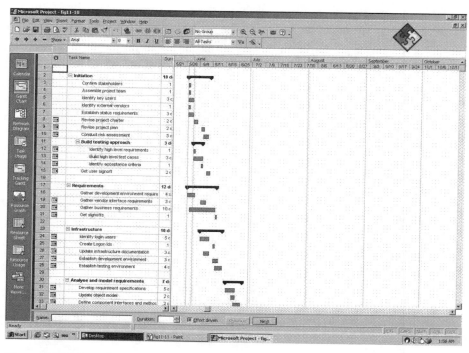

Figure 11.10 Project timeline (window 1 of 3).

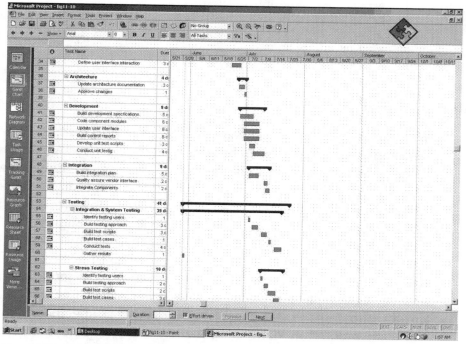

Figure 11.11 Project timeline (window 2 of 3).

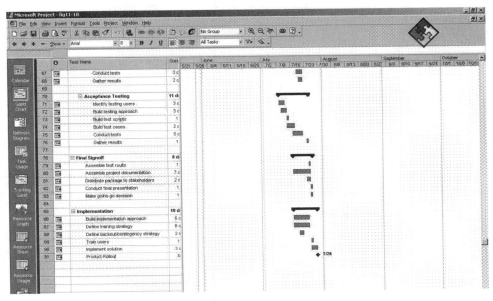

Figure 11.12   Project timeline (window 3 of 3).

conducted in parallel and will assume that the developers are in close communication with each other during the process.

Managing Resources

Once the project manager has an opportunity to understand the overall project plan, a reasonable project team can be assembled. One approach is to build a complete project team's role definitions and then find resources to fill them. Another approach is to begin with a core team of practitioners you've already worked with and then identify the roles that remain to be filled. Figure 11.13 shows the team roles that are required for the project.

Resource names can be allocated to the roles on the project team organization chart. The number of resources required per role are also identified. The total team complement is 13 (including the project manager) on a full-time basis and 2 resources on a part-time basis. Figure 11.14 shows the actual resource names allocated to each role.

The team names can be entered into the resource sheet in Microsoft Project to make them available for assignment to specific tasks. Figure 11.15 shows the appearance of the resource sheet after the team members have been added to it.

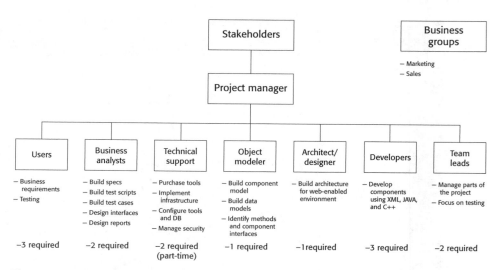

Figure 11.13 Project team roles.

Resources can be allocated to tasks using the Resources tab in the Task Information panel. There is a one-to-many relationship between a task and its resources. Resources can be allocated to a task using an item selection list that appears when you click in the Resource Name row. The number of Units that a resource is allocated to a task for can also be specified in the same tab. Leaving the column entry blank defaults it to a value of 100%, representing full-time involvement in the task. A percentage can also be entered into the column as well, say 10%. If a day has been specified as containing 8 hours, this translates to 80 minutes for the task. The percentage values should be used if there is an intent to use the resource

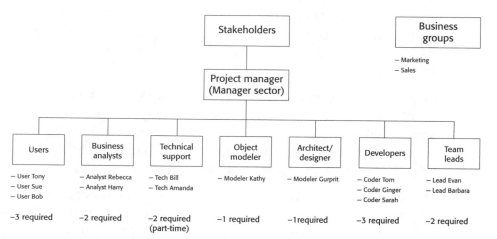

Figure 11.14 Project team.

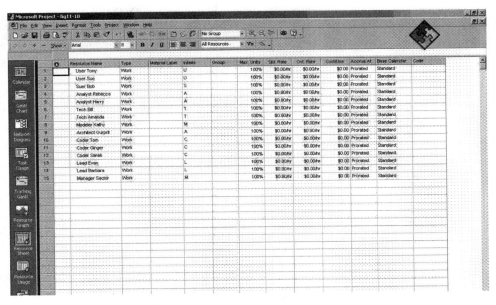

Figure 11.15   Resource sheet.

capabilities to track usage and cost on the project. Figure 11.16 provides a view of the Gantt diagram with the addition of resources to the tasks. Displaying the resource sheet shows the resources that are overallocated in their duties.

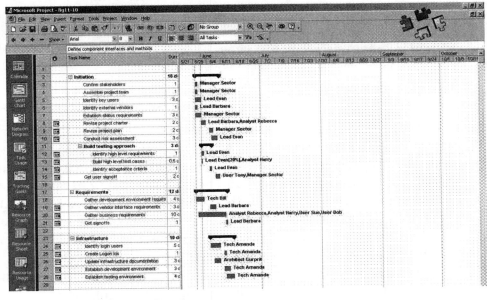

Figure 11.16   Resource allocation.

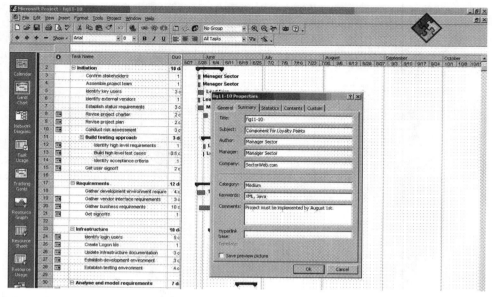

Figure 11.17 Project Properties.

Entering Project Administrative Information

The File, Properties option allows project administrative information to be entered for the project in the summary tab. As shown in Figure 11.17, this includes providing the filename, subject, author, manager, and comments. This information appears on printed copies of the project plan and in other miscellaneous views as well.

Saving a Baseline

Saving a project plan as a baseline allows it to be used to track progress against the original estimates. A baseline can be saved for a project plan at anytime. A common approach is to build a project plan with a reasonable degree of thoroughness and then to save it as a baseline to support tracking activities. This can then be used to compare actual numbers received from the project teams. At some point, there may be a need to adjust a fairly high number of dates in the plan. A new baseline can be saved and used to continue tracking the project, but with a new state for comparison. For new project files, the save option allows a baseline to be saved at anytime. New baselines can be saved using the Tools-Tracking, Save Baseline option from the main menu.

Import/Export Plans

Export functionality is available from the File, Save As menu option. A "Save as type" value must also be specified, for example as a "Text (Tab delimited)." Project supports a diverse set of export maps including a "Who Does What" report, Compare to Baseline, Default task information, Task "Export Table" map, and Top Level Tasks list.

New Import/Export maps can also be created using tasks, resources, and assignments. For example, selecting task allows specification of a combination of columns from a fairly large list, including Actual Cost, duration, %Complete, Actual Finish, Milestone, Priority, Predecessors, IDs, Name (for Task Name), under a "Task Mapping" tab, as shown in Figure 11.18. The delimiter value can also be varied (e.g., tab, space, comma).

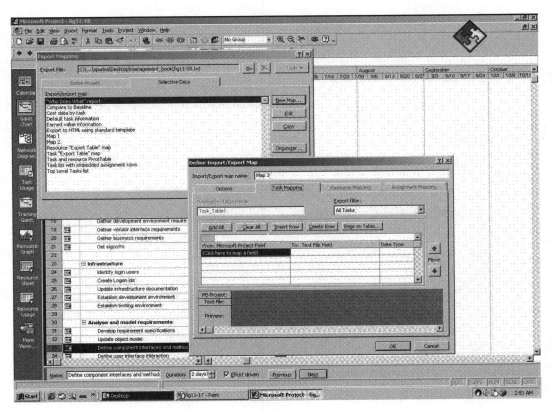

Figure 11.18   Define Import/Export Map.

GanttChartWizard

The GanttChartWizard can be used to customize the appearance of the Gantt chart. It is available under the Format pull-down menu and also appears as an icon in the toolbar with a surface picture that includes three horizontal bars and a magic wand. This wizard leads you through several steps that begin with a standard wizard panel, shown in Figure 11.19. Some of the steps are skipped, depending on the selections that are made. For example, if you select "Critical Path" in step 2, the wizard jumps straight into step 9. However, if you select "Custom Gantt Chart," the wizard proceeds to step 3.

The first interactive panel of the wizard is also step 2 in the process. It allows you to specify a type of filter for the information you want to display in your Gantt chart. This includes whether the view should be standard, critical path, or baseline. A lot of additional options are available in the pick list under the "other" option. Selecting a "Custom Gantt Chart" leads you through steps 3 to 8. These allow you to specify the separation of critical from noncritical tasks, and the color and patterns of critical tasks. They also allow you to specify the styles of normal, summary, and milestones tasks. Standard is the default option in step 2.

Step 9 of the wizard allows you to specify the type of information you want displayed in your Gantt chart. This includes a combination of resources, dates, and custom information. Selecting the custom option takes you through steps 10 to 13. These allow you to select the type of information to display on the left or right of a taskbar. You can also dis-

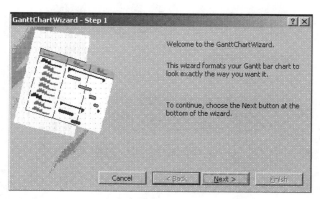

Figure 11.19 Using the GanttChartWizard.

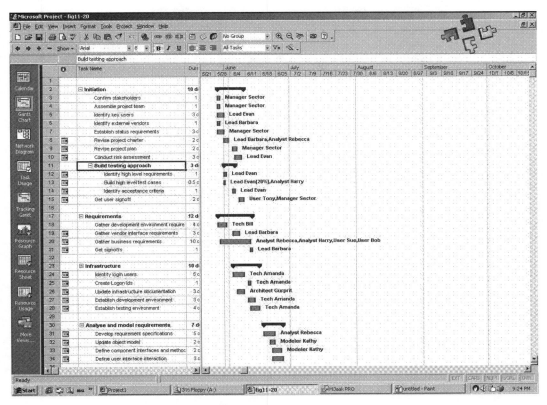

Figure 11.20 Visual results of GanttChartWizard.

play information inside a bar. The information that can be selected for display includes %complete, constraint date, duration, finish, name, priority, resource names, start, and total slack. Displaying resources and dates is standard. The customization option also allows you to select the information that appears with the status bars and the milestones. The milestones appear as diamonds. Essentially the same list of options is available for this step as well.

Step 13 allows you to link dependent tasks. Step 14 allows you to format the Gantt chart according to the options that were selected. Figure 11.20 shows the results of executing the wizard with the following options selected for steps 2 through 13:

```
Step 2: select Custom Gantt Chart
Step 3: select No, Thanks (which makes the wizard skip directly to step 5)
Step 5: select Color = Lime, Pattern=accept the default value, end
   shapes=• (a circle)
Step 6: accept the default values
```

```
Step 7: accept the default values
Step 8: select Total slack
Step 9: select Resources and dates (which makes the wizard skip directly
   to step 13)
Step 13: select Yes, please
```

The results are applied to the Gantt chart and displayed. The Gantt-ChartWizard can be reapplied to change the appearance of the Gantt chart. However, the original defaults are applied in each of the steps, so it is necessary to reenter all the information again. For example, the choices above are difficult to read, and so it's possible to relaunch the wizard to make the changes contained in the following steps, with the results shown in Figure 11.20:

```
Step 2: select Custom Gantt Chart
Step 3: select No, Thanks (which makes the wizard skip directly to step 5)
Step 5: select Color = blue, Pattern=accept the default value, end
   shapes=■ (a rectangle or bar)
Step 6: accept the default values
Step 7: accept the default values
Step 8: select None, thanks
Step 9: select Resources and dates (which makes the wizard skip directly
   to step 13)
Step 13: select Yes, please
```

Summary

This chapter focused on implementing the project planning and tracking concepts discussed earlier in this book. The new release of Microsoft Project was used as a tool to accomplish this. This release contains many improvements and enhancements that center on making the tool more effective for project management and project tracking in environments that are Web-enabled. These were itemized in this chapter within specific categories.

The primary views of the Project interface, its areas, and its functions were examined in the context of a sample project plan for constructing a Web component. Readers were shown how to begin with a statement of a business problem and to iteratively build a project plan through several steps. A project team was defined using a role-based approach. These resources were allocated to the project plan.

Methods of adjusting task information and timelines were also examined in the chapter using dialog boxes and panels. The project plan was saved

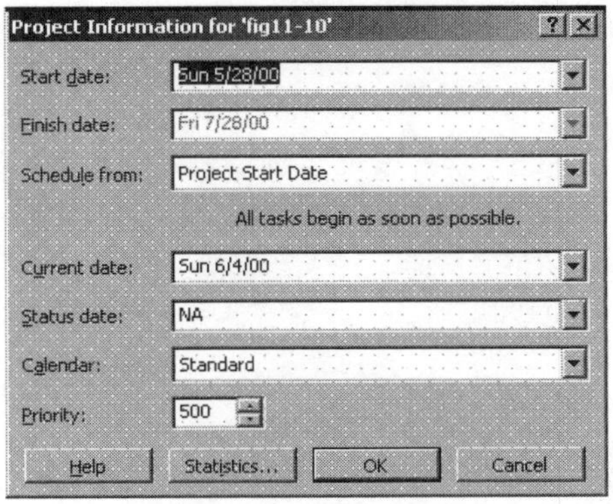

Figure 11.21   Project information.

as a baseline to support the project manager's future tracking efforts. This chapter also provided examples for exporting parts of a project plan as a delimited flat file. A set of views can be established for a variety of export formats. Project level information can be maintained using the File, Properties dialog box. This contains a variety of tabs, including General, Summary, Statistics, Contents, and Custom. Some of this information is also visible under the Project, Project Information option, as shown in Figure 11.21. This dialog box can be used to enter a project Start date, Current date, base calendar, and scheduling approach. The project start date is important because a lot of scheduling is done from this point.

The GanttChartWizard was used to modify the appearance of a Gantt chart. This wizard contains 14 steps that allow customization of the taskbars, the way they interact, and the information that appears around them and inside them. The wizard can be rerun at any time to modify the appearance of a Gantt chart.

CHAPTER 12

Project Tracking and Reporting Using Microsoft Project

I n this chapter the reader will learn how to use some of Microsoft's functions for establishing and formatting its environment. The reader will also be shown how to manage additional information for project plans at the task level, including the following:

- Recurring tasks
- Inserting columns
- Planning by milestones
- Task panel information
- Options management
- Calendar management
- Letting the tool plan for you
- Task linking
- Critical tasks
- Managing resources

Enhancing the Project Plan

The project plan developed in chapter 11 could be expanded several ways to capture management activities. Including a few more milestones in the plan would demonstrate the importance of some key dates to the project team. These will also support the project tracking process and give an early warning if there is danger of missing the project's delivery date. Another useful addition to the project plan is the inclusion of a recurring task that shows the timing of weekly status meetings. For example, these may occur every Monday for a couple of hours. Prior releases of Project made this difficult to represent on the Gantt chart without adding unnecessary time to the project plan. The task representing the project status meetings appeared as a solid line for the duration of the task. The current release of Project allows an activity to be divided into segments that more accurately represent a weekly status meeting. This option is available under Insert, Recurring Task from the toolbar. Figure 12.1 shows a panel that can be used to schedule a weekly status meeting very Monday for the duration of the project.

Figure 12.2 shows the result of adding a weekly status meeting to be held every Monday. Resources are not yet assigned, but the assumption is that the whole project team will attend parts of the meeting. The figure also shows the addition of several key milestones that can be used to track the important events. A recurring task is represented by an icon showing two circular arrows in the ID column.

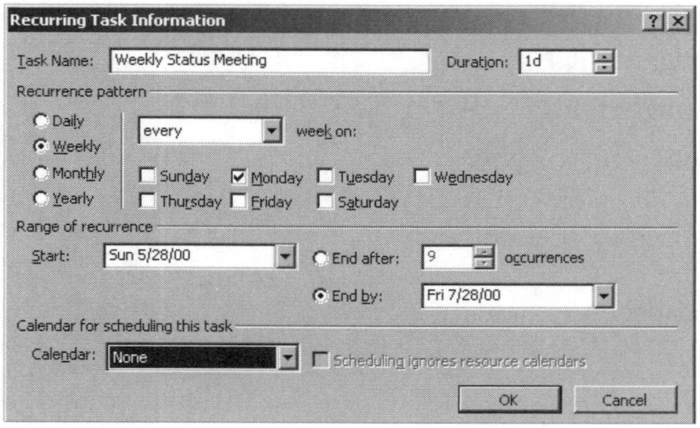

Figure 12.1   Creating a recurring task.

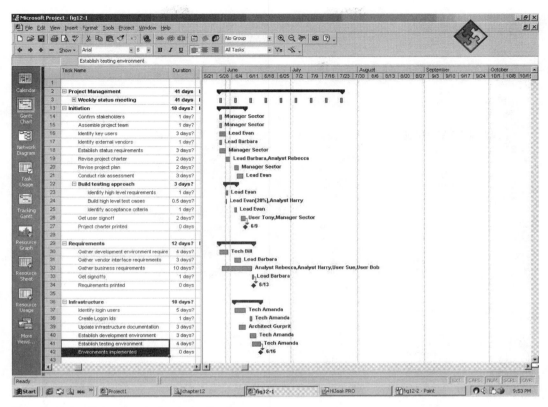

Figure 12.2 Recurring tasks and milestones.

Filling Out the Task Panel

In chapter 11, the task name column in the Gantt chart was primarily used to create and manage tasks. As shown in Figure 12.3, there is a dialog box that can be used to manage significantly more information about a task. This dialog box can be accessed by double-clicking on a task name, pressing shift-F2, or selecting Project, Task Information from the taskbar. The dialog box contains five tabs, as explained in this section.

General Tab

Use this tab to specify basic information about a task. The name field contains the name of the task. Entering information into the duration, dates, and priority fields can affect the tool's ability to generate the plan automatically. For example, the duration field can affect the start and

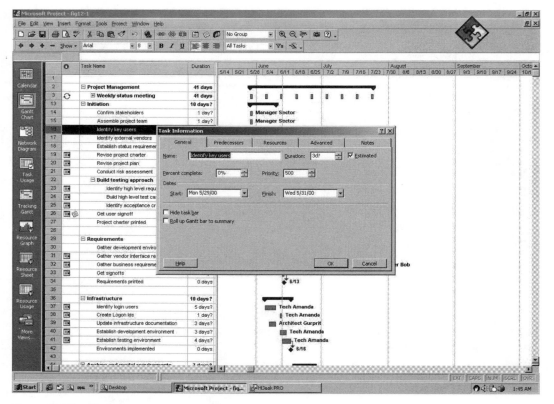

Figure 12.3 Task management panel.

end dates, or entering start and end dates will calculate a duration. The duration then continues to be generated by any changes made to either of these fields. The duration field contains the length of the task. A new feature in the new product release allows a duration to be entered as an estimate (shown by the ? sign). The Percent complete field is used for tracking purposes. A value of 0 means that the task has not started. A value of 100 means the task is completed. The Priority field can hold a number between 0 and 1000. This value is used by project to set the priority of tasks so that the project plan can sequence them appropriately. The Start and Finish dates specify the start of a task and its completion date, respectively. The tool generates a warning if the Start date is given before the project start dates specified under the Project, Project Information option from the toolbar.

Predecessors Tab

Use this tab to specify or remove dependencies between tasks. The task-linking functionality is also available, but to a more limited extent, from the Edit, Link Tasks toolbar option. When using the toolbar approach, the process of linking tasks involves highlighting adjacent rows in the Gantt table and selecting the option. The results can be seen by connecting lines between task rows in the Gantt chart. The result can also be seen in this tab, as shown in Figure 12.4, where the ID field contains the ID of the predecessor task. The Task Name field contains the name of the predecessor task. The Type and Lag columns are derived from the properties of the predecessor task. You can also specify the Predecessor task(s) by entering IDs directly under this tab.

Resource Tab

Use this tab to select the resources being allocated to a task. This function was demonstrated in chapter 11. The resource allocation selected in the dialog box shown in Figure 12.5 can be modified at any time and will take effect immediately after the OK button is processed. Resources can be selected from a pick list by clicking on a line in the Resource Name column. If the desired name has not already been allocated to Microsoft Project, you can either enter it through the Resource Sheet dialog box, or you can enter a new name in the line above the Resource Name in Figure

Figure 12.4 Task Information—Predecessors.

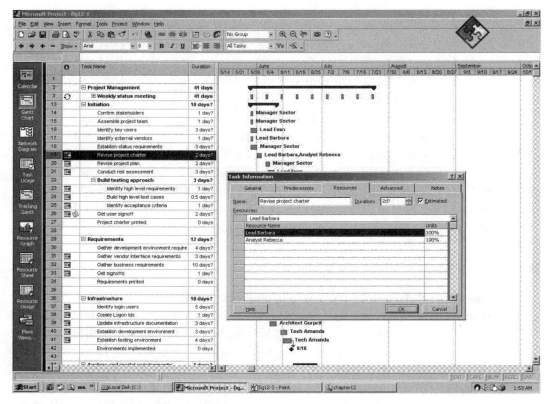

Figure 12.5 Allocating resources to a task.

12.5. This name will be saved in the resource table or sheet, and can be edited in the Resource Sheet.

Advanced Tab

Use this tab when you want to let the tool do the planning for you. This is done by establishing constraints and priorities on tasks and then allowing the tool to determine the overall project plan. The two fields that chiefly enable this process are Deadline and Constraint type. Figure 12.6 shows the information that can be entered in this tab.

The Deadline field offers a calendar that is used to specify the date by which a task must be completed. This will act as an important priority for the task relative to other ones. The Constraint type field operates within two parameters. The first of these specifies the type of constraint on the task; the second is the Constraint date, that is, when the constraint

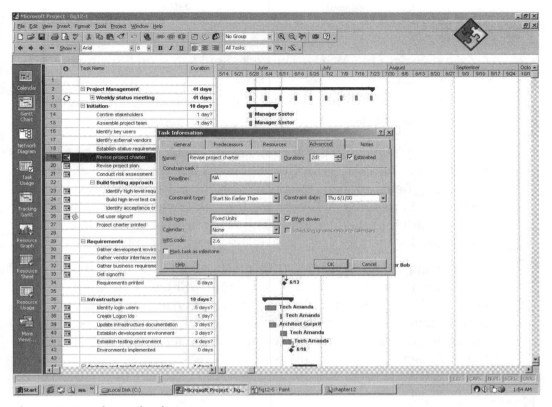

Figure 12.6 Advanced task usage.

comes into effect. Constraints are described as flexible and inflexible. Flexible constraints allow Project to recalculate a date when a task is moved when the plan is automatically built. Inflexible constraints are based on the hard-coded date value. Constraint type can take on the following values:

☐ **Start No Earlier Than (SNET).** The task should not start before the value specified in the Constraint date field.

☐ **As Late As Possible (ALAP).** The task should start as late as possible to meet the task deadline.

☐ **Finish No Earlier Than (FNET).** The task should be completed no earlier than the constraint date.

☐ **Finish No Later Than (FNLT).** The task should be completed no later than the constraint date.

❑ **Must Finish On (MFO).** The task should finish on the constraint date.

❑ **Must Start On (MSO).** The task should start on the constraint date.

❑ **Start No Later Than (SNLT).** The task should start no later than the constraint date.

The Task type field and the accompanying check box are used to specify whether the duration, effort, or resources are fixed. The calendar and scheduling fields are used to specify specific calendars, for example, if a night shift is required. WBS (or work breakdown structure) identifies a task's position in the hierarchy. The Mark task as milestone check box can be used to identify a task as a milestone without entering a 0 duration.

When using the constraints in this panel, avoid specifying the start and end dates in the General panel. The tool will calculate these for you. Hard-coding values in the General tab can override the constraints specified in this panel. The constraint can also be negated by specifying an environment parameter available on the Schedule tab in the Options dialog box discussed later in this section.

Notes Tab

The notes tab offers a Word-like environment to enter additional text about a task. Limited text formatting and object embedding is supported in this environment. The ID column shows a yellow Post-it-like icon to indicate that a note is saved with the task line.

Options Dialog Box

The options dialog box is available from the toolbar under Tools, Options. If Project is displaying information (e.g., help on startup) or using formats that you'd rather do without, this is the place to make the environment changes. This is supported by the panels shown in Figure 12.7, which are described below:

❑ **General tab.** Use this tab to establish startup options, such as the size of the recently used file list, autofilter option, whether to automatically display help, and whether to open the last file being edited. The PlanningWizard can be customized from here. You can also

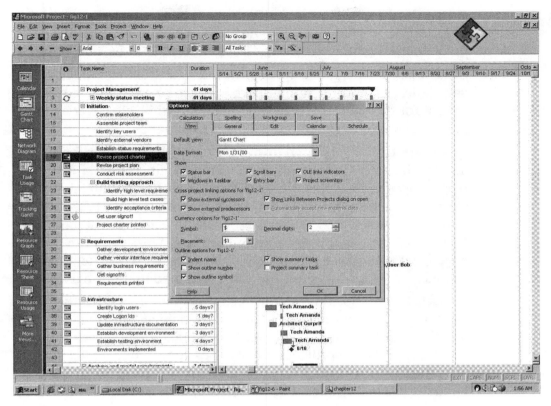

Figure 12.7 Options dialog box.

establish a blended standard rate for resources, as well as an overtime rate. These rates are used in the Resource List by default and can be overridden there.

☐ **Calendar tab**. Use this tab to specify the working schedule used by the project team. This includes specifying the start of the week, the start of the fiscal year, daily start time, and the default end time. The standard hours in a working day and week are specified here, as well as the number of days in a standard month.

☐ **View tab**. Use this tab to establish default formats and to control some of the information that is displayed. This includes establishing a default view that is displayed on startup. Default formats for date and currency are specified in this tab. The tab is also used to specify whether certain information is displayed. This includes successors/predecessors, summary information, and specific symbols.

- **Edit tab**. Use this tab to specify edit options, view options, and the appearance of hyperlinks. The view options focus on time and date units, including Minutes, Hours, Days, Weeks, Months, and Years.

- **Save tab**. Use this tab to specify the automatic extension of the saved files, save file locations, auto save parameters, and storage format for the disk. You may want to change this whenever a new project is started to keep related plans together as a set.

- **Schedule tab**. Use this tab to specify scheduling options for Project and for the active project plan. Assignment units can be specified as percentages or decimals. New tasks can start on the official project start date or the current date. A duration unit can be established as Minutes, Hours, Dates, Weeks, or Months. A task type can be specified as Fixed Units, Fixed Duration, or Fixed Work. You can also specify whether tasks must or should honor their constraint dates. Default values for tasks estimates are specified in this tab as well.

- **Calculate tab**. Use this tab to specify calculation options that are used by the tool to generate results. This includes specifying whether calculations should be calculated automatically or manually. Open or active projects can also be processed from this tab with the Calculate button. Options for task and resource usage are included as check boxes. Fixed costs can be prorated over a wider base from this tab. Task criticality can be derived by the value of slack time available to a task.

- **Spelling tab**. Use this tab to establish the scope, hints, and operation of the spelling tool. For example, you can specify the fields that should be examined by the spell checker. You can also choose to ignore uppercase words and words containing numbers. The tab allows a dictionary suggestion to be displayed by the spell checker.

- **Workgroup tab**. Use this tab to establish defaults for workgroup options. This includes specifying a mechanism for sending messages (e.g., Web, email), a URL for the central server, and identification for the central server. Account information for the central server can be established from this tab.

Insert

The Insert option from the toolbar offers several functions that are useful for improving the appearance and information content of project plans. These are discussed in this section.

Figure 12.8 Column Definition dialog box.

Inserting Columns

The Insert, Column option from the toolbar displays the dialog box shown in Figure 12.8. The Field name offers a pick list that can be used to insert a column into the Gantt table. The title field is used to specify a label for the column. The Align title and Align data fields specify the positioning of the text and data. The Width field specifies the size of the column. Figure 12.9 shows the results of adding a new column, titled "Variance," into the Gantt table.

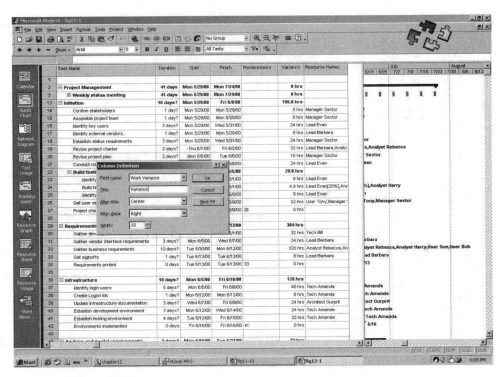

Figure 12.9 Inserted column.

Inserting Drawings

The Insert, Drawing option displays the drawing toolbar, which is used to draw figures, in the graphical views supported by the tool. Figure 12.10 shows an example where an arrow and box are drawn beside a task to highlight it. These figures were drawn with the toolbar. The drawn figure also gets saved with the view and the project plan.

Inserting Objects

The Insert, Object option can be used to insert an object into various views of the project plan. The objects can be created or imported from an existing file. The object type can belong to a large list, including HiJaak Images, Adobe Acrobat Documents, Media clips, Microsoft Clip Gallery images, and Microsoft Office files. Figure 12.11 shows a Project file pasted into a bitmap object.

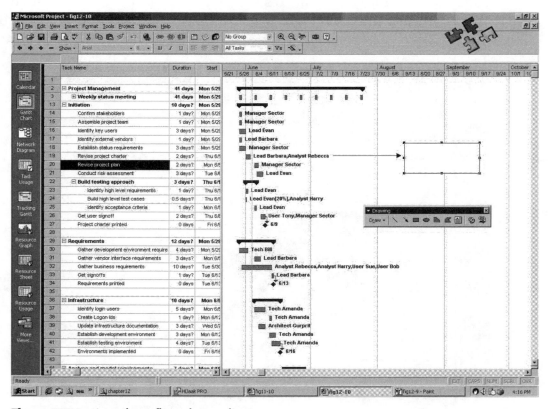

Figure 12.10 Inserting a figure into a view.

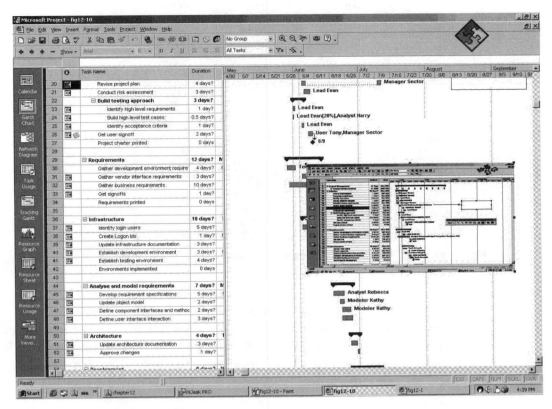

Figure 12.11 Inserting an object.

Inserting Project Plans

The Insert, Project option is used to insert a project plan within another project plan. The tool offers an opportunity to use a browser to select Project files to include in the current project plan that is open. The project plan that is selected from the browser is inserted at the cursor. The tool will accept multiple project plan inserts. An inserted project plan can be identified by a Microsoft Project icon in the ID column. Changes can also be saved back to the project plan file that was inserted.

Further Calendar Management

The calendar options specified in the Options panel can be augmented with functionality offered in the Change Working Time dialog box. This dialog box is available under Tools, Change Working Time from the toolbar, and is shown in Figure 12.12. Calendars can be created and cus-

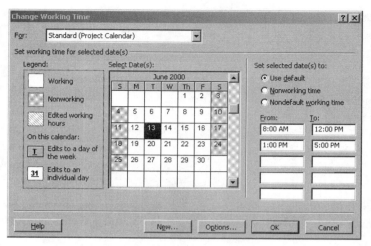

Figure 12.12   Change Working Time dialog box.

tomized using this dialog box. Nonworking time can be specified by using the radio button and then selecting a day. Dates that are underlined have associated customized information for the specific date. Using the "For" field, various calendars can be created and customized by different categories (e.g., individuals).

Letting the Tool Do the Planning

Allowing the tool to do the planning for you involves using the Advanced tab in the Task Information panel. This approach can save you a lot of time and will use important functionality in the tool. As a general guideline, it is better not to get too fancy when you start to allow the tool to do the planning for you. For example, do not enter hundreds of tasks with their constraints and expect the tool to build an appropriate plan for you. It is not unusual to want to save time upfront and let the tool do part of what it's designed for, namely, assist in the planning efforts. However, the decisions it makes will not necessarily be the ones that an experienced manager would make. The results generated from a lot of activities will be difficult to understand and more difficult to modify. We have seen many examples where complex project plans were built using this technique, only to be ignored when they proved to be difficult to understand and maintain. The replacement was often a project plan that was hard-coded with specific start and end dates in Project or even in a spreadsheet. Though less elegant and requiring more upfront planning time, the results were easier to understand and track.

The planning features of the tool work well when used iteratively. This involves starting with an overall project plan and validating it before moving to more progressive levels of detail. This has the benefit of retaining control over the plan, and also of becoming intimately aware of the lower-level tasks. Relying on the tool exclusively to do the planning for you often results in a superficial understanding of the plan's dependencies and critical timelines. The iterative approach mixes the best of both worlds.

As a demonstration of the tool's planning capabilities, consider this limited project. The business requirements are to conduct an assessment of an application currently in beta testing within three weeks or 15 working days. Assuming a start date of June 5, the project would then end on June 22. The first iteration of the project plan could consist of the following high-level tasks:

```
Project initiation
Review background materials
Prepare for interviews
Conduct interviews
Prepare final presentation
Conduct final presentation
Deliver final report
```

Working backwards from the three-week deadline results in the following durations for each of these high-level tasks, based on experience:

```
Project initiation                2 days
Review background materials       2 days
Prepare for interviews            1 day
Conduct interviews                5 days
Prepare final presentation        2 days
Conduct final presentation        1 day
Deliver final report              2 days
Project done (milestone)          0 days
```

These high-level tasks can be entered with a constraint of "As soon as possible." A dependency exists on the preceding task right down the task list. This results in the project plan shown in Figure 12.13, once the dependencies are represented. These dependencies are fairly straightforward and can be highlighted as a group and linked from the Edit option in the toolbar. Now suppose that another activity is required to make a go/no go decision by a specific date, say on May 13, because key stakeholders are only available on that day. The dependency of the "Conduct interviews"

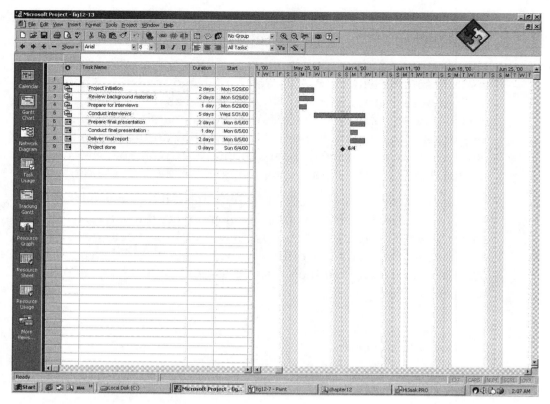

Figure 12.13 Application assessment—Iteration 1.

task changes to this new task. The "Go/No Go discussion" task should be entered using a "must finish on" constraint. You should temporarily ignore any warning or messages that inserting this task causes. You will eventually fix all of these. There should be no predecessor to this task, as the constraint in the task information dialog box is supplying this information. Figure 12.14 shows the results of adding this new task to the list. A day of slack time is now available on Monday for the first three tasks. However, notice the automatic impact on the end date—which is now shifted to June 26 from June 22. There are several approaches for a project manager to deal with this situation. The first one is to negotiate a new end date due to the fixed go/no go decision. The stakeholders may accept a delivery on June 26. However, if this is impossible, perhaps due to a management board meeting that requires an answer and which is taking place before June 26, there are several other approaches to try, as follows:

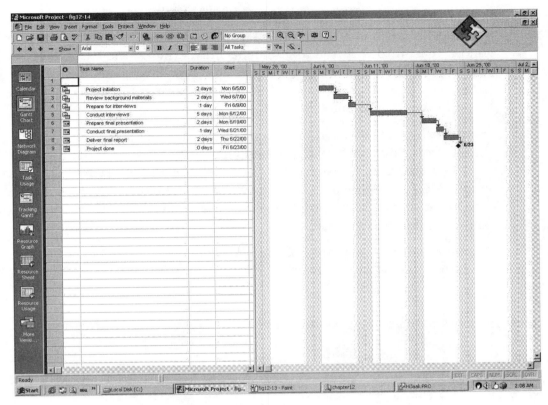

Figure 12.14 Application assessment—Iteration 2.

1. Reduce the time available for some of the tasks. Some choices are to reduce the interview period from five days to four days. Another option is to reduce the report presentation time to one day from two.

2. Conduct some of the tasks in parallel. This could mean starting the final presentation before the interviews are completed. Another option is to keep the dependency between the Conduct interviews task and the Prepare for interviews task, instead of the Go-No-Go discussion task.

The risk of the first option involves running out of time and affecting the quality of the final deliverable. The risk of the second option involves doing some duplication or unnecessary work. Our preference would be to change the dependencies so that work continues until a go-no-go decision is made. The risk of not finishing the project on time easily outweighs the cost of doing some unnecessary work. Our assumption, also, is that the checkpoint date is too soon to really allow the steering committee to find a reason to stop the assessment. Furthermore, the assessment is needed for a board meeting and has a lot of high-level sources pushing it forward. Figure 12.15 shows a view of some tasks running in parallel to support the original end date.

Some resources still need to be added to the project plan. These will be drawn from three sources. The assessment team consists of one manager and two analysts. There are also five resources to interview from the application project team. There are three stakeholders reporting to the corporate board and sponsoring the assessment. These groups are shown in the following list:

☐ **Assessment team.** Assessment Manager, Senior Assessment Analyst, Junior Assessment Analyst

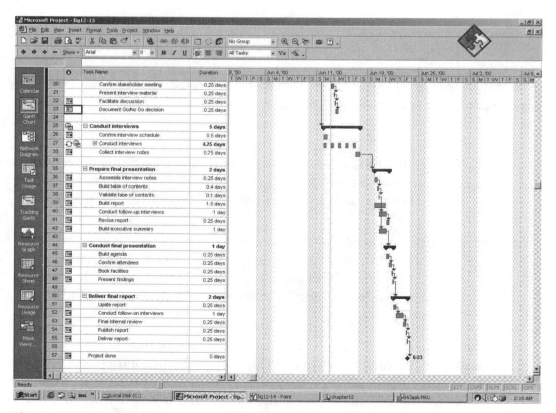

Figure 12.15 Application assessment—Iteration 3.

□ **Application project team.** Project Manager, Senior Architect, Business User 1, Business User 2, Systems Analyst

□ **Stakeholders.** Business Director, Vice President Operations, CIO

The next iteration of the project plan could involve adding a prime resource to each high-level task. It may also become appropriate to drive down to subtasks, as follows:

```
Project initiation                2 days    Assessment Manager
     Assemble project team
     Document assessment criteria
     Construct project charter

Review background materials       2 days    Senior Assessment Analyst
     Gather application project material
     Build list of documents
     Prioritize documents
     Review and understand documents

Prepare for interviews            1 day     Senior Assessment Analyst
     Confirm interview list and time
     Establish interview agenda
     Prepare interview material
     Distribute interview material

Go/No Go Decision                 1 day     Assessment Manager
     Confirm stakeholder meeting
     Present interview material
     Facilitate discussion
     Document go/no go decision

Conduct interviews                5 days    Senior Assessment Analyst
     Confirm interview schedule
     Conduct interviews
     Collect interview notes

Prepare final presentation        2 days    Senior Assessment Analyst
     Assemble interview notes
     Build table of contents
     Validate table of contents
     Build report
     Conduct follow-up interviews
     Revise report
     Build executive summary

Conduct final presentation        1 day     Assessment Manager
     Build agenda
     Confirm attendees
     Book facilities
     Present findings
```

```
Deliver final report              2 days    Senior Assessment Analyst
        Update report
        Conduct follow-on interviews
        Final internal review
        Publish report
        Deliver report

Project done (milestone)          0 days
```

On more complex subtasks, the prime resources could assist in allocating resources. In this case, the number of tasks is not onerous, so the project manager can pretty much allocate time to each subtask and the corresponding resources. Figure 12.16 shows these details and the final form of the project plan for this assessment. The plan can be saved as a baseline and then tracked over the course of the assessment. Various reporting views can also be generated from this information. These topics are discussed in chapter 13.

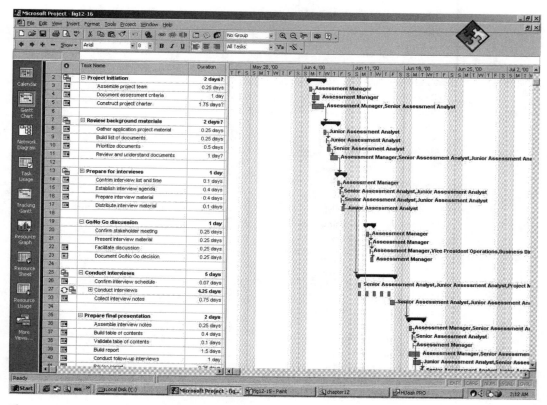

Figure 12.16 Application assessment—Iteration 4.

Planning by Dependencies

The high-level tasks from the previous example can be combined with dependencies and constraints in many ways to build workable project plans. The following table shows some reasonable dependencies between the tasks. Figure 12.17 shows an example of a project plan that was built

ID#	TASK	DURATION (DAYS)	DEPENDENCIES
1	Project initiation	2	
2	Review background materials	2	1
3	Prepare for interviews	1	1
4	Conduct interviews	5	3
5	Prepare final presentation	2	4
6	Conduct final presentation	1	5
7	Deliver final report	2	6
8	Project done	0	7

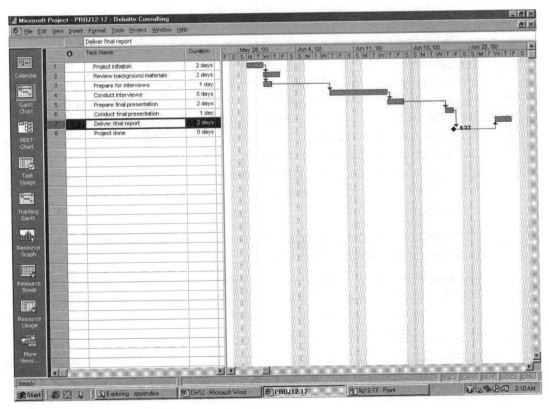

Figure 12.17 Planning by dependencies.

using dependencies that has slack/lag values in some of the tasks. The project report can be delivered within a specific amount of time after the final presentation. The project milestone that needs to be met is the final presentation.

Linking Tasks

While the simplest method of linking adjacent tasks is available from the pull-down menu under Edit, Link Tasks or by pressing Ctrl-F2 for a highlighted task list, the task panel offers four options of linking tasks. These are available from the Predecessor, Type pick list. The options are differentiated in the position of the link between the first and the second task(s). The basic method is to select a task that will serve as a base within a set of tasks. The other tasks in the set can use the base as a common predecessor task. In general, these are useful options; however, we recommend constructing your project plan using one or two options that work well for you. This makes it easier to maintain the project plan on an ongoing basis. Using too many options in the same plan works well for a time; however, it quickly adds a lot of overhead that keeps your plan from being lean, mean, and effective. Another issue about task linking is the limitation that this places on staggering tasks. Some tasks can be started before others are completed. A hard link does not allow this to be represented accurately. Microsoft provides a solution to this by providing a lag time (or lead time) value that can be specified in the same panel that accepts a link option. This value allows a buffer to be established for tasks. However, going this route requires more time and also starts to hard-code values (e.g., time it takes to print a report) into a generated plan. The following list discusses the link options that are available, including none (no link):

☐ **None.** This option removes a predecessor task/link that has already been established between tasks.

☐ **Finish-to-start.** This is the common task linkage and the normal default value. The link exists between the end of the first task and the start of the second task.

☐ **Start-to-start.** This involves starting the linked tasks on the same date. This is useful when a series of tasks are required to begin, but the deadlines are not dependent on when they finish.

☐ **Finish-to-finish.** This involves ending the linked tasks on the same date. This is useful when a specific implementation date is established. For example, training material acceptance testing must be completed by a specific date before a go/no go decision is made to implement a solution.

☐ **Start-to-finish.** This involves using a task start date as a predecessor constraint for the end date of another task. It is an opposite of the "Finish-to-start" option, but in this case, subsequent tasks are positioned earlier than the predecessor as the gate for a first task. This is useful when a task must end on the start date of another task. This approach can be used to build a set of tasks from a known end date and sequence them out to a logical start date.

Do not specify specific start and end dates for tasks that are being linked. Removing tasks between links will cause Microsoft to generate default task dates that are based on the project start date, as opposed to those belonging to a specific task. Figure 12.18 shows three tasks that are

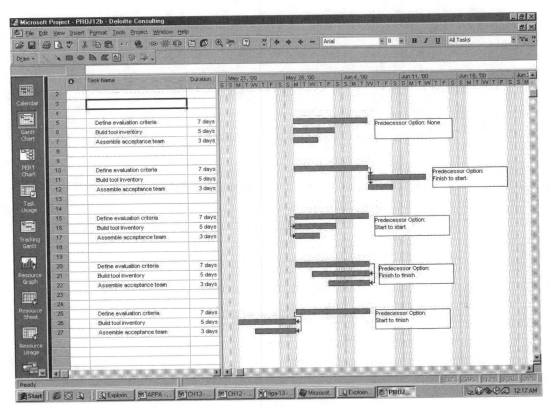

Figure 12.18   Application assessment—Iteration 4.

linked using these options in the order in which they are presented above.

Critical Path Planning

Critical path planning is important for ensuring the on-time delivery of a project. The critical path is the sequence of tasks that must be completed for a project to be successful, and also it ends on the last date of the project plan. This means that any delay in the activities in this path will immediately affect the project end date. If this end date, as on most projects, is the last possible date to deliver the project, there is no slack available in the critical path. For example, consider the following example, which involves implementing a development environment to support a known technical architecture.

ID#	TASK	DURATION (DAYS)	DEPENDENCIES
1	Identify technical requirements	3	
2	Determine load	2	
3	Purchase components	3	1, 2
4	Establish environment	2	3
5	Build communication plan	2	
6	Process payment	2	3
7	Development environment established	0	4

On the basis of this task list, the priority list will consist of the longer of task 1 or 2, 3, and 4. Task 5 must be completed before task 4, but can start independently. Process payment is certainly not a priority to project completion at all. Figure 12.19 shows a high-level linked project plan that was generated by Project based on this basic information.

Figure 12.20 shows a PERT view of the project plan. Any changes to the tasks in the critical path will delay the project completion date. The "build communication plan" and "process payment" tasks can be adjusted in duration and for start/end dates within a slack period without affecting the completion date. Changes made to the PERT view are propagated to the other views.

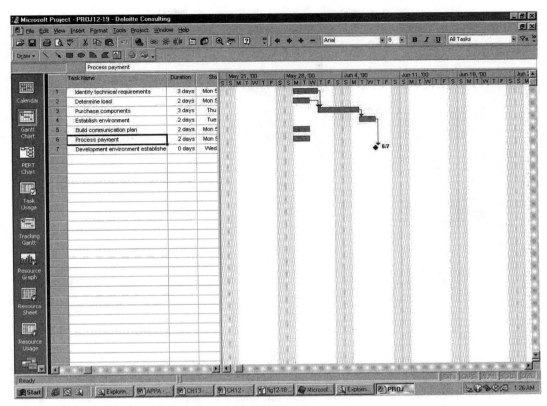

Figure 12.19 Implement development environment.

Resource Management

Now that the critical path is understood, we can begin to add our resources. For now, we are not anticipating our resources to be bottlenecks to the project; however, this may change as the planning continues. The initial approach will be to keep the resources at a minimum. Given the requirements of the project, we need a lead, a technical administrator, and an analyst. Their roles on the project are as follows:

☐ **Project leader.** This resource will assume leadership of the initiative, planning, resource allocation, and scope control. Budget decisions and communication will be authorized by this resource.

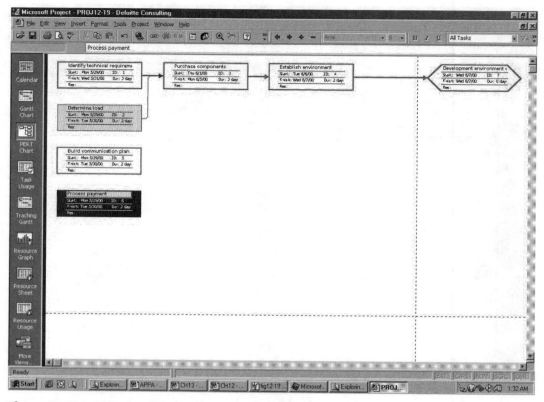

Figure 12.20 PERT chart for the development environment project.

- ☐ **Technical administrator.** This resource will be responsible for all technical aspects of the engagement, including capturing the technical requirements, validating the equipment, and implementation.
- ☐ **Analyst.** This resource will be responsible for all documentation on the project. Typically the analyst will build the documentation, while the project leader will approve and distribute it.

For the purpose of this example, we can assume that three individuals are identified for the project, named leader1, technical1, and analyst1. The following table shows the resource allocation across the tasks:

ID#	TASK	DURATION (DAYS)	DEPENDENCIES	RESOURCES
1	Identify technical requirements	3		Technical1
2	Determine load	2		Technical1
3	Purchase components	3	1, 2	Leader1
4	Establish environment	2	3	Technical1
5	Build communication plan	2		Analyst1, Leader1, Technical1
6	Process payment	2	3	Leader1
7	Development environment established (MILESTONE)	0	4	

A resource list can be created relatively quickly for these resources by selecting the resource sheet icon. They can then be allocated to the tasks using the task panel. Suppose we want to determine which resources are overburdened and which ones have too little to do. A resource graph can be used to determine this information. In this short example, we would expect to see that the technical1 lead is the busiest resource. Figure 12.21 validates this situation, but also shows that leader1 is also overburdened. In the default settings, the amount of time allocated to a specific resource shows up as red on a color display. In fact, the leader's time on the project shown in Figure 12.21 is not a true representation of actual involvement on the initiative because project management activities have not been captured. This will show even more red in the allocation view. Page through the view to see the allocation of other resources on the project. Note that each of these resources has been allocated to tasks on a full-time basis or for 100% of the time represented as a full day in the calendar.

In many real-life projects, managers use the plan to track resource responsibilities and involvement in tasks, but not necessarily the hours spent at the test level. This means that although resources are shown as overallocated in the project plan, they are expected to manage their own

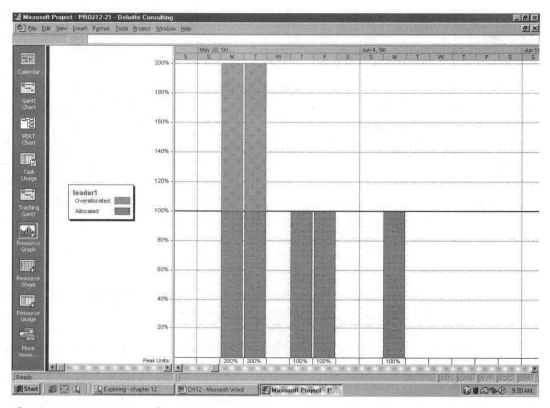

Figure 12.21 Resource allocation.

time and support the dates and tasks that require their involvement. In other projects, this is not a reasonable assumption. In this specific example, the effort required for a task may not require 100% involvement. For example, although all three resources are working on the communication plan, the analyst is doing most of the work. The technical resource is only providing information. This may require an hour a day on average, which, assuming an 8-hour day, translates into 12.5% of the day. Similarly the leader is only reviewing and validating the communication plan and documentation, so may only have a 2-hour commitment to the task on a daily basis. One approach for managing the resource overallocation problem is to represent true time on the Gantt chart. In general, the following approaches are available to make this adjustment:

☐ Show true time on the Gantt chart

☐ Experiment with shifting start/end dates for noncritical tasks

☐ Delay the start of some tasks

☐ Add more resources

☐ Allow Project to level the resources for you

☐ Encourage resources to work longer hours

It is not unusual to leverage more than one of these approaches to get an acceptable resource allocation. Figure 12.22 shows the Gantt view of the project plan with true values represented. As you adjust the units column in the Task, Resource tab to represent the true time allocation, Project will adjust the task duration to preserve the original time estimates. This will have the effect of stretching the taskbars. In a situation where resources are bottlenecks and are only available on a part-time basis, this

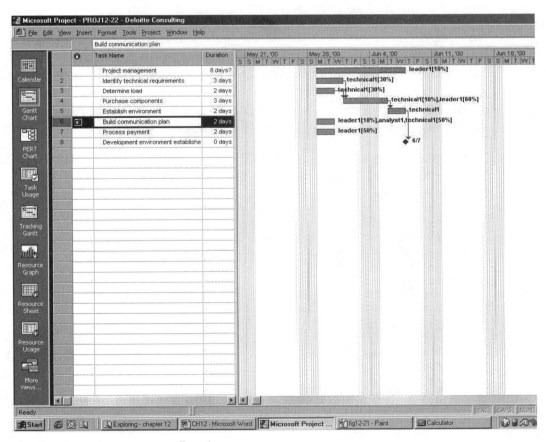

Figure 12.22 True resource allocation.

may be a valid decision for Project to enforce. The result will be to push the implementation out (or to the right on the Gantt chart). However, we have already concluded that the resources are not required on a full-time basis for the original duration estimates. In fact, the original durations represented elapsed time, as opposed to true effort. This is not unusual, since certain tasks require a specific period of time to finish, but may not require dedicated resources for the duration. As an example, consider a task that generates reports after user sign-off. While printing, collating, and binding the reports may take two days, the actual batch submission of the work may only require 25% of that time.

In the example we are developing, the original task durations can be used to override Project's automatic tasks duration generation. A quick review of all the resources in the resource graph view shows that all the resources are no longer overallocated during the project.

Now suppose that we decide that the technical resource is needed for a larger percentage of time during the communication plan tasks—say for 50% of the time. This will create an overallocation problem early in the project. One or more of the options described previously can be used to correct this new problem. Since the process payment task is not a priority, its start date can be delayed appropriately.

The previous examples focused on the high level of the task hierarchy. In order to better manage this project, another level of tasks can be identified as follows:

```
Identify technical requirements
     Review proposed architecture
     Determine linkage with existing infrastructure
     Assemble shopping list
Determine load
     Determine number of resources
     Define development platforms
     Update shopping list
Purchase components
     Place order
     Arrange priority delivery
     Accept delivery
     Validate shipment
Establish environment
     Install hardware
     Implement software
     Configure environment
```

```
Build communication plan
        Document rules and regulations
        Distribute documentation
Process payment
        Validate invoice
        Mail invoice
        Update GL
```

This project will be used to develop further examples in the next chapter.

Summary

This chapter reviewed Microsoft Project's features for establishing the tool's environment and standards. It also examined methods of maintaining more detailed information for tasks. Other topics reviewed in this chapter included recurring tasks, planning by milestones, managing options, managing the calendar, and letting the tool plan for you.

A project plan was developed for conducting an assessment of a project plan within a period of three weeks. This plan was developed iteratively, using some of the tools planning facilities to generate parts of the plan. The first iteration established the overall plan based on a specific delivery date. Subsequent iterations pulled out some of the details and added a resource team at the task level. This example demonstrated how Project can be managed to do some of the work for you.

Another project plan was developed to implement a development environment without an enforced implementation date. This example was used to demonstrate how various task-linking options can be used to let project suggest a suitable end date for you. The example was also used to demonstrate several resource-leveling options. Resources were initially allocated to the project based on an elapsed time basis. However, this resulted in overallocation in the early parts of the project plan. Several solutions were considered to correct this issue. An approach that represented resource allocation as true time during an elapsed period in a task was used to resolve the issue.

Microsoft Project clearly has substantial functionality for managing project plans. On larger engagements, although the project manager owns the overall plan, it is not unusual to have a full-time resource allocated to the project and dedicated to maintaining the plan by collecting information from the project team and making weekly updates.

CHAPTER 13

Reporting, Tracking, and Customizing Projects

T his chapter focuses on retrieving information from Microsoft Project through a variety of tools. It also focuses on tools that allow specific information to be peeled away from the project plan and presented in different views. The following topics are examined in this chapter:

- Project reporting
- Project tracking
- Data filters
- Data sorting
- Data grouping
- Resource leveling

Reporting

Microsoft Project supports a diverse set of reports that can be used throughout the project lifecycle. These are easily accessible from the View, Reports option from the main pull-down menu. Reports are similar to views in that information is presented in a variety of formats. Although the line separating the two formats can be hazy, depending on the definitions you proceed with, a primary differentiator is that views essentially provide data in different formats to support effective data management using the input dialog boxes. Conversely, reports are commonly used to gather and present data to provide an overall status for a project.

Figure 13.1 shows the six essential report categories that are available to users. These can be selected by double-clicking on the large icon to display another level of report choices. Reports are generated when a selection is made and displayed in the window. The report preview window has its own active toolbar. Among the useful options available to you from here are functions to page through a report (the number of pages in the report is shown in the bottom-left message field), to shift it left or right, and to establish page options. The Zoom, One Page, and Two Page options are used to manipulate the details that are visible in the online report. You can zoom into a particular spot on the report and then zoom out again to see the big picture. The mouse also offers this capability. Clicking on the mouse at a particular point enlarges the area under the cursor. Clicking on it again zooms the view back out. The report can, of course, be printed.

Each of the report categories contains a set of reports that can be selected for generation by the tool. Some of these reports offer options to significantly alter their visual appearance before they are generated. The Edit option allows some of the header information on a report to be customized. Fonts and colors can also be modified for the report. The set of report options, by report category, are discussed in this section.

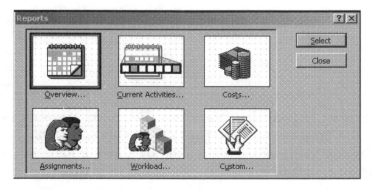

Figure 13.1   Reporting dialog box.

Overview Reports

The Overview report category offers a set of reports that can be used for retrieving the information entered into the project plan, as follows:

☐ **Project Summary.** This report shows the overall project information, often at a summarized level. The major blocks of information include the key dates, durations, work effort expended, costs, task status (e.g., tasks not started, total tasks), and the resource status (e.g., working resources and overallocated resources). The header information contains the name of the project, project manager, and effective date of the report.

☐ **Top-level Tasks.** This report shows key information for the high-level tasks in the project plan. This includes the task duration, start date, finish date, percentage complete, and cost of the task.

☐ **Critical Tasks.** This is a more complicated report that contains critical tasks, sequencing, and successor names.

☐ **Milestones.** This is a useful report for showing the project milestones, especially if you choose a style of project planning that includes identifying key milestones that can be tracked throughout a time stream.

☐ **Working Days.** This is a simple report that shows the base calendar, including standard hours and nonworking days.

Current Activities Reports

The Current Activities report category offers the following reports that are focused primarily at the task level:

☐ **Unstarted Tasks**. This report shows a list of unstarted tasks and detailed information about them.

☐ **Tasks Starting Soon**. This task report captures a start and end date range in a dialog box. Project performs some rudimentary editing on the dates that are entered and displays error messages. The date value can be in the form "month day, year" (e.g., July 30, 2000).

☐ **Tasks in Progress**. This task report shows a list of tasks that are in progress mode. The report does not appear if tasks are not found to fit the qualification criteria.

☐ **Completed Tasks**. This task report shows a list of tasks that are complete or which have a 100% completion value assigned to them in the task dialog box.

☐ **Should Have Started Tasks**. This task report captures a "should start by" date and displays the tasks that should be started by that date.

☐ **Slipping Tasks**. This task report shows a list of tasks that are slipping as of the current date.

Cost Reports

The reports in the Cost category are meaningful only if the rate information is accurate and if resource allocation is leveled and detailed. Keeping these up to date can be highly complicated and time-consuming. The tool provides this functionality for you if you want to combine the project plan with the budget. It is not unusual to use Project for planning and to use a spreadsheet to track the budget. The Cost category offers the following reports:

☐ **Cash Flow**. This report shows the projected cash flow as of the current date for the tasks in the project plan. Cash flow is shown for three successive weeks.

☐ **Budget**. This report shows the budget at the task level as a function of fixed cost, accrual, baseline, and variance.

☐ **Overbudget Tasks**. This report generates a list of tasks that are over their assigned budget.

☐ **Overbudget Resources**. This report generates a list of resources that are over their assigned budget.

☐ **Earned Value**. This report generates earned value at the task level. This includes columns for BCWS, BCWP, ACWP, SV, and CV.

Assignment Reports

The Assignment reports are useful in the early stages of a project to get team members committed to their roles and responsibilities. Reports can be generated on a weekly basis and passed out to team members to show them exactly what needs to be done and what they are accountable for on the project. This category offers the following reports:

☐ **Who Does What**. This report groups on resource name. All the tasks that a resource is responsible for are grouped on the report under the resource name. Information is shown by task, similar to the format of the resource template.

☐ **Who Does What When**. This report also groups on resource name. Tasks owned by the resource are grouped under the name, but also scheduled out by week. The amount of effort required by the resource is shown by week.

☐ **To-do List**. A dialog box with a pick list on resources is available to select a name. The report shows the activities that are on that resource's to-do list by week. Each line of the report shows a task name, duration, start date, and finish date.

☐ **Overallocated Resources**. This report groups on resource name and shows resources that are allocated along with detailed task information.

Workload Reports

The Workload category contains two reports that provide information on usage at the task level and the resource level, as follows:

☐ **Task Usage**. This report shows resources allocated to a task. The time dedicated by a resource to the task is also shown, separated into weekly time periods.

☐ **Resource Usage**. This report takes a resource view of usage by showing tasks owned by resources. The time that a resource needs to devote to a task is shown, separated into time periods.

Custom Reports

The Custom category contains a lengthy list of reports, including the Base Calendar, Cash Flow, Critical Tasks, Earned Value, CrossTab, Overbudget Resources, and Overbudget Tasks. The Edit function with the custom report dialog box offers the opportunity to select a table, filters, summary information, and a date period for the report. Formatting information can also be customized.

Project Tracking

Project tracking generally involves collecting actual resource usage on a project and recording it in the project plan. The Tools, Tracking option from the toolbar provides a set of functions that can be used for project tracking. These include the following:

☐ **Update Tasks**. This function provides access to a dialog box that allows % complete, actual start date, actual finish date, notes, and an actual duration to be specified for a selected task.

☐ **Update Project**. This function provides a global method of updating task information, usually as complete, up to a certain point in time. It also allows unscheduled tasks to be shifted to another date. Instead of a global scope, a range can also be specified.

☐ **Progress Lines**. This function is used to establish progress lines against the actual plan or the baseline plan.

☐ **Save Baseline**. This function can be used at any time to save the plan with a new baseline.

☐ **Clear Baseline**. This function can be used to clear the baseline at any time.

As shown in Figure 13.2, the tracking process is part of the overall process for using Microsoft Project in an end-to-end lifecycle. Project

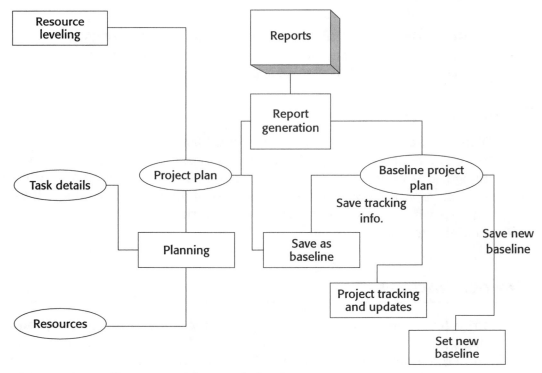

Figure 13.2   Tracking as part of the overall planning process.

tracking can involve comparing actual work done to a plan, or actual work done as well as modifications, both of which are compared to an earlier version of the project plan. The earlier project plan is referred to as a baseline. Project allows a plan to be saved in this format. Saving a plan as a baseline actually creates another set of buckets that are used to store changed information. Any changes made to the project plan (e.g., shifting a task to start three weeks later) can then be compared to the baseline. At some point, so many changes could be made to a plan that the baseline is no longer relevant. In this case, the project plan can be saved with a new baseline. This causes the buckets to be reinitialized to zero, and the current plan replaces the original baseline.

Once a project starts, it's highly likely that the original plan will be modified to keep it accurate on a regular basis. This may involve modifying allocated resources, changing the duration of a task, adjusting a start/end date, adjusting priority, and modifying the list of predecessors and dependencies. These changes can be done in several ways in Microsoft Project; however, the common ones include using the graphical format of the Gantt chart, using drag and drop, as well as the Task Information dialog box.

In addition to managing the ongoing accuracy of the project plan, it is also useful to track progress against the original plan. A common way of doing this is to use the Percent Complete field, as shown in Figure 13.3, to specify how much of a task is complete. For example, if the task was scheduled for a duration of 10 days for 1 resource, and 4 days have been

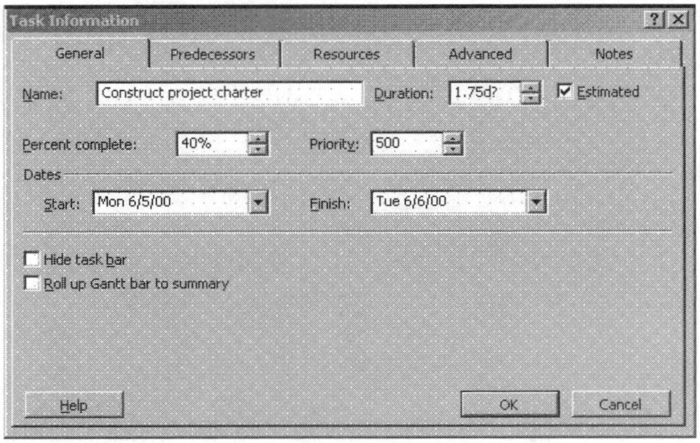

Figure 13.3 Task update dialog box.

completed, a value of 40 can be entered into the Percent Complete field. This will show up as a dark line on the Gantt chart within the taskbar. The value can be subsequently modified in either direction, either for a correction or as an update to an existing task. It is common practice to continue to update this field on a weekly basis, usually showing an increase in the percentage complete value. A value of 100 means that a task has been completed.

The combination of modifying a project plan and using the Percent Complete field to track tasks is effective for most projects. However, the earlier generation of planning estimates gets lost when using this approach. Using the baseline comparison approach offers an opportunity to combine the best of both worlds. The baseline view is visible in the Tracking Gantt view. Figure 13.4 shows that task 5 "Construct project charter" is 70% complete and task 11 "Review and understand documentation" has shifted start/end dates.

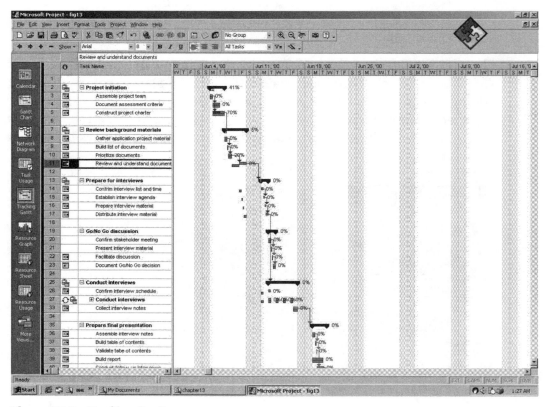

Figure 13.4   Tracking Gantt.

Reporting and Tracking: Another Example

We want to demonstrate some tracking cycles, costing, and reports for another project plan that was developed in chapter 12. The objective of this plan, which consists of seven high-level tasks, is to implement a development environment. The expanded version of the plan contains durations and resources by task, with a few tweaks from the original, as shown in Table 13.1.

Figure 13.5 shows the Gantt view of this project plan. There are about eight working days on the project. The implementation date is on 6/7. This plan will be used to support some of the examples in the subsequent sections of this chapter.

Table 13.1   Plan for Implementing a Development Environment

PHASE LEVEL 1	PHASE LEVEL 2	RESOURCES	DURATION
Project management		Leader1	Entire length of the project
Identify technical requirements		Technical1, Leader1	3
	Review proposed architecture	Technical1	1
	Determine linkage with existing Infrastructure	Technical1	1
	Assemble shopping list	Technical1, Leader1	1
Determine load		Technical1	2
	Determine number of resources	Technical1	.5
	Define development platforms	Technical1	.5
	Define development software and tools	Technical1	.5
	Update shopping list	Technical1, Leader1	.5
Purchase components		Leader1	3
	Place order	Leader1	.5
	Arrange priority delivery	Leader1	.2
	Accept delivery	Leader1	1.8
	Validate shipment	Technical1, Leader1	.25

Table 13.1 (*continued*)

PHASE LEVEL 1	PHASE LEVEL 2	RESOURCES	DURATION
Establish environment		Technical1	2
	Install hardware	Technical1	1
	Implement software	Technical1	.5
	Configure environment	Technical1	.5
Build communication plan		Analyst1, Leader1, Technical1	2
	Document rules and regulations	Analyst1, Leader1, Technical1	1.5
	Distribute documentation	Analyst1	.5
Process payment		Leader1	2
	Validate invoice	Leader1	.5
	Mail invoice	Leader1	.5
	Update GL	Leader1	1
Development environment implemented			0

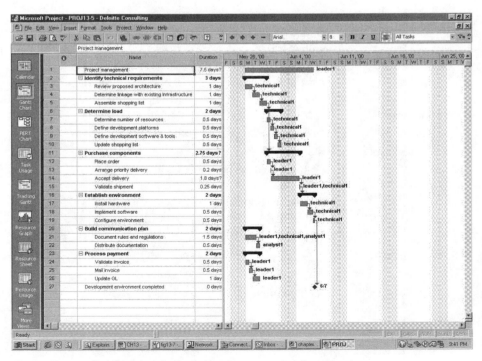

Figure 13.5 Detailed development environment Implementation.

Establish and Track Project Costs

Project costs are established and tracked using the resource panels and the costing reports available from the pull-down menus. Both of these are reviewed in this section.

Establishing Project Costs

Microsoft Project supports project cost management and tracking through the resource sheet, tracking options, and specific costing reports. Although many managers separate the accounting function from project management, it is worthwhile to examine some of the features the tool offers in this area. Maintaining cost information in Project requires you to establish fees or costs for resources, using the resource sheet. You can enter a standard rate and an overtime rate for every resource, as shown in Figure 13.6. Project can now use this information along with the project plan to calculate the budget of the project. The

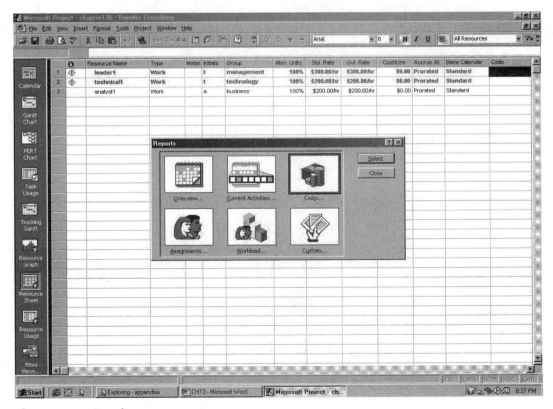

Figure 13.6   Entering resource rates.

costing reports are available under View, Reports from the primary pull-down menu.

Save the project plan with the resource cost information as a baseline, from the Tools, Tracking, Save Baseline option. This allows Project to compare actual information against the original plan. It is a good idea to archive this version of the baseline for future reference. Anytime a baseline is saved, the current version is overwritten. The archive will allow you to go back and retrieve the original plan if it is needed. Figure 13.7 shows a basic cost report for the project, which is accessible from the Reports dialog box under the Costs, Budget option. Notice that the baseline and cost columns are equivalent because we saved the baseline plan before generating the budget report. Future reports thus allow you to track changes to this budget information.

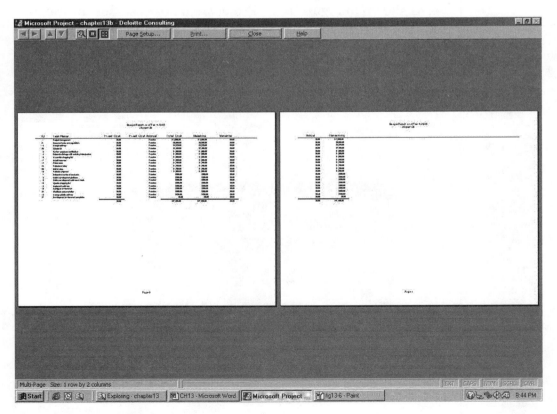

Figure 13.7   Project budget.

The cost/use column in the resource list sheet is reflected in the total cost and baseline columns. The accrued column can take on one of three basic values: prorated, start, and end, reflecting the costs as processed in the calculations and at what values as a function of time. The actual and remaining columns are used to track the actual amount of the budget that is consumed versus what is left over. This report will be revisited after a tracking iteration later in this chapter.

Figure 13.8 shows a cash flow report that is available from the same Reports dialog box as the project budget report. This report projects the cash available by task across weeks and for the project as a whole. Cash is identified at the task level that identifies resources. In this example, this is level 2. This report is based on current, as opposed to historical, information.

Cash Flowas of Tue 4/25/00
chapter13b

	5/28/00	6/4/00	Total
Project management	$12,000.00	$6,000.00	$18,000.00
Identify technical requirements			
Review proposed architecture	$1,600.00		$1,600.00
Determine linkage with existing Infrastructure	$1,600.00		$1,600.00
Assemble shopping list	$1,600.00		$1,600.00
Determine load			
Determine number of resources	$800.00		$800.00
Define development platforms	$800.00		$800.00
Define development software & tools	$800.00		$800.00
Update shopping list	$800.00		$800.00
Purchase components			
Place order	$1,200.00		$1,200.00
Arrange priority delivery	$480.00		$480.00
Accept delivery	$3,120.00	$1,200.00	$4,320.00
Validate shipment		$1,000.00	$1,000.00
Establish environment			
Install hardware		$1,600.00	$1,600.00
Implement software		$800.00	$800.00
Configure environment		$800.00	$800.00
Build communication plan			
Document rules and regulations	$5,600.00		$5,600.00
Distribute documentation	$800.00		$800.00
Process payment			
Validate invoice	$1,200.00		$1,200.00
Mail invoice	$1,200.00		$1,200.00
Update GL	$2,400.00		$2,400.00
Development environment completed			
Total	$36,000.00	$11,400.00	$47,400.00

Figure 13.8 Cash flow report.

Tracking Project Costs

Tracking against the project plan will also provide a current financial picture for you at any given time. Given the short timeframe of the project, it may be advisable to track the project plan on a daily basis. Assuming normal progress, after four days, tasks with dates ending on 6/1 or before will be complete. The others will be completed to a prorated percentage of the entire task duration on 6/1. For example, the project management function is about half completed, but a status report is still outstanding—so a value of 47% complete can be entered for this task. Similarly, the "review proposed architecture" task is a one-day activity that started and ended on 5/29. This should be shown as 100% complete. Figure 13.9 shows a tracking Gantt chart view with this updated information.

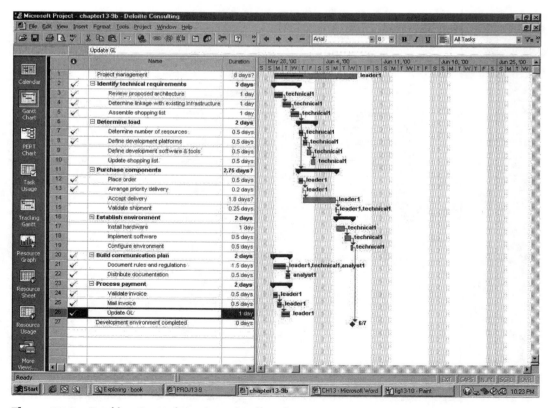

Figure 13.9   Tracking Gantt chart view after four days.

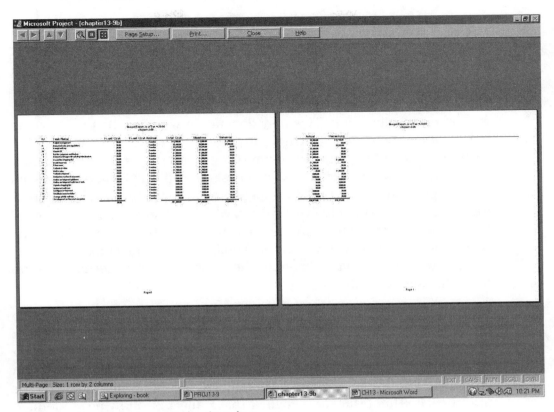

Figure 13.10 Budget report after four days.

Figure 13.10 shows the budget report reflecting money that has been spent, some variance against the baseline, and the amount of budget remaining in the project. The variance amount against the baseline was caused by stretching the duration of the project management task so that it matches the end of the implementation day. The original budget was based on having the project management task end halfway during the implementation day. This variance will continue to be tracked in the report against the baseline.

Updating the Baseline

Saving the project plan with another baseline resets the variance values to 0 throughout the project plan. For example, the budget report appears with a 0 variance value in the fields that were showing up with values reflecting the task changes.

Resource Leveling

Project's resource leveling functionality can be used to ensure that resources are not overbooked on tasks. It's the responsibility of the project manager to determine the level of tolerance the project has for resource overallocation. This may depend on whether the plan is going to be used to track budgets. On some projects, resources are allocated to a set of tasks, but the amount of time they actually spend on a particular one is not known up front. In such a case, the allocated time represents time elapsed and not actual time spent, and so leveling may end up shifting dates inappropriately or unnecessarily. It is good practice to review the results of any reallocation process to ensure that the results of the operation are in line with what is acceptable to the project manager. Leveling functions are available under the Tools, Resource Leveling option from the main toolbar.

Priorities indicate which tasks to level first, with a priority of 0 being the first task to be leveled. Leveling is a process whereby Project follows a set of rules to remove resource overallocations. Resource leveling can be set to automatic or manual entry. Pressing the Level Now button when the manual option is selected levels the resources in the order of their priorities. It is important to recognize that Project is following predefined rules and will not necessarily provide the most optimized solution. Always inspect the results after a leveling transaction.

Figure 13.11 shows a dialog box that can be used to automatically or manually level resources on a project plan. Overallocations can be assessed under different levels of detail, such as to the minute, hour, day, week, or month. Leveling can also be done for the whole project or for a specific date range.

Several reports and views are available to see the current resource status. Chapter 12 examined the resource status at a higher task level. Generating a resource report at two levels of task detail yields the results shown in Figure 13.12. In this example, a report called Overallocated Resources, from the Assignments report option, shows that two resources are overallocated, along with the tasks that reflect their involvement.

Now suppose that we realize that we need the analyst's assistance in several other tasks. Making these adjustments overallocates this resource as well, as shown in Figure 13.13. Other reports and views, such as the

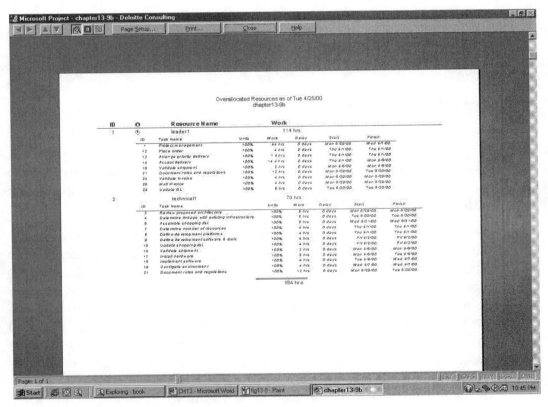

Figure 13.11 Resource leveling options.

Figure 13.12 Overallocated resources report.

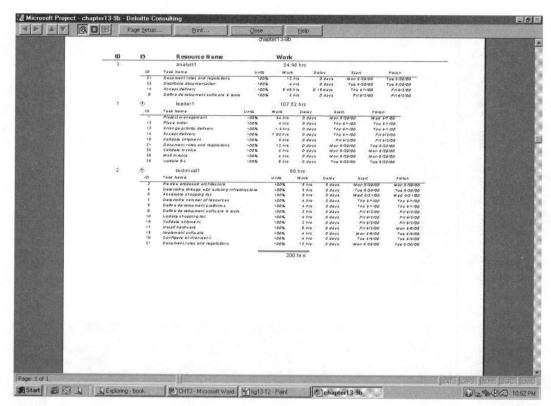

Figure 13.13 Overallocated analyst.

resource graph and the resource sheet, can also be used to identify resources that are overallocated. These are identified by Project with a different color from the other text—say red.

As mentioned in chapter 12, resolving resource overallocations is not a science, but a combination of both science and art. In this example, we should consider using percentage values for the resource allocation to get a more accurate picture of their time involvement across tasks. This is a more accurate process at a lower level of task detail, compared to working at the high-level task view. Applying this technique is useful when you are tracking information that has not yet been entered at the task level. Going through the project plan and making these adjustments—after moving any percentage complete values back to 0—identifies a few more places where another resource can pick up slack, while freeing up overallocated resource time. Making these adjustments, as

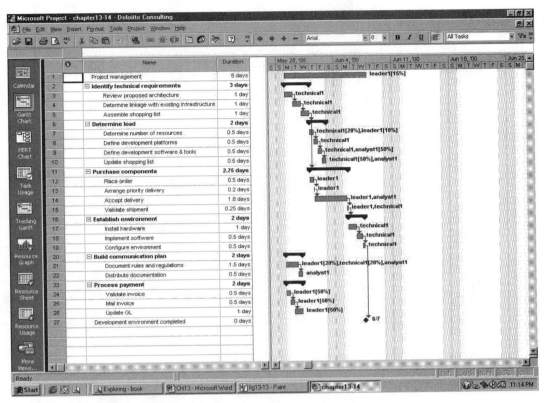

Figure 13.14   Resource percentages.

shown in Figure 13.14, improves the situation somewhat, but the resources are still overallocated across the board.

Attempting to use the resource leveling features, the results of which are shown in Figure 13.15, improves the situation. Only leader1 is overallocated, as can be seen in a copy of the overallocated resources report. Examining the Resource Graph view quickly shows that leader1 is overallocated during the week of May 28, specifically on Thursday and Friday, at 115% and 125%, respectively, as shown in Figure 13.16. Since project managers tend to have some discretionary time in their schedule, as well as the requirement to work until an assignment is completed, this situation might be tolerable and the project plan might be ready for tracking. However, being a stickler and removing all resource overallocations in this case can be accommodated by some straightforward reallocation of responsibilities. For example, on the Friday in question, leader1 is

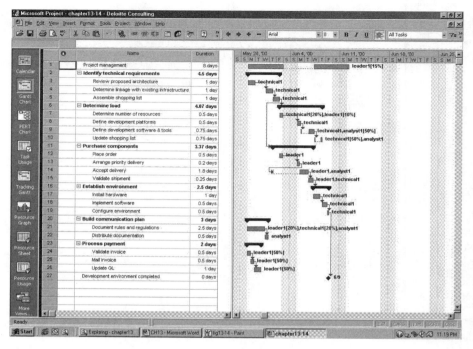

Figure 13.15 Leveled resources.

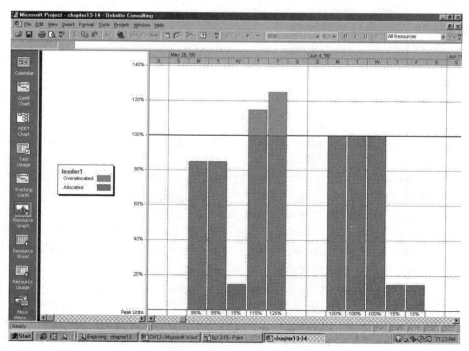

Figure 13.16 Overallocated time for Leader1.

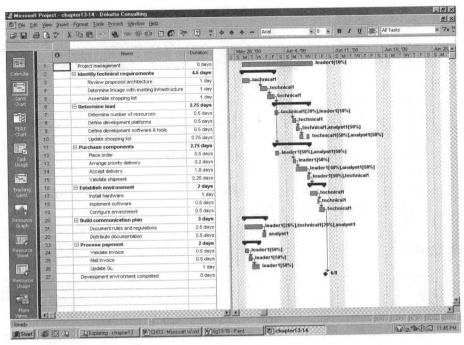

Figure 13.17   Overallocation corrected.

100% allocated to placing an order. Some of this time can be split with the analyst who is still underutilized on the project. Moving 50% of the work effort to this other resource brings leader1 to 75% utilization on that day. The analyst is busier than before, but still not overallocated. The simplest method of seeing which resources are overallocated is to look at the resource sheet. This will show you which resources are overallocated, but not when. This information can be drawn from the Resource Graph view. You can make adjustments and use Level Now again at any time. Figure 13.17 shows a Gantt chart view with the overallocations fixed for all the resources. The shifted dates are acceptable to the users.

Avoiding Information Overload

Microsoft Project can easily overwhelm users with information overload. Reports and views offer good approaches for massaging specific information to focus on specific data. Several additional options are also available to do this, as discussed in this section.

Filtering Tasks

Another method of reducing the amount of information that is visible in any Project view (e.g., Gantt Chart, Tracking Gantt) is to use the filtering function that is available from the Project, Filtered for: All Tasks option from the main toolbar. Selecting a filter option causes it to be processed immediately. The basic filters that are available include the following: All tasks, Completed Tasks, Critical, Date Range, Incomplete Tasks, Milestones, Summary Tasks, Task Range, Tasks With Estimated Durations, and Using Resource. Some of the filters (e.g., Using Resource) will prompt you for additional information. An additional filter set is also available under Project, Filtered For, More Filters.

Sort Option

The sort option, available from the Project, Sort option from the toolbar, can be used with different display views to reshuffle the order of the data that is displayed. Sort options can be specified by Start Date, by Finish Date, by Priority, by Cost, and by ID. A Sort dialog box is also available to specify a specific set of fields to act as a sort key.

Group by Option

The group by option, available from the Project, Group by option from the toolbar, can be used to group task types together. This includes No Group, Complete and Incomplete Tasks, Constraint Type, Critical, Duration, Duration then Priority, Milestones, Priority, Priority Keeping Outline Structure, and Team Status Pending.

Summary

This chapter examined some of the more useful reports that extract and format information from a project plan. These reports fit into six basic categories and offer a great deal of customization to the user. Another topic that was examined in this chapter was project tracking through a percentage-completed value or through a baseline. This was examined in the context of cost tracking and management.

A dialog box for leveling resources was also discussed in this chapter and used at a lower level of detail than in chapter 12. A variety of techniques were used to resource level a project plan to implement a development environment that initially had several overallocated resources. The leveling process with Project's estimation and project management experience was used to adjust the plan until the resource overallocation was eliminated.

Several approaches for reducing the amount of information that is visible in the reports or views were also examined in this chapter. This included a set of filters, sort fields, and methods of grouping tasks.

Sample Project Plans

This appendix contains a selection of project plans that can be used as templates for your projects. It also collects the key plans started in chapters 10, 11, 12, and 13 and includes the completed versions in one spot. These are sample project plans that satisfy the requirements of the initiatives they were created for. You will need to customize them in terms of durations and resources for your initiatives. It will also be necessary to determine the level of detail required for your projects and to adjust the task lists accordingly.

Project Plan 1: Conducting an IT Strategy and Plan

This plan essentially coordinates setup activities, interviews in multiple locations, and assembly of the results. The major activities, showing several levels of tasks in the hierarchy, are as follows:

```
IT Strategy & Plan
    Define Overall Approach and Interview Schedule
    Interview New York City Resources
        Mike John
        Bill Paul
```

```
        Tom Jones
        Paul Rose
Compile Interview Results
Interview New Jersey Resources
        Bob P
        Sue T
        Kathy M
        Gina K
        Henry R
        Tony R
        Tony M
Compile Interview Results
Interview Orlando Resources
        Erin I
        Joe I
Compile Interview Results
Interview Memphis Resources
```

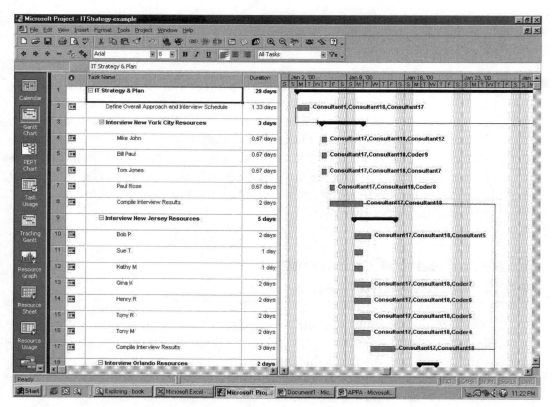

Figure A.1 IT strategy and plan part A.

```
                    George G
                    Corey P
              Compile Interview Results
              Develop Draft Project Synopsis for 100 enhancements
              Distribute Draft project synopsis for Review by Interviewees
              Analyze Resource Requirements and Create Full Resource Plan
                    Including Project Phasing and Relative Priorities
        Develop IT Strategy and Plan Presentation and Supporting Detailed
        AnalysisConduct Planning Workshop
```

Figures A.1 and A.2 show the resources and durations attached to these tasks. The major scale timeline is set to weekly, while the minor scale is set to daily because of the short duration of this project. Figure A.3 shows one part of the project, with a major scale of monthly and a minor scale of weekly as a contrast.

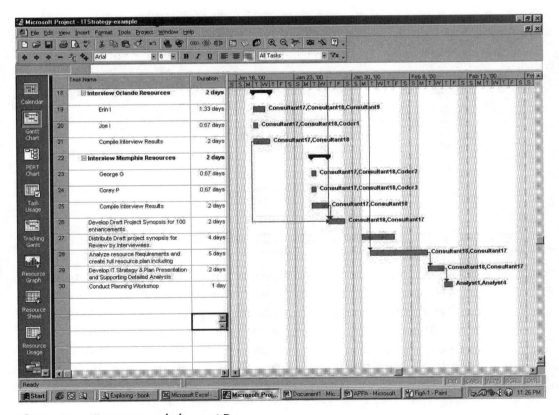

Figure A.2   IT strategy and plan part B.

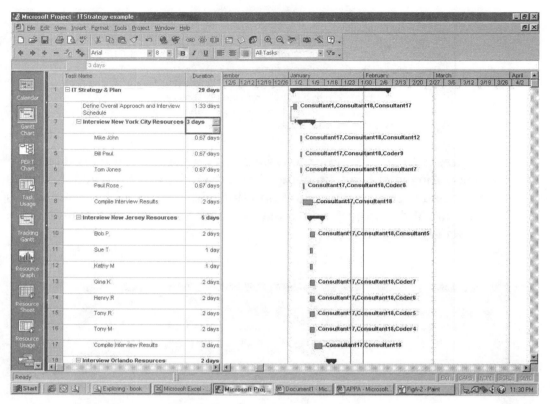

Figure A.3 IT strategy and plan reduced timescale.

Project Plan 2: IT Systems Review

Here is an example of a project plan for conducting an IT systems review. This was built using a top-down management technique, whereby specific time durations are predefined and the plan is built to accommodate these constraints. Slack time is left within the major activities. Table A.1 shows the task names, durations, and some of the roles that are required to conduct such a process. Figure A.4 shows a Gantt chart view of these activities mapped to a timescale and showing some of the dependencies between the tasks.

Table A.1   IT Systems Review Plan

TASK NAME	LEVEL	DURATION	RESOURCE
Internal Systems Review	1	15d	
Develop Application Inventory	2	3d	Integrator
Gather Internal Systems Background Documentation	2	5d	Designer 2
Review Internal Systems Background Documentation	2	1d	"Project Manager 2,Consultant 2"
Schedule Interviews with Internal Systems Managers	2	3d	"Project Manager 2,Consultant 2"
LAN/WAN	1	5d	
Conduct Interviews	2	1d	"Project Manager 2,Consultant 2"
Compile Interview Results	2	1d	"Project Manager 2,Consultant 2"
Help Desk	1	5d	
Conduct Interviews	2	1d	"Project Manager 2,Consultant 2"
Compile Interview Results	2	1d	"Project Manager 2,Consultant 2"
Accounting & Administrative Systems	1	15d	
Conduct Interviews	2	1d	"Project Manager 2,Consultant 2"
Compile Interview Results	2	1d	"Project Manager 2,Consultant 2"
Customer Relationship Management Systems	1	15d	
Conduct Interviews	2	1d	"Project Manager 2,Consultant 2"
Compile Interview Results	2	1d	"Project Manager 2,Consultant 2"
ISN	1	15d	
Conduct Interviews	2	1d	"Project Manager 2,Consultant 2"
Compile Interview Results	2	1d	"Project Manager 2,Consultant 2"
Prepare Draft of Internal Systems Review	1	1d	"Project Manager 2,Consultant 2"
Revise Internal Systems Review Based on Feedback	1	1d	"Project Manager 2,Consultant 2"
Deliver Internal Systems Review	1	1d	"Project Manager 2,Consultant 2"

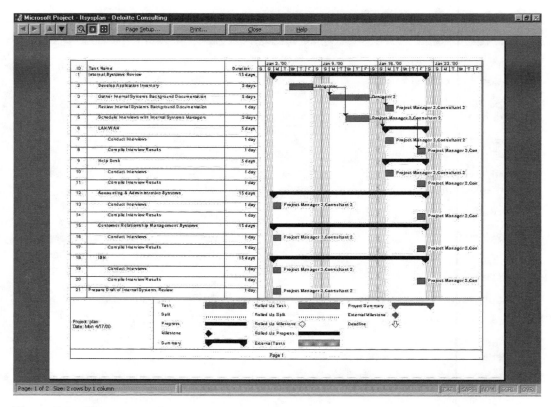

Figure A.4 IT systems review.

Project Plan 3: Component Development and Integration with the Web

This project plan shows activities for constructing a set of components according to business requirements, and the process for testing and integrating them into an existing Web-based solution. This plan has arranged some tasks in parallel in order meet an aggressive fixed end date. The Gantt view of this plan is shown in Figures A.5, A.6, and A.7.

```
Project Management                                    41d
   Weekly status meeting                              41d
Initiation                                            10d?
  Confirm stakeholders         Manager Sector         1d?
  Assemble project team        Manager Sector         1d?
  Identify key users           Lead Evan              3d?
```

Identify external vendors	Lead Barbara	1d?
Establish status requirements	Manager Sector	3d?
Revise project charter	"Lead Barbara,Analyst Rebecca"	2d?
Revise project plan	Manager Sector	2d?
Conduct risk assessment	Lead Evan	3d?
Build testing approach		3d?
Identify high-level requirements	Lead Evan	1d?
Build high-level test cases	"Lead Evan[20%],Analyst Harry"	5d?
Identify acceptance criteria	Lead Evan	1d?
Get user sign-off	"User Tony,Manager Sector"	2d?
Project charter printed		0d
Requirements		12d?
Gather development environment requirements	Tech Bill	4d?
Gather vendor interface requirements	Lead Barbara	3d?
Gather business requirements		
"Analyst Rebecca, Analyst Harry,User Sue, User Bob"		10d?
Get sign-offs	Lead Barbara	1d?
Requirements printed		0d
Infrastructure		10d?
Identify logon users	Tech Amanda	5d?
Create Logon IDs	Tech Amanda	1d?
Update infrastructure documentation	Architect Gurprit	3d?
Establish development environment	Tech Amanda	3d?
Establish testing environment	Tech Amanda	4d?
Environments implemented		0d
Analyze and model requirements		7d?
Develop requirement specifications	Analyst Rebecca	5d?
Update object model	Modeler Kathy	2d?
Define component interfaces and methods	Modeler Kathy	2d?
Define user interface interaction	Modeler Kathy	3d?
Architecture		4d?
Update architecture documentation	Architect Gurprit	3d?
Approve changes	Manager Sector	1d?
Development		12d?
Build development specifications	"Analyst Rebecca,User Tony"	5d?
Code component modules	"Coder Tom,Coder Sarah"	6d?
Update user interface	Coder Sarah	6d?
Build control reports	Coder Sarah	6d?
Develop unit test scripts		
"Coder Tom,Coder Ginger,Coder Sarah,User Sue"		3d?
Conduct unit testing		
"Coder Tom,Coder Ginger,Coder Sarah"		4d?

```
Integration                                                      9d?
  Build integration plan      "Lead Evan,Lead Barbara,User Bob"   5d?
  Quality assure vendor interface        Analyst Rebecca         2d?
  Integrate Components       Coder Tom                           2d?


Testing                                                         16d?
  Integration & System Testing                                  15d?
  Identify testing users      Manager Sector                    1d?
  Build testing approach       "Lead Evan,Analyst Harry"        1.5d?
  Build test scenarios        "User Sue,User Bob"                2d?
  Build test cases            "Modeler Kathy,Analyst Harry"     3d?
  Build test scripts       "Coder Sarah,Lead Evan"              1d?
  Conduct tests         "Lead Evan,User Tony,User Sue,User Bob" 4d?
  Gather results         Lead Evan                               1d?

Stress Testing                                                  10d?
  Identify testing users        Manager Sector                  1d?
  Build testing approach
          "Manager Sector,User Bob,Tech Amanda,Lead Barbara"  0.5d?
  Build test cases         "Tech Amanda,User Bob"                1d?
  Build test scripts       Tech Amanda                          3d?
  Conduct tests            Tech Amanda                          3d?
  Gather results         "Tech Amanda,Lead Barbara"             1d?

Acceptance Testing                                              11d?
  Identify testing users        Manager Sector                  3d?
  Build testing approach
        "User Sue,Manager Sector,Lead Evan,Architect Gurprit" 2.25d?
  Build test cases
              "User Tony,User Sue,User Bob,Analyst Rebecca"    0.5d?
  Build test scripts       "Coder Tom,Coder Ginger"             2d?
  Conduct tests
          "User Tony,User Sue,User Bob,Analyst Rebecca"       3.75d?
  Gather results         "Lead Evan,Analyst Rebecca"            1d?

Final Sign-off                                                   8d?
  Assemble test results        Analyst Rebecca                  1d?
  Assemble project documentation     Analyst Harry              7d?
  Distribute package to stakeholders   Analyst Rebecca          2d?
  Conduct final presentation
              "Manager Sector,Lead Barbara,Lead Evan"          1d?
  Make go/no go decision                                        1d?

Implementation                                                  10d?
Build implementation approach
              "Architect Gurprit,Lead Barbara,User Bob"        6d?
Define training strategy
              "Analyst Rebecca,Analyst Harry"                  6d?
Define backout/contingency strategy    Tech Bill               2d?
Train users              "Analyst Harry,User Tony"             1d?
Implement solution        "Tech Amanda,Tech Bill"              3d?
Product Rollout                                                 0 d
```

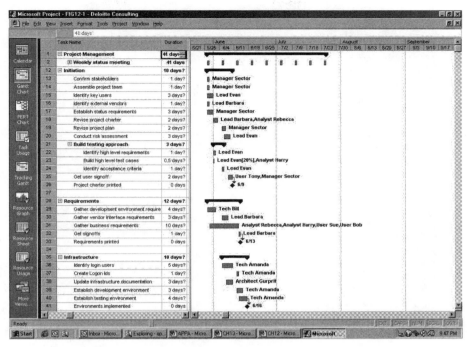

Figure A.5   Web-based component development—Part A.

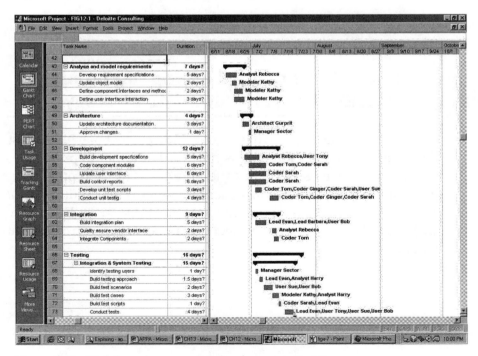

Figure A.6   Web-based component development—Part B.

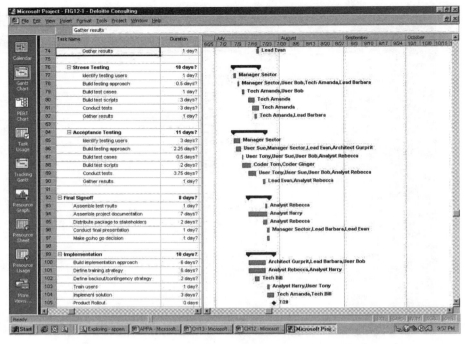

Figure A.7   Web-based component development—Part C.

Project Plan 4: Component Development and Integration with the Web—Alternate Strategy

This is an alternate approach to building the project plan in the last example. If an implementation date is not fixed, another approach would be to use dependencies to fill out the timeline. This will push out the implementation date and, consequently, support the reduction of some resources as well as reducing the load on individuals. Figures A.8, A.9, A.10, and A.11 show the project plan recut with stronger intertask dependencies.

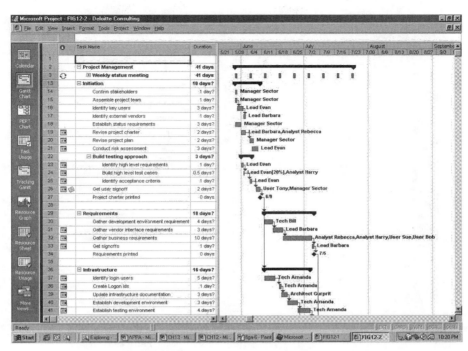

Figure A.8   Web-based component development with dependencies—Part A.

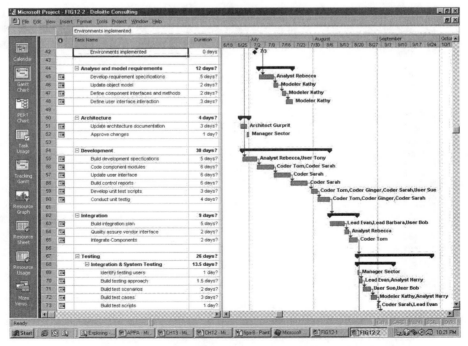

Figure A.9   Web-based component development with dependencies—Part B.

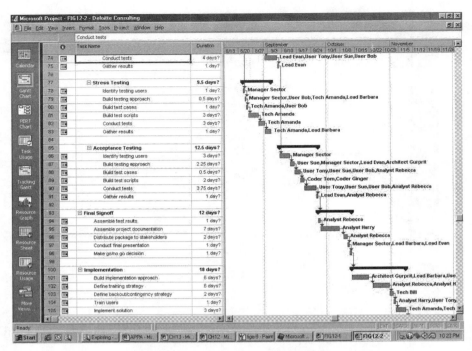

Figure A.10 Web-based component development with dependencies—Part C.

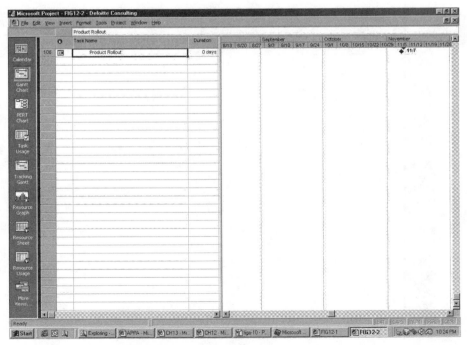

Figure A.11 Web-based component development with dependencies—Part D.

Project Plan 5: Project Audit

This project plan was built iteratively when we demonstrated the capabilities of Microsoft Project in chapters 11 through 13. This plan supports an audit or review of another project. Figures A.12 and A.13 show the Gantt view of the following activities:

```
Project initiation
    Assemble project team              Assessment Manager
    Document assessment criteria       Assessment Manager
    Construct project charter          "Assessment Manager,
                                       Senior Assessment Analyst"


Review background materials
    Gather application project material  Junior Assessment Analyst
    Build list of documents              Junior Assessment Analyst
    Prioritize documents                 Senior Assessment Analyst
    Review and understand documents      "Assessment Manager,
                                         Senior Assessment
                                         Analyst, Junior
                                         Assessment Analyst"

Prepare for interviews
    Confirm interview list and time    Assessment Manager
    Establish interview agenda         "Senior Assessment
                                       Analyst,Junior Assessment
                                       Analyst"

    Prepare interview material         "Senior Assessment
                                       Analyst,Junior Assessment
                                       Analyst"

    Distribute interview material      Junior Assessment Analyst


Go/No Go discussion
    Confirm stakeholder meeting        Assessment Manager
    Present interview material         Assessment Manager
    Facilitate discussion              "Assessment Manager,
                                       Vice President
                                       Operations, Business
                                       Director, CIO"
    Document go/no go decision         Assessment Manager


Conduct interviews
    Confirm interview schedule         "Senior Assessment
                                       Analyst, Junior
                                       Assessment Analyst,
                                       Project Manager, Senior
                                       Architect,Business User
```

                                              1,Business User 2,Systems
                                              Analyst"

Conduct interviews
    Collect interview notes   "Senior Assessment
                                              Analyst, Junior Assessment
                                              Analyst"

Prepare final presentation
    Assemble interview notes   "Assessment Manager,
                                              Senior Assessment
                                              Analyst,Junior Assessment
                                              Analyst"

    Build table of contents   Senior Assessment Analyst
    Validate table of contents   Assessment Manager
    Build report   "Assessment Manager,Senior
                                              Assessment Analyst,Junior
                                              Assessment Analyst"

    Conduct follow-up interviews   "Junior Assessment
                                              Analyst,Senior Assessment
                                              Analyst"

    Revise report   "Senior Assessment
                                              Analyst,Junior Assessment
                                              Analyst"

    Build executive summary   "Assessment Manager,Senior
                                              Assessment Analyst,Junior
                                              Assessment Analyst"

Conduct final presentation
    Build agenda   "Assessment Manager,Senior
                                              Assessment Analyst"

    Confirm attendees   Senior Assessment Analyst
    Book facilities   Junior Assessment Analyst
    Present findings   Assessment Manager

Deliver final report
    Update report   "Senior Assessment
                                              Analyst,Junior Assessment
                                              Analyst"

    Conduct follow-on interviews   Project Manager
    Final internal review   "Assessment Manager,Senior
                                              Assessment Analyst,Junior
                                              Assessment Analyst"

    Publish report   Junior Assessment Analyst
    Deliver report   Assessment Manager

Project done

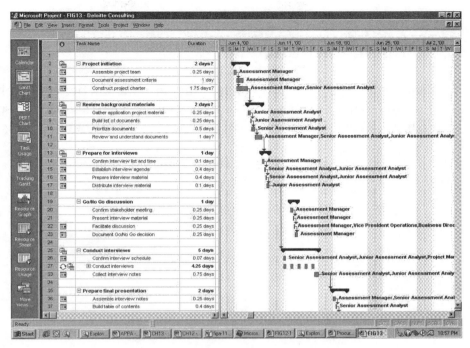

Figure A.12   Audit and assessment of an existing project—Part A.

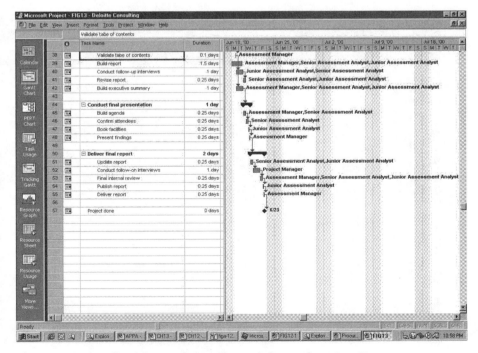

Figure A.13   Audit and assessment of an existing project—Part B.

Project Plan 6: Implement Development Environment

This project plan identifies some of the major activities involved in upgrading a development environment with a limited number of resources: Figure A.14 shows the Gantt chart view of this project plan.

```
Project management                                    7.5d?
Identify technical requirements                         3d
   Review proposed architecture                         1d
   Determine linkage with existing Infrastructure      1d
   Assemble shopping list                              1d

Determine load                                          2d
   Determine number of resources                       0.5d
   Define development platforms                         0.5d
   Define development software and tools                0.5d
   Update shopping list                                0.5d
```

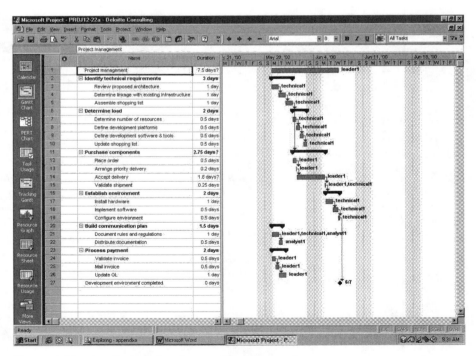

Figure A.14 Implement development environment.

```
Purchase components                    2.75d?
   Place order                          0.5d
   Arrange priority delivery            0.2d
   Accept delivery                      1.8d?
   Validate shipment                    0.25d

Establish environment                   2d
   Install hardware                      1d
   Implement software                    0.5d
   Configure environment                 0.5d

Build communication plan                1.5d
   Document rules and regulations        1d
   Distribute documentation              0.5d

Process payment                         2d
   Validate invoice                      0.5d
   Mail invoice                          0.5d
   Update GL                             1d

Development environment completed       0d
```

The Management Questionnaire

We used two versions of the management questionnaire to gather information from a pool of managers. The full management questionnaire was sent to over 50 managers and executives in order to collect their experiences on what works on a project and what does not work well. A simplified version of the questionnaire was sent to 100 managers, and their responses were collected, primarily by email, over the phone, and in person (in a limited number of cases). Both versions of the questionnaire are reprinted in this appendix, beginning with the long form.

An Interview Guide for Project Managers—Long Form

Part I General Information

Name: _____   Title: _____

Organization: _____   How long with the Organization: _____

Interview Date: _____

Part II Project Management

1. Briefly describe typical projects managed in the past three years.
   a. Large projects (include project size in person-years, $)

      Project   Size ($ & PYs)   Complexity   I.T. Environment
   b. Small Projects
2. How was the project initiated? (e.g., part of the I.T. strategic plan)
3. Was a business case prepared for the above projects?

   Yes _____   No _____

   If yes, what were the key benefits identified as part of project justification.
4. Who were the stakeholders for the project?
5. Which application development tools were used?
6. How was the project managed?
   a. regular reporting to the steering committee (how frequently)
   b. project management tools used
   c. project management methodology used
   d. use of external resources to supplement project team
   e. exclusively external resources
7. How would you rate the success of this project?

   _____ Very successful
   _____ Moderately successful
   _____ Not successful

   Explain:

8. Based on what you know now, how would you have managed the project?

9. Based on your experience in managing projects, would you manage small projects differently than large projects? Explain.

10. What are the five key attributes of successful project management?

11. What are five ingredients to watch for to ensure that projects do not fail?

12. A project manager should spend more time as a hands-on person and not planning and directing the project. Agree or disagree?

13. Any comments you wish to make about project management techniques or tools that could be of benefit to others?

14. Please rank the typical reasons for project failure in a descending order by placing a number at the right (we are interested in the top 7):

Typical Reasons for Project Failure:

Reason	*Ranking*
Insufficient funding	
Lack of technical skills	
Insufficient time to complete the project	
Lack of a project plan	
Project team politics	
Organizational politics	
Lack of communication	
Requirements not clearly understood	
Lack of flexibility to accommodate changing requirements	
Insufficient testing	
Lack of postimplementation support	
Technological limitations	
Unrealistic expectations from stakeholders	
Lack of project leadership and management	
Other _____	
_____	
_____	

An Interview Guide for Project Managers—Short Form

Project Management Questionnaire

Part 1: General Information

Name: _____   Title: _____

Organization: _____   Time with organization: _____

Interview Date: _____

Part II: Project Management Questions

Out of the projects you have completed in the last 5 years, how many fit into each of the following categories?

Very Successful (e.g. all objectives met, on budget, on time): _____

Moderately Successful: _____

Not Successful: _____

What are the five key attributes that a successful project manager should have?

What are five indicators that a project is going to fail?

Please rank the top 7 reasons for project failure in descending order of impact by placing a number from 1 to 7 to the left of a description:

_____ Insufficient funding

_____ Lack of technical skills on the project team

_____ Lack of other skills on the project team

_____ Insufficient time to complete the project

_____ Lack of a project plan

_____ Project team politics

_____ Organizational politics

_____ Lack of communication

_____ Requirements not clearly understood

_____ Requirements repeatedly being changed

_____ Lack of flexibility to accommodate changing requirements

_____ Insufficient testing

_____ Lack of postimplementation support

_____ Technological limitations

_____ Unrealistic expectations from stakeholders

_____ Lack of project leadership and management

_____ Other: _____

_____

Management Survey Results—Why Projects Fail

O ver 100 managers were surveyed by the authors for this book to collect a broad base of project experiences. The survey gathered empirical information about reasons for project success, project failure, and other project issues. Responses to two questions on why projects fail are summarized in this section.

The following questions were included on the survey:

1. What are five indicators that a project is going to fail?
2. Please rank the top seven reasons for project failure in a descending order of impact by placing a number from 1 to 7 to the left of the description. [The complete list of possible reasons is shown in Table C.1.]

Responses to Question 3

Because of the open-ended nature of the question, responses were diverse. There was no attempt to rank or prioritize the responses. A summary of indicators contributing to project failure are described here.

☐ Scope creep, lack of funding, unrealistic constraints on project schedule and deliverables

□ Little or no commitment from stakeholders and management

□ Unclear business goals and changing project objectives

□ Slippage in meeting project milestones

A significant number of respondents felt that organizational and team politics were key contributors to project failure. Others felt that a lack of project direction—exemplified by a lack of executive commitment—fuzzy project deliverables, and poor project management were also key hindrances.

Responses to Question 4

Table C.1 tabulates the number of respondents who selected a particular reason for project failure to be a top-six candidate:

Table C.1 Reasons for Project Failure

TYPICAL REASONS FOR PROJECT FAILURE	RANKINGS					
	1	2	3	4	5	SUM
1 Insufficient funding	3	3	4	3		13
2 Lack of technical skills on the project team	2		4	3	8	17
3 Lack of other skills on the project team	1	1	1	3	4	10
4 Insufficient time to complete the project	3	2	2	4	2	13
5 Lack of a project plan	4	8	7	24	23	66
6 Project team politics		3	1	2	1	7
7 Organizational politics	6	3	4	14	24	51
8 Lack of communication	3	4	15	20	6	48
9 Requirements not clearly understood	27	37	10	8	5	87
10 Requirements repeatedly being changed	2	3	36	3	3	47
11 Lack of flexibility to accommodate changing requirements		1	4	1	3	9
12 Insufficient testing				3	2	5
13 Lack of postimplementation support	1				1	2
14 Technological limitations			2	1		3
15 Unrealistic expectations from stakeholders	2	4	11	11	14	42
16 Lack of project leadership and management	48	33	1	5	3	90
Total Responses	102	102	102	102	102	510

The top six reasons for project failure selected by the respondents to this survey were:

1. Lack of project leadership and management (selected by 90 respondents)
2. Requirements not clearly understood (selected by 87 respondents)
3. Lack of a project plan (selected by 66 respondents)
4. Organizational politics (selected by 51 respondents)
5. Lack of communication (selected by 48 respondents)
6. Requirements repeatedly being changed (selected by 47 respondents)

Interpretation

Interestingly, a lack of technical skills was not selected enough times to appear in the top six, despite the fact that many employers spend a great deal of time asking prospective employees about their technical skills in painstaking detail. This observation is consistent with the successful projects discussed in chapter 6, since projects using new technology succeeded with teams that needed to be trained on software/hardware after being hired.

Another observation is that organizational politics was selected in the top five 51 times, while project team politics was selected 7 times. Politics, on the whole, was selected 58 times. As mentioned in chapter 4, politics is a non-value-added activity that draws energy away from constructive project activities. Professionals who are preoccupied with trying to protect themselves, marketing their abilities, or playing sparring matches with others are not focused on achieving a project deliverable. At a more insidious level, professionals who are engaged in playing the political game sometimes sabotage the project's potential for success if someone else appears to be getting the credit. After observing, and at times playing, the political game, it seems that the game is difficult to eliminate entirely. There are not enough positions to go around, so team members will compete for advancement. Management at all levels should insist that this competition be played, within some definite boundaries that will not allow the political game to degenerate into a free-for-all. All too often management does the opposite by rewarding those who play the game well, and by overlooking those who do not choose to participate. Is it any wonder that many projects are plagued by too much politics?

Another key area that was viewed as a major contributor toward project failure was "Requirements not clearly understood," which was selected 87 times, and the related "Lack of flexibility to accommodate changing requirements," selected 47 times. This is hardly surprising, considering some of the team dynamics at this particular phase of the project. Typically, IS has the skills and tools but not the business know-how, while the business community has the business knowledge but lacks the skill to pull this knowledge together to form a proper business requirements document. Also typical is the ongoing tension between the business and IS communities. This gap is slowly closing as organizations evolve into operations where business planning skills are becoming embedded in the business environment and IT professionals provide services on an as-needed basis. This type of approach often results in a project that is managed jointly by IS and the business community. Though a bit awkward at first, this method of managing a project is quite successful, and a number of large organizations are evolving toward this mode of operation.

Table C.2 provides a cross-reference of chapters the reader should consult in order to avoid each of the top six failure factors.

Other chapters in the book deal with the other factors of failure that were identified in the management survey.

Table C.2 Top Six Failure Factors

FAILURE FACTOR	REFER TO CHAPTER(S)
1 Lack of project leadership and management	1, 2, 5, 6, 7
2 Requirements not clearly understood	5, 6, 7
3 Lack of a project plan	4
4 Organizational politics	5
5 Lack of communication	5, 6
6 Requirements repeatedly being changed	5, 6, 7

Management Survey Results— Why Projects Succeed

The key ingredients for attaining project success—as noted by the respondents to our two management surveys—included executive support, a good project plan, and strong project management. Specific responses to the survey question are included in this section. These are grouped into categories to allow for easier comprehension.

Specific Responses

Commitment

☐ Organizational support, executive support

Human Skills

☐ Skill-sets, competent team, competent users

☐ Ability to identify problems quickly and resolve them

☐ Excellent facilitation/coordination

☐ Coaching ability

☐ Good communication

☐ Good interpersonal skills

- ☐ Able and cooperative participation of project members and clients
- ☐ Ensure scope is clear; get the right people involved/committed

Management

- ☐ Project plan
- ☐ Good project management
- ☐ Expectation management
- ☐ Conflict management
- ☐ Monitoring and following effectively throughout project lifecycle
- ☐ Ability to separate funding from deliverables/resources
- ☐ Accurate planning and budgeting
- ☐ Full application of sufficient resources
- ☐ Accurate tracking of progress

Requirements

- ☐ Clear understanding of objectives
- ☐ Full understanding of objectives

Planning

- ☐ Agree on acceptance criteria
- ☐ Contingency planning
- ☐ Prioritization
- ☐ Establish critical success factors

Resources

- ☐ Adequate human and budget resources
- ☐ Resource management

Standards

- ☐ Ability to deliver quality

Interpreting Survey Results

It has been said that the project manager is quite a unique individual. This person has to understand the technical intricacies of a project, have a keen understanding of human behavior, and be well organized. Not only is this person expected to deal with the daily gauntlet of project-related issues, but he or she is also expected to understand and provide encouragement to the staff whose personal problems have overflowed into the work environment. The results from the survey were not surprising and were consistent with the responses received for why projects fail. Projects succeed when:

☐ The project manager possesses superior management and human skills.

☐ The project manager takes the time to understand the dynamics of his or her working environment. This includes the players—their relationships, strengths, and weaknesses.

☐ The project manager takes the time to become familiar with his or her staff, and understand their individuality and orientation. This is crucial in motivating staff members.

☐ Project sponsorship is unequivocal.

☐ The project is funded adequately.

Of particular importance is that players get along, share a common goal, have talents and experience, and have a burning desire to succeed. Many successful projects also have a high-ranking champion who plays a pivotal role in ensuring that the project gets the attention and resources it needs. Such a champion is usually talented, has a mind for the big picture and details (where appropriate), and is highly regarded within the organization.

A clear understanding of a project's deliverables, how to reach them, and continuous monitoring are also strong contributors toward project success.

Development Lifecycle Forms

This appendix contains sample forms and templates that are loosely bundled under the full project lifecycle phases. They are also available for downloading on the companion Web site at www.wiley.com/compbooks/purba. The following categories are examined in this appendix:

- **Project initiation.** This template bundle contains a project charter, estimate by components, project risk, streamlined quality plan, resource needs table, and role requirements across systems.

- **Project management.** This template bundle contains a milestone checklist (lifecycle), milestone checklist, data conversion project plan, weekly status report, monthly status report, monthly timesheet, issue and concern log, issues list, issues log, planning checklist, and status meeting agenda.

- **Change requests.** This template bundle contains a scope change and a project change request.

- **Testing.** This template bundle contains a testing variance, test scenario, and problem report.

- **Requirements.** This template bundle contains a requirements checklist and requirements statement.

☐ **Architecture.** This template bundle contains architecture checklists.

☐ **Communication.** This template bundle contains a letter for wide distribution before implementing a project, issue memo, and project newsletter.

☐ **Sign-offs.** This template bundle contains a project deliverable and a project acceptance form.

☐ **Costing.** This template bundle contains estimating project costs, project cost report—deliverable based, project cost report—resources, and calculating a budget.

☐ **Other.** This template bundle contains a resource evaluation, short evaluation form, project evaluation matrix, and a project history form.

The remaining sections of this appendix contain forms to reflect these bundled templates. Forms are contained within categories. The name of the form precedes the template, which is delimited within two horizontal lines.

Project Initiation Template Bundle

Deliverable templates that are relevant to project initiation activities are included in this section.

Form: Project Charter

Provide details under each of the following headings to build a project charter. Use an iterative approach to complete the details, as not all the information will be known at the start of the project.

Project Definition

Project Scope

Project Objectives

Project Deliverables

Approach

The milestone deliverable dates for this project are as follows:

Jan 30, xxxx	Complete xxxx;
Feb 29, xxxx	Complete xxxx;
March 18, xxxx	Complete xxxx;
April 20, xxxx	Complete xxxx;

Resources, Their Roles and Responsibilities

User Sign-off

Critical Success Factors

Project Plan

Dependencies

Outstanding Issues

Form: Estimate by Components

A table can be used to build first cut estimates for the project charter by dividing the number of components involved in the initiative into effort categories, such as simple, moderate, and complex. For example, the following table would be used to store the total number of windows expected in the solution. Each window is added to one of the effort columns. The total work effort is calculated by assigning a value to each of the effort columns (e.g., simple = 5 days, moderate = 10 days, and complex = 20 days). The total work effort is calculated by multiplying the effort value by the number of components under the effort column.

COMPONENT	EFFORT COLUMNS			TOTAL
	SIMPLE	MODERATE	COMPLEX	
Windows				
Interfaces				
Reports				
Navigation				
Business Components				
Documentation				
Toolbars				
Workflow				
Tables				

Form: Project Risk

This questionnaire can be used to capture the relevant risks across categories and to define a mitigation strategy for each one. Some risk categories are shown, but these should be reviewed and customized with input from your organization's risk manager.

PROJECT INFORMATION	MANAGEMENT INFORMATION
Project Name:	Project Manager:
Project Number:	Sponsor/Stakeholder:
Project End Date:	PMO Office:
Date of Assessment:	Risk Manager:

Risk Management Questionnaire Objectives:

describe

Understanding the grades:

describe

Instructions: Complete the table for each of the risk categories defined below. Project managers can identify and include additional categories.

Risk Categories:

☐ Business Risks

☐ Project Risks

☐ Project Management Risks

☐ Technology Risks

RISK	DESCRIPTION	OCCURRENCE	IMPACT	SCOPE	MITIGATION APPROACH	STATUS

Form: Streamlined Quality Plan

Fill in the relevant details under each of the following headings to start a quality plan for the organization. From an ISO9001 quality perspective, it is necessary to follow the processes that are defined in this plan. Even if your organization is not ISO-compliant—and is not interested in becoming compliant—it is sound policy to ensure that at least minimal quality requirements are followed during the project lifecycle.

Project Methodology

Describe the methodology to be used.

Project Team

Describe project team roles, responsibilities, and authorization levels.

Project Management

Describe project management approach and occurrence of status meetings and generation of status reports.

Escalation Procedures

Describe issue escalation and resolution procedures. Identify resources with final authority.

Project Documentation

Describe storage and location of documentation.

Risk Assessment

Describe risk assessment manager, expectations, and involvement.

Project Closeout

Describe project acceptance procedures, final sign-offs, and next steps.

Form: Resource Needs Table

In the following table, need is expressed in terms of percentage effort, based on full-time involvement (e.g., 0.5 for half-time environment, 1 for full-time involvement). The resource column contains the names of individuals who can satisfy the requirements. The gap column is used to identify any skill gaps that remain in the role and still need to be filled. The description column can be used for a variety of purposes, including the indication of when the resource is required to start or how a gap is going to be filled. Do not hesitate to include different types of data in the description column as long as it is relevant. This is a good method of ensuring that key "to do" items are not lost.

	NEED	RESOURCE	GAP	DESCRIPTION
Sign-off				
Leader/Manager				
Finance Users				
Business Users (operations)				
Business Analyst				
Developers				
Designers				
Analysts				
Architects				
System Testers				
Other				

Form: Role Requirements across Systems

This form captures the roles required across systems under an engagement. This is used to track shared resources.

ROLE	SYSTEM 1	SYSTEM 2	SYSTEM 3
IT Owner			
Business Owner			
Test Architect			
Test Team Coordinator			
Business Team Lead			
Systems Analyst (QA/UAT)			
Systems Developer			
DBA			
UNIX			
Tester(s)			

Project Management Template Bundle

Some of the deliverable templates that are relevant to project management are included in this section.

Form: Milestone Checklist (Lifecycle)

This checklist is used to capture the completion of key milestones from requirements gathering to implementation. It is a highly useful tool for ensuring that the proper dependencies are met. We've seen many projects in which development is expected to finish before the requirements are even completed. This checklist makes it easy to track and discuss the key dates in their relevant sequence.

SYSTEM	REQUIRE-MENTS	DESIGN	DEVELOP-MENT	UA TESTING	INTE-GRATION TESTING	FINAL USER SIGN-OFF	IMPLEMEN-TATION	TRAINING WORKFLOW

Form: Milestone Checklist (Milestone Filled In)

The following table demonstrates how the lifecycle milestone checklist can be used with some data values filled in the columns. Milestones that have been met are marked DONE in the appropriate cell.

SYSTEM	REQUIRE-MENTS	DESIGN	DEVELOP-MENT	UA TESTING	INTE-GRATION TESTING	FINAL USER SIGN-OFF	IMPLEMEN-TATION	TRAINING WORKFLOW
System 1	Done	Done	Done	Done	April–June 15 June 30-July 15 (Parallel test)	July 15 (Parallel test)	July 15–July 31 Pilot	TBD
System 2	Done	Done	May–July 7	July 1–July 31	July 19–Aug 10	Aug 11	Aug 12	TBD
System 3	Done	Done	Ends June 14	July 14	July 19–Aug 10	Aug 11	Aug 12	TBD
System 4	Done	Done	June 30 July 21		End-to-End Test July 15–July 28 July 21–Aug 21 Mid August start	July 29 Aug 21	July 31 Aug 30	TBD

Form: Milestone Checklist

This milestone checklist is slightly different from the earlier one. It focuses on providing more contact information, as well as key dates. This format is useful in distributed development projects where communication is not going well. Including the key contact information in this form allows questions to be quickly escalated and resolved.

SUBPROJECT NAME	OWNER	DATE REQUIRED	SPECS END DATE	DEVELOPMENT END DATE	TESTING END DATE	TRAINING REQUIRED	SYSTEMS CONTACT	BUSINESS CONTACT	COMMENTS

Form: Data Conversion Project Plan

This form can be used to schedule a set of data conversion tests. The cycle scope row is used to identify the data that is being converted—generally in terms of volume. The other rows capture cycle start dates.

ACTIVITY	CYCLE 1	CYCLE 2	CYCLE 3	CYCLE 4	PRODUCTION
Cycle Scope					
Download Starts					
Conversion Starts					
Reconciliation Begins					
Reconciliation Results Reported					
Development/Fixes					
Go/No Go Decision					

Form: Weekly Status Report

> NOTE: *The information contained in this report is based on work that is in progress. Any questions, discrepancies, or differences of opinion should be directed to xxxxxxx at xxx-xxx-xxxx so that they can be dealt with immediately.*

Project Name: _____ Week Ending: _____

PROJECT SPONSOR	PROJECT MANAGER	STATUS INDICATOR
		Red
		Yellow
		Green

Project Start Date: Planned Project End Date:

Project Description:

Milestone Dates:

Revision History:

Key Decisions that were made this period:

Key Decisions Still Outstanding:

The Current Status and Planned Activities:

Describe:

Form: Monthly Status Report

A monthly status report is prepared by the project manager for the benefit of the project sponsor and the stakeholders. The monthly report includes the following sections:

Project Identification. This section will contain project-identifying information, including project name, project number (if applicable), project manager, and names of the project team.

Project Summary. This section will include a brief summary of the project, including scope.

Project Resources. This section includes project budget and actuals, planned project completion date, and percentage project completion. The dollar variance will also be included.

Accomplishments. This section includes key project accomplishments such as completion of a prototype, completion of logical design, and completion of integration testing.

Obstacles. This section includes any obstacles encountered by the project team, such as resignation of two programmer analysts, changed specifications, delay in the delivery of hardware, and so on.

Objectives for the Next Period. This section includes objectives for the next month, such as completion of physical design, completion of acceptance testing, and installation of software.

Form: Monthly Timesheet

This form can be used to collect time information from resources.

Organization:

Project Name:

Project Number:

Team Member's Name:

Key Project Activities:

Regular Hours Worked

	MONDAY	TUESDAY	WEDNESDAY	THURSDAY	FRIDAY	OVERTIME	TOTAL
Week 1:							
Week 2:							
Week 3:							
Week 4:							
Week 5:							
Total							

Remarks:

Team Member's Signature

Authorized Signature

Form: Issue and Concern Log

SYSTEM NAME	DOCUMENTED REQUIREMENTS & FILE LAYOUTS REQ.	FILE	ISSUE DESCRIPTION	RESPONSIBILITY	DATE RAISED	RESOLUTION DATE	STATUS

Form: Issues List

Date of List:

CURRENT STATUS	ISSUE #	ISSUE NAME	DATE FOUND	OWNER	SEVERITY	DESCRIPTION	UPDATE

Please contact xxxxxx at xxxxx if there are any changes or modifications to this list.

Form: Issues Log

Project Name:

Date of List:

ISSUE NO	ITEM DESCRIPTION	WHO'S IMPACTED	STATUS	RESPONSIBILITY	REMARKS
1					
2					
3					

Please contact xxxxxx at xxxxx if there are any changes or modifications to this list.

Form: Stakeholders' List Of Deliverables and Sign-off

This template is used to track sponsor sign-off of specific issues. This list can be saved within a project status report and extracted for meetings. This straightforward table ensures that expectations are clearly communicated to anyone involved in the inspection and sign-off process. The sign-off column contains the name of a group or specific individuals and their contact information. A couple of examples have been left in the template as a reference.

ISSUE	ESTIMATED DATE	SIGN-OFF
Test Converted Database Upload to Mars Process	July 10	Data Conversion Team
Technical Validation	?	John Bill
Conversion Team Validation	July 31	Data Conversion Team
User Validation and Corrections	August 10	?

Form: Planning Checklist

This document contains a checklist for the subprojects that are within scope of the project. It focuses on subjects within specific categories. A resource is given the responsibility to lead a category. Resources are also allocated at the subject level and have ownership and responsibility for the subjects they are assigned.

General:

SUBJECT	DELIVERABLE/ACTIVITY	DUE DATE	WHO	DONE	LEFT TO DO/COMMENTS

Notes:

Production Environment: Subproject Responsibility – xxxxxxxx

SUBJECT	DELIVERABLE/ACTIVITY	DUE DATE	WHO	DONE	LEFT TO DO/COMMENTS

Notes:

Data Conversion: Subproject Responsibility – xxxxxxxx

SUBJECT	DELIVERABLE/ACTIVITY	DUE DATE	WHO	DONE	LEFT TO DO/COMMENTS

Notes:

(continues)

Data Reconciliation: Subproject Responsibility – xxxxxxxx, xxxxxxx, xxxxxxxx

SUBJECT	DELIVERABLE/ACTIVITY	DUE DATE	WHO	DONE	LEFT TO DO/COMMENTS

Notes:

Business Sign-offs: Subproject Responsibility – xxxxxxxx, xxxxxxx, xxxxxxxx

SUBJECT	DELIVERABLE/ACTIVITY	DUE DATE	WHO	DONE	LEFT TO DO/COMMENTS

Notes:

Interfaces: Subproject Responsibility – xxxxxxxx, xxxxxxx

SUBJECT	DELIVERABLE/ACTIVITY	DUE DATE	WHO	DONE	LEFT TO DO/COMMENTS

Notes:

(continues)

Form: Planning Checklist (*continued*)

Organization: Subproject Responsibility – xxxxxxxx, xxxxxxx, xxxxxxxx

SUBJECT	DELIVERABLE/ACTIVITY	DUE DATE	WHO	DONE	LEFT TO DO/COMMENTS

Notes:

Training and Documentation: Subproject Responsibility – xxxxxxxx

SUBJECT	DELIVERABLE/ACTIVITY	DUE DATE	WHO	DONE	LEFT TO DO/COMMENTS

Notes:

Testing: Subproject Responsibility – xxxxxxxx, xxxxxxx, xxxxxxxx

SUBJECT	DELIVERABLE/ACTIVITY	DUE DATE	WHO	DONE	LEFT TO DO/COMMENTS

Notes:

Operations: Subproject Responsibility – xxxxxxxx

SUBJECT	DELIVERABLE/ACTIVITY	DUE DATE	WHO	DONE	LEFT TO DO/COMMENTS

Notes:

Form: Status Meeting Agenda

Date: ddmmyyyy

<u>Conference Call Number:</u>   number, passcode

2:00–2:30 P.M.   Meeting 1

2:30–3:30 P.M.   Meeting 2

3:30–4:30 P.M.   Meeting 3

Facilitator Name and contact information—please report any omissions

<u>Attendees:</u>
<u>Meeting 1:</u>
<u>Meeting 2:</u>
<u>Meeting 3:</u>

<u>AGENDA:</u>

2:00–2:30 P.M.	Category Name	facilitator
	Topic 1	speaker
	Topic 2	speaker
2:30–2:45 P.M.	Category name	facilitator
	Topic 1	speaker
	Topic 2	speaker
2:45–3:30 P.M.	Category name	facilitator
	Topic 1	speaker
	Topic 2	speaker
3:30–4:30 P.M.	Category name	facilitator
	Topic 1	speaker
	Topic 2	speaker

Change Requests Template Bundle

Some of the deliverable templates that are relevant to managing change requests on a project are contained in this section. Change requests can refer to modifications to accepted requirements, a scope change, or an enhancement to a project after it is completed.

Form: Scope Change

Current Date
Contact Name
Title
Company
Address

SCOPE CHANGE TO PROJECT XXXX

Dear Sirs/Madam:

It has been our pleasure to continue to work with you on the XXXXX project. Earlier in the engagement, it was agreed that the approach was XXXXXXX. The new approach is XXXXXXXX.

We sincerely hope that you have been pleased with the progress of the project to date. Once again, thank you for the opportunity to be of assistance to you in the important initiative. Should you have any questions, please do not hesitate to call me at (XXX) XXX-XXXX.

Yours truly,

Name
Title
Cc: xxxxxxx

Form: Project Change Request

Organization:
Project Name:
Project Number:
Client Contact:
Description of the Proposed Change:

Reason for Change (provide supporting documentation):

Impact of Change:
a) Cost impact:
b) Time impact:

Type of Change Required:

_____ Program Change   _____ Report Change

_____ Screen Design Change   _____ Documentation Change

_____ Other (explain) _____

_____

Requested by: Approved by:

Testing Template Bundle

Some of the deliverable templates that are relevant to the testing phases are included in this section.

Form: Testing Variance

ID#	Tester name: User name: Assigned by: Logged by:	Log Date: Deadline:
Description:		Test Scenario / Case:
Results:		
Impact:		Review Status: Resolution Date:
Description:		
Next Steps:		

Sign-off:

Tester:_____

Business Owner:_____

Form: Test Scenario

Test Scenario: Test Case:	Date Executed:
Testers:	Other Resources:
Test Script:	Setup Instructions:
Inputs:	Outputs:
Test Case:	Expected Results:
Results:	Comments:

Form: Problem Report

Organization:

Project Name:

Project Number:

Client Contact:

Problem Number:

Problem Reported by:

Problem Description (provide relevant supporting documentation):

Problem Resolution:

Date Problem Reported: Date Problem Resolved:

Resolved by: Latest Status:

Requirements Template Bundle

Some of the deliverable templates that are relevant to requirements gathering are shown in this section:

Form: Requirements Checklist

ISSUE NO.	ISSUE NAME	REQUESTER	DATE IDENTIFIED	PERSON RESP.	ISSUE STATUS	DATE RESOLVED

Form: Requirements Template

Description and Purpose:

Systems(s) Affected:

Windows(s) Affected:

Major Impacts:

Owners:

OWNERSHIP	NAME	DIVISION	PHYSICAL LOCATION	CONTACT INFORMATION
Owner:				
Technology:				
Business:				

Requirement Description:

Window Layouts (if applicable):

Maps/Layouts:

Interfaces:

Comments:

Issues:

Architecture Template Bundle

Some of the deliverable templates that are relevant to the architecture phase are shown below:

Form: Architecture Checklists

Production and Development Environments

Desktop

	APP1	APP2	APP3	APP4
Win 2000		X	X	X
Win NT 3.51		X		X
Win NT 4.0+		X		X
486				
Pentium		X	120	X
RAM (MB)			32 64	
ODBC/JDBC (not used on client)				
Oracle 8 Client	X		X	
PowerBuilder DDDK 6.5			X	
PowerBuilder 6.5			X	
Netscape 4.x/IE 4.x	X	X		X
Oracle 7.3 driver				
Excel v5+				
MSWORD				
Adobe Acrobat Reader		X		X
Actuate & Infomaker				
Report Writers		Crystal		
Version Control Tools	PVCS			
TCP/IP				
FTP/IP				
TI				
Distribution Software				

Place an "X" where an application uses the designated technology.

(continues)

Form: Architecture Checklists (*continued*)

Server

TECHNOLOGY	APP1	APP2	APP3	APP4	APP5
HP9000					
Sun Workstations					
HP/UX UNIX 10.20 OS					
Other OS					
Java Virtual Machine					
Oracle Web Application Server 3.0					
Java/JavaScript					
Oracle 8.x					
Exchange 5 (email)					
Oracle 8 pack					
Oracle 8 Network/Web pack					
PL/SQL, PRO*C					
Version Control Tools					
Distribution Software					

Installation Locations

	APP1	APP2	APP3	APP4
Source Physical Locations				
Server Physical Locations				
User Physical Locations				

User Distribution
  New York City
   San Francisco
   Houston
   Seattle
   Dallas				

Availability				
Batch Cycle				

(*Continues*)

Comments

	DESCRIPTION
Application 1	
Application 2	
Application 3	
Application 4	

Communication Form Template Bundle

Some of the deliverable templates that are relevant for communicating with the project team, sponsors, and the organization are included in this section.

Form: Letter for Wide Distribution before Implementing a Project

Memorandum

To:
From:
Date:
Subject:

Background description/benefits of project

What to expect in the future

Upcoming activities

    <u>List of dates and activities</u>

During this time, if you have any concerns or questions, feel free to contact any of the following individuals:

    <u>Name, phone number, email</u>

A "help desk" will also be available to assist you after implementation

Thanks for support

Yours truly,

    Signature

Executive
Title
cc:

Form: Issue Memo

```
Author:
Date:
Priority: Urgent
Receipt Requested
TO:
TO:
TO:
Subject:
```

———————————————— Message Contents ————————————————

Here are some issues regarding the project that require immediate attention. Solutions are suggested later in this memo:

ISSUES:

Describe.

SUGGESTED SOLUTIONS (select several):

Describe.

Signature

Form: Project newsletter

Project XXXX Newsletter

Who we are

What we are doing

Short-term objectives

Who's affected

Benefits

Timeline

Photos

Next newsletter date

Sign-offs Template Bundle

Some of the deliverable templates that are relevant for obtaining final sign-off and approval for project deliverables are included in this section.

Form: Project Deliverable Signoff

Organization:

Project Name:

Project Number:

Client Contact:

Project Manager:

Authorization is hereby given to proceed with the conversion and implementation activities for the project. We confirm that the specifications and details contained within this document meet all deliverables and requirements outlined for the system integration test phase.

Requested by: Approved by:

Form: Project Acceptance Form

Organization:

Project Name:

Project Number:

Client Contact:

We have reviewed the project deliverables and agree that:

☐   The project meets the acceptance test previously set forth.

☐   The documentation meets the criteria previously set forth.

Reviewed by: Approved by:

Costing Template Bundle

Some of the deliverable templates that are relevant for costing components and resources on a project are included in this section.

Form: Estimating Project Costs

Project Name: Project Manager:
Project Number: Project Cost Summary
Project Sponsor:

1. People costs

POSITION	PERSON–DAYS	COST/DAY	TOTAL COST
Project Manager			
Data Analyst			
Business Analysts			
Systems Analysts			
Programmers			
Testers			
Documentation specialist			
Total			

2. Equipment costs (expressed monthly over the duration of the project)

TYPE	COST
Hardware	
Software	
Communications	
Maintenance	
Total	

3. Travel and other costs (expressed monthly over the duration of the project)

TOTAL PEOPLE	EQUIPMENT	TRAVEL AND OTHER COSTS

Form: Project Cost Report—Deliverables Based

DELIVERABLE	TARGET DATE	ACTUAL DATE	PLANNED BUDGET ($)	ACTUAL BUDGET ($)	VARIANCE ($)	REMARK
Data Collection						
Data Analysis						
Logical Design						
Functional Specs						

Form: Project Cost Report—Resources

Time and Cost Analysis				
Report for the month of:	December 200x			
	Plan	Actual	Variance	Totals to Date
(a) Resources (Hours)				
1) Programmer				
2) Programmer Analyst				
3) Systems Analyst				
4) Data Analyst				
5) Project Manager				
(b) Resources ($)				
1) Programmer				
2) Programmer Analyst				
3) Systems Analyst				
4) Data Analyst				
5) Project Manager				

Form: Calculating Budget

INITIATIVE/ STAFFING	LEVEL	FULL RATE (PER DIEM)	DISCOUNTED RATE	EFFORT	DAYS	FEES	EXPENSES
Resource 1							
Resource 2							
Resource 3							
Resource 4							

Conversion Rate:

Discount Rate:

Hours/Day:

Other Templates

Some of the deliverable templates that are relevant in the general project development lifecycle are included in this section.

Form: Resource Evaluation

This form can be used to evaluate a resource at the conclusion of a project. It is good management practice to complete a similar form at the start of an engagement to ensure that each resource's objectives, career goals, and development needs are established. They can then be met over the lifecycle of a project. Several evaluation forms should be completed for resources allocated to a project for more than six months. An evaluation frequency of four to six months is common practice.

Project Name:	Evaluation Period:
Employee's Name: Project Manager's Name: Reviewed by:	Comments:
Resource Objectives: Major Accomplishments: Areas for Development/Improvement:	

SIGNATURES:

Reviewer: _____   Date: _____

Employee: _____   Date: _____

(continues)

Form: Resource Evaluation (*continued*)

Please rate resource in the following areas with specific examples where available:

Communication Skills:

_____

_____

Technical Skills:

_____

_____

Leadership Skills:

_____

_____

Business Knowledge:

_____

_____

Conflict Management:

_____

_____

Responsiveness:

_____

_____

Professionalism:

_____

_____

Other:

_____

_____

Form: Short Evaluation Form

This form can be used to quickly collect feedback from managers and clients who are busy, but who are likely to respond to email. The form is quick to complete and documents feedback quite effectively. It also quickly lays out a yardstick for performance on a project.

Dear xxxxxx,

I want to take this opportunity to thank you for working with me in the past six months in a constantly changing environment. You have demonstrated a keen ability to understand the impact of the business, technical, and process issues facing the IT Integration process. You have also demonstrated an ability to effectively manage multiple responsibilities and project teams to deliver on time. The documentation and training teams consist of a combination of permanent and contract staff. The training video has thus far received strong reviews. You were also successful in building the training environments and training material, while the organization has been facing constant change. I have also valued your upward feedback and the fact that you escalate concerns at the right time.

I would also like to take this opportunity to provide you with feedback in a number of standard areas. Please feel free to use this at review time, and do not hesitate to call me at xxxxxxxx if you have any questions. In the rating score below, 1 or greater is considered to be positive feedback and a job well done.

Note: 0 - Needs improvement
       1 - Fair performance
       2 - Good Performance
       3 - Excellent performance

Technical Ability:	3
Business Knowledge:	2
Professional:	3
Communication:	2
Interpersonal Skills:	3
Teamwork:	3
Initiative:	3
Creativity:	2
Adaptability:	2
Judgment:	3
Leadership:	3
Maturity:	3
Integrity:	3
Sense of Humor:	2
Intensity and Energy Level:	3

Form: Product Evaluation Matrix

This form is used to evaluate a set of products against some common criteria. The criteria list should be customized to your organization.

	PRODUCT 1	PRODUCT 2	PRODUCT 3	PRODUCT 4
Vendor				
Costs				
Functionality				
Warranty				
Cultural Fit				
Vendor Stability				
Vendor Support				
Market Presence				
Strengths				
Weaknesses				
Other				

Form: Project History Form

This form should be completed by the project manager on project acceptance.

Project Name:

Project Number:

Brief Project Description:

Key Project Data:

Project Size (in person years):   Planned: _____ person years
                                  Actual: _____ person years

    Project Size (in $):   Planned: $_____   Actual: $_____

    Project Metrics: Lines of code _____

                      # of screens _____

                      # of reports _____

                      # of users _____

Key Project Deliverables:

Did the project meet its goals and objectives?

List three areas that contributed to project success.

List three areas where you could have done things differently.

Status. Specify the contents of status reports, agenda of status meetings, and timing issues.

Workshops and meetings. Specify how these should be conducted and documented.

Documentation. Specify the minimum amount of documentation that is required in the project and provide a format for each document. This must include a business case, business requirements, architecture diagram, test cases, and a communication plan.

Technical. Specify formats for coding, screen layouts, and walk-throughs.

Issues. Specify the format for reporting an issue, how issues are tracked, and how issued are resolved.

A Generic Project Lifecycle

A typical project development lifecycle consists of four to six standard phases that are referred to by many different names. Many of the customized methodologies offered by management tool vendors and consulting firms are based on these standard phases. The methodologies are augmented by linkages to technologies that become mainstream, such as Web-based solutions, the Internet, and object-oriented technology. Techniques such as prototyping and iteration are also embedded in the methodologies. In general, transition from one phase to another has overlap and is not a solid boundary. For example, testing activities are likely to begin in the gather and analyze phase, even though full testing will not begin until a much later phase. The standard phases in the development lifecycle are shown in Figure F.1 and are described here:

☐ **Plan/initiate.** These activities involve building a project charter, getting executive support, building consensus and assembling a project management and a data-gathering team.

☐ **Gather and analyze.** These activities involve identifying key users and gathering information. The information is analyzed and modeled to ensure that it is valid.

☐ **Develop.** These activities develop the application using a variety of tools and techniques.

☐ **Test.** These activities test the application in a variety of ways, including unit, stress, functional, performance, and acceptance testing. The results must be signed off by the project sponsors before proceeding to the next phase.

☐ **Implement.** These activities implement the application in a pilot, in a series of pilots, or as a single large solution. This includes building and implementing a communication plan and training for the users.

☐ **Maintain.** These activities support the ongoing operation of the application production environment, enhancements, bug fixes, and feedback to the project manager.

The generic project development lifecycle is rarely implemented as shown in Figure F.1. It is usually customized by an organization—if only to a small degree. For example the generic plan can be translated into the following steps for a medium-sized organization:

1. Establish initial staffing (architect, manager, data modeler, business analyst, steering committee).
2. Conduct feasibility study to establish a business need. This includes a cost/benefit analysis.
3. Build the project team.
4. Capture business requirements.
5. Confirm business requirements.
   ☐ Prototype
   ☐ Documentation
   ☐ JAD sessions
6. Establish pilot project (requirements and functionality).
7. Establish/design technology infrastructure.
8. Expand project team.
9. Establish milestones and project plan.
10. Build pilot.
11. Iterative testing.
12. Confirm audit/control requirements.
13. Implementation.

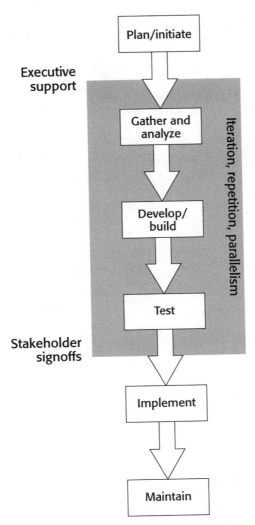

Figure F.1 Generic project development lifecycle.

14. Review of important lessons.

15. Design of support infrastructure.

16. Postimplementation review.

17. Expand scope of pilot to include other business functions.

Several phases can be conducted at the same time. For example, development can be started before analysis is complete. If this is done, management must be handled skillfully to avoid missing business requirements or creating other types of chaos on a project.

Bibliography

Alter, Steven. 1999. *Information Systems: A Management Perspective.* 3rd ed. MA: Addison-Wesley.

Band, Williams A. 1991. *Creating Value for Customers.* NY: John Wiley & Sons.

Bender, Paul S. 1983. *Resource Management.* NY: John Wiley & Sons.

Booch, Grady. 1996. *Object Solutions: Managing the Object-Oriented Project.* MA: Addison-Wesley.

Brooks, Frederick P. 1995. *The Mythical Man-Month.* Anniversary ed. MA: Addison-Wesley.

Carson, William M. Spring 1994. "Strategic Planning and the Anatomy of Change." *Journal of Management Consulting*, 30–39.

Champy, James. 1995. *Reengineering Management: The Mandate for New Leadership.* NY: HarperCollins.

Connell, John, and Linda Shafer. 1994. *Object-Oriented Rapid Prototyping.* NJ: Prentice-Hall.

Cummings, Thomas, and Christopher Worley. 1997. *Organizational Development and Change.* 6th ed. OH: International Thompson.

Cusumano, Michael, and Richard Selby. 1995. *How the World's Most Powerful Software Company Creates Technology, Shapes Markets, and Manages People.* NY: Free Press.

Davenport, Thomas H. 1993. *Process Innovation, Reengineering Work through Information Technology.* MA: Harvard Business School Press.

Davis, Alan. 1990. *Software Requirements: Analysis and Specification.* NJ: Prentice-Hall.

Donaldson, Scott, and Stanley Siegel. 1997. *Cultivating Successful Software Development: A Practitioner's View.* NJ: Prentice-Hall.

Gibbs, W. Wayt. September 1994. "Software's Chronic Crisis." *Scientific American,* 86–95.

Gilbreath, Robert D. 1986. *Winning at Project Management.* NY: John Wiley & Sons.

Grady, Robert. 1993. *Practical Software Metrics for Project Management and Process Improvement.* NJ: Prentice-Hall.

Hammer, Michael, and James Champy. 1993. *Reengineering the Corporation: A Manifesto for Business Revolution.* NY: HarperCollins.

Humphrey, Watts. 1997. *Introduction to the Personal Software Process.* MA: Addison-Wesley.

Jacobson, Ivar, Grady Booch, and James Rumbaugh. 1999. *The Unified Software Development Process.* MA: Addison-Wesley.

Jacques, Elliot, and Stephen Clement. 1991. *Executive Leadership: A Practical Guide to Managing Complexity.* MA: Cason Hall & Co.

Johns, Gary. 1996. *Organizational Behavior: Understanding and Managing Life at Work.* 4th ed. NY: HarperCollins.

Jones, Capers. 1994. *Assessment and Control of Software Risks.* NJ: Yourdon Press.

Keyes, Jessica, ed. 1999. *Internet Management.* NY: Auerbach.

Kliem, Ralph, and Irwin Ludin. 1998. *Project Management Practitioner's Handbook.* NY: American Management Association.

McCarthy, Jim. 1995. *Dynamics of Software Development.* WA: Microsoft Press.

McConnell, Steve. 1998. *Software Project Survival Guide.* WA: Microsoft Press.

Microsoft Project 2000 Product Documentation, Microsoft Corporation.

Payne, J. 1998. "Five Steps toward Transformation." *Datamation.*

Reynolds, George W. 1992. *Information Systems for Managers.* NY: West Publishing Company.

Satzinger, John, et al. 2000. *Systems Analysis and Design in a Changing World.* MA: Thomson Learning.

Thomsett, Rob. 1993. *Third Wave Project Management.* NJ: Prentice-Hall.

Walker, Royce. 1998. *Software Project Management: A Unified Framework.* MA: Addison-Wesley.

Walton, Mary. 1990. *Deming Management at Work*. NY: G.P. Putnam's Sons.

Whitten, Neal. 1995. *Managing Software Development Projects*. 2nd ed. NY: John Wiley & Sons.

Wood, Jane, and Denise Silver. 1995. *Joint Application Development*. 2nd ed. NY: John Wiley & Sons.

Yourdon, E. 1989. *Modern Structured Analysis*. NJ: Prentice-Hall.

Yourdon, E. 1997. *Rise and Resurrection of the American Programmer*. NJ: Yourdon Press.

Index

Page references followed by italic *t* indicate material in tables.

DATE DUE

0 6 AUG 2001	
MR 11 '04	

DEMCO, INC. 38-2931